The

Bible Handbook

The Essential Bible Handbook

A GUIDE FOR CATHOLICS

With Prayers and a Glossary of Key Terms

A REDEMPTORIST PASTORAL PUBLICATION

Liguori
LIGUORI, MISSOURI

Imprimi Potest: Richard Thibodeau, C.Ss.R.
Provincial, Denver Province
The Redemptorists

Imprimatur: Most Reverend Timothy M. Dolan
Auxiliary Bishop, Archdiocese of St. Louis

Written and compiled by Thomas M. Santa, C.Ss.R.
Published by Liguori Publications
Liguori, Missouri
www.liguori.org

Library of Congress Cataloging-in-Publication Data

Santa, Thomas M.
The essential Bible handbook : a guide for Catholics : with prayers and a glossary of key terms / written and compiled by Thomas M. Santa, C.Ss.R.
p. cm.—(A Redemptorist pastoral publication)
ISBN 978-0-7648-0836-4 (pbk.)
1. Bible—Hermeneutics. 2. Bible—Criticism, interpretation, etc. 3. Bible—Study and teaching—Catholic Church. I. Title. II. Series
BS476 .S26 2002
220'.088'22—dc21 2002067148

Liguori Publications, a nonprofit corporation, is an apostolate of the Redemptorists. To learn more about the Redemptorists, visit *Redemptorists.com.*

Printed in the United States of America
11 10 09 08 07 7 6 5 4 3

Contents

Introduction

When I was growing up in the fifties, in a traditional Catholic family, our family routinely participated in a regular schedule of activities associated with our local Catholic parish. We attended Sunday Mass as a family and returned to church on Tuesday evenings to attend devotions in honor of the Blessed Mother under the title of Our Mother of Perpetual Help. We made it a point to go to confession on most Saturday afternoons and, of course, prayed the rosary together as a family each evening while kneeling in a circle in the living room. Ours was a family that believed, and my mother probably believed it the most, that "the family that prays together, stays together," and so we participated in all that was expected of us.

In our neighborhood most of the Catholic families engaged in the same rituals as did our family. Not for a moment did any one of us even question what we were doing because each of us understood that somehow "this is what a good Catholic family does." Meanwhile, across the street and on either side of our house, the good families that were formed in another Christian tradition experienced other family rituals. They attended services on Sunday morning and on Sunday evening, returned to church on Wednesday evening for yet another service, then spent a portion of their time each evening gathered together as a family reading the Bible.

One Christian family, formed in the Catholic tradition, prayed and found their guidance and nourishment in the devotions and the rituals that had been handed down to us. The other Christian family, formed in a Protestant tradition, prayed and found their guidance and nourishment in the Bible. Although our Christian families were neighbors, living in close proximity to one another, we could not have been further apart in our spiritual understanding and in our faith experience.

Although our Catholic family owned a Bible, and the Bible had a prominent place in our living room, we were never inclined to open it either for family prayer or at any other time for that matter. The thought never even occurred to us, at the time of prayer or perhaps at the moment of decision-making or personal challenge, to select a passage from Scripture and to "break open the Word." I sincerely doubt if any of us, had we been so challenged or inclined, would have been able to easily find the passages in the Scripture that would have reflected the mysteries of the rosary, for example, that we would have prayed together. Each of us would have assumed that the mysteries of the rosary could be found in the Bible, because we understood the rosary to tell the story of Jesus and the Blessed Mother, but none of us would have had a clue to where to look.

It wasn't because we didn't believe that the Bible was an essential Christian resource and the Word of God, but rather we possessed an attitude, a perception, that all that was important for us was given to us by the Church. Each of us believed that all we needed could be found in the traditions and the pious devotions that we were encouraged to practice and incorporate into our daily life.

Catholics looked to their leadership for guidance in what was expected and encouraged and there was very little deviation from the norm. With this beginning assumption, I suppose if we were instructed to read the Bible, and if it was promoted from the pulpit with the same vigor and enthusiasm as were our other spiritual practices, we would have complied. Obedience to the leadership of the Church and the representatives of that Church in the person of our priests and sisters was also very important to us. As it so happened this value played a very important role in what happened next.

What occurred after the reforms of the Second Vatican Council was that the emphasis changed rather quickly from a spiritual practice that was highly devotional to practices that encouraged biblical reading and study. Bible-study classes, scriptural prayer services, and other practices were promoted and recommended while traditional devotional practices became less and less important. Probably the single most important change was the emphasis on the Liturgy of the Word at Mass, distinct from the Liturgy of the Eucharist. It was not that Catholics did not read the Scripture at Mass before the Second Vatican Council, but rather that it seemed not to be emphasized and highlighted. After the Council that changed very dramatically.

The emphasis on the Liturgy of the Word, and a complimentary emphasis on the preached word as homily, explaining and interpreting the readings from Scripture just proclaimed as opposed to the traditional sermon that could be on almost any spiritual subject or discipline in a sense introduced most Catholics to the Bible. The lectionary cycle of assigned readings "broke open the Word" of God and the history of God's salvific action for us all.

These changes in emphasis seemed to accomplish that which was intended. Today, long after the reforms of the Council have been implemented, we have a situation in which most Catholics are more conversant with the Bible, but still relatively few incorporate the praying or the study of the Bible into their daily lives. For an older generation the Bible is much more a part of their lives, but not as comforting as perhaps the more traditional prayers and devotions from their youth. For still others, especially men and women who have been formed and educated in the spirit of the Second Vatican Council, there is a different situation. Although they are more familiar and comfortable with the Bible, and most of the traditional devotions and prayers are unknown to them, they are possessed with a certain frustration, a frustration that is reflective of the core experience of Catholicism.

For a Catholic to go to the Bible with the expectation that all that is important to them in their faith journey will be easily discovered and explained, disappointment soon sets in. They discover the power of the Word of God, but they do not clearly discover the dogmas, doctrines, and practices of Catholicism. The reason is, of course, that Catholicism has been constructed on the twin pillars of Scripture, but also of tradition. The tradition is present in the Scripture, but not as clearly as some might assume it would be.

For Catholics searching for direction and explanation, a further frustration sets in when they attempt to educate themselves about their spiritual tradition. If they go to a bookstore and pick up a book on the Bible, more often than not the book will help them understand the Bible, but it will be from a non-Catholic perspective, and much of what is important to Catholics in their journey—such as the sacraments, the teaching authority of the Church, and moral theology—will not be explained.

It is into this vacuum, in answer to this frustration, that *The Essential Bible Handbook* is positioned. It is in this spirit that this book is offered as a helpful companion and tool for the Catholic who feels called to study and reflect on the Bible, but who wants to do so with a Catholic sense and feeling to what is being read and reflected on. This book is intended to be a helpful guide and, as such, will be distinctly different from other potential Bible-study books that may appear on the shelves of the local bookstore.

Catholic readers will be guided throughout this handbook in the use of the essential references which have been consulted. The primary reference that will be provided is the appropriate Scripture reference. The Scripture reference provides the name of the book, along with the appropriate chapter and verse, for example, "the Gospel of John, chapter 5, verse 11" (Jn 5:11). A review of abbreviations used is provided in section two of this handbook. In addition to the references provided from Scripture, references to the *Catechism of the*

Catholic Church are also provided. Catechism references include the specific paragraph reference point, for example, "*The Catechism of the Catholic Church,* paragraph 135" (CCC 135). Within the text proper, whenever "catechism" is referenced, it is always a reference to the *Catechism of the Catholic Church.*

Because this book is part of the "Essential Catholic Handbook" series published by Liguori Publications, the reader should expect that the book will cover what Catholics *believe* about the Bible; the *practices* that are incorporated into our Catholic tradition and identity as a result of biblical study and reflection; and, finally, the *prayer* forms and experiences that are scripturally based. The reader of this essential handbook will not find those resources that are typical of other Bible books, especially those which are anchored in the evangelical Protestant tradition and which are readily available for those who desire to use this approach in their faith journey.

The last word in this introduction includes the reminder that this *Essential Bible Handbook* is by no means complete. Biblical study and reflection offers a wealth of opportunity for the reader who wants to pursue any biblical topic in depth. Men and women scholars have devoted their entire lives to the study and exploration of the Bible and there are many fine resources available for anyone who desires to learn more. A good place to continue your education and reflection is often found in the Bible-study groups that are well established in most Catholic parishes. If a Bible-study group is not something that you are interested in, perhaps another approach that you might find nourishing and helpful for your spiritual journey is to approach Bible study thematically. For example, choose to read books that reflect on a single subject such as the synoptic Gospels, the teachings of the apostle Paul, or perhaps a book on the psalms or the prophets from the Old Testament. Resources that lend themselves to a thematic study of Scripture are readily available and identifiable.

For those readers who will be using this handbook as an introduction to the Bible a process for using this book might include the following points. If you are not familiar with the stories and the theology of the Bible, or if you feel that you might need a refresher, begin by reading section four, an abbreviated presentation of salvation history, the story of God's relationship with humanity. After reading this section, proceed to read the first three sections that speak about how the Bible was formed and how it is understood as both the inspired and the revealed Word of God. The concluding sections of the book offer a sampling of ways that you can use the Bible for your own spiritual journey. The sections on praying with the Word of God and with some of the major personalities of the Bible are appropriate for times of retreat and other times of personal reflection. All in all this handbook should prove to be a helpful companion as you break open for yourself the Word of God.

STUDIUM, DECEMBER 2001
ST. BENEDICT'S MONASTERY
ST. JOSEPH, MINNESOTA

PART ONE

Beginnings

It would seem that a book about the Bible, especially a book that claims to be about the essentials of the Bible, would begin with a discussion about something like "the Bible and its origin." Admittedly, there are many books about the Bible that would use this approach. However, since this book is also identified as the essential *Catholic* book about the Bible, we take our guidance from the *Catechism of the Catholic Church.* The catechism is the primary educational resource that is available to us, and the catechism begins with an explanation of the context or "the big picture" of what it means to be a Catholic, and what it therefore means to be a person of faith within the Catholic tradition (CCC 5–7). It is only after we come to an understanding and appreciation of the contextual experience of our faith tradition that we can then move to the particulars.

In and of itself this starting point illustrates a very important point about Catholicism, and what it means to be a person of faith within the Catholic tradition. By choosing to begin our study and reflection by admitting the need to look at the "big picture" means that we accept the concept that the fundamentals of faith go beyond the Bible; this is an assertion that many non-Catholics would not be inclined to accept. Again, we look to the catechism for clarification, and when we do so, we discover that there are other experiences of God's presence in our world that we need to consider.

The catechism teaches that if we intend to understand the essential and fundamental content of the Catholic faith, we need to look to four sources for our point of reference: the sacred Scriptures, the Fathers of the Church, the liturgy, and the Church's magisterium (CCC 11). A study and appreciation of these four sources will lead us to the four "pillars" on which Catholic catechesis is constructed: "the baptismal profession of faith (the *Creed*), the sacraments of faith, the life of faith (the *Commandments*), and the prayer of those who believe (the *Lord's Prayer*)" (CCC 13).

It is beyond the scope of this book to examine in detail each of the four sources and four pillars of Catholicism; our intent and purpose is to study the Bible. However, it would not be very helpful to attempt to study one source of our tradition without at least making necessary references to our other sources when such an application would be important and would complete the "big picture." For this reason, every effort to provide the necessary cross references are included whenever possible.

1. Creation, The Work of God

Catholics believe, as do all Christians, that the world was created according to the wisdom of God (CCC 295). Sacred Scripture teaches us in the very first words of the book of Genesis: "In the beginning when God created the heavens and the earth" (Gen 1:1). This assertion means that we believe that everything proceeds from God, because God has intended it to be so. Or in other words, we believe that creation was a deliberate act of God—it was not something that occurred as a result of fate or chance.

Not only do we believe that creation is the work of God, we also believe that creation is the work of the Holy Trinity—Father, Son, and Spirit. Both the Old Testament and the New Testament suggest, at least from a Christian perspective, the creative activity of the Son and the Spirit with the Father (Ps 33:6; 104:30; Gen 1:2–3). Of course the New Testament goes beyond simple suggestion and clearly asserts the essential role of the Son, "In the beginning was the Word...and the Word was God....All things came into being through him..." (Jn 1:1–3) (CCC 291–292).

As creator, God made the world, in the words of Saint Bonaventure (1221–1274), "not to increase his glory, but to show it forth and to communicate it" (CCC 293). This creative activity of God, this communication of the glory of God, finds its most dramatic emphasis in the human person, in "man fully alive" (CCC 294).

2. The Human Person

In God's plan of creation, the human person has been created "in the image of God" (Gen 1:27; Col 1:15). This creation is "good" (Gen 1:4), and has been blessed by God with an abundance of gifts. Perhaps the greatest gift that God has given to his creatures is the fact that he is present to them in every imaginable way, "in him we live and move and have our being" (Acts 17:28) (CCC 330).

In all of God's creation, it is only the human person who is capable of self-knowledge. Only the human person is capable of freely entering into relationships with other persons (CCC 357). This ability and this freedom have also been given to us by God; it is not the result of our own talents or abilities, but the gift does come with certain responsibilities. The primary responsibility of the human person is to live in friendship with the Creator, in harmony with other human persons and all of creation (CCC 374). Sacred Scripture teaches that this harmony, or what the catechism identifies as "divine intimacy" (CCC 376), was experienced by the human person at the beginning of time in Paradise (Gen 2:5—3:24), but was lost by sin:

> The account of the fall in *Genesis 3* uses figurative language, but affirms a primeval event, a deed that took place *at the beginning of the history of man*. Revelation gives us the certainty of faith that the whole of human history is marked by the original fault freely committed by our first parents (CCC 390).

3. The Human Person Desires to Know God

Because the human person has been created by God, and once enjoyed "divine intimacy" with God, he or she craves a restoration of this original and intimate relationship with God. This desire for God is "written in the human heart" (CCC 27) and has been expressed throughout history, in religious beliefs, practices, rituals, prayers, and sacrifices (CCC 28). This desire for God is nourished by the honest use of the gift of intelligence and by the example and witness of other people of faith who teach others to seek an intimate and life-giving relationship with God (Ps 105:3) (CCC 30).

Although the human person desires to know God and to live in relationship with God, it is also possible (because of the gift of freedom that the human person has been given by the Creator) for the human person to forget, overlook, ignore, or even explicitly reject this primary relationship with God (CCC 29). It is possible for the human person to try and live without a relationship with God, but regardless of the actions of humanity, God continues to call the human person to the fullness of life and happiness (CCC 30).

4. How Can We Know God?

The human person arrives at a beginning knowledge of the existence of God in two ways: the first is by observing the created world; the second is by becoming fully aware of their own humanity. The catechism identifies these "ways of approaching God" as "converging and convincing arguments" (CCC 31).

A person can begin to know about God by observing and meditating on the order and beauty of creation. In the words of Saint Augustine, "Question the beauty of the earth, question the beauty of the sea...question the beauty of the sky...question all these realities" (CCC 32). It is in the questioning that a person can then arrive at the point when they *confess* and *profess* that someone greater than themselves is responsible for all that surrounds us. Of course, in order to make this profession, it is necessary to be aware of your own humanity, the second argument.

The human person, if they are open to truth and to beauty, to the longings within for infinite happiness, or as the catechism teaches, if they are open to the "spiritual soul," arrives at the conclusion that all of creation can have its "origin only in God" (CCC 33). The human person realizes that they cannot be, nor have they ever been, the creative power/life that has first caused all of creation to come into being. The human person also realizes that they are not the final end of all things, and so they are left, in their observation and meditation, to the conclusion that Saint Thomas Aquinas (1226–1274) identifies as the reality "that everyone calls God" (CCC 34).

As wonderful as it is to know that the human person can arrive at a beginning knowledge of the existence of God through experience and reason, it must also be stated that this is not enough. Experience and reason have been provided by the Creator to the human person, not as an end in themselves, but rather to create within the human person the capacity to "welcome God's revelation" (CCC 36). In other words, experience and reason can predispose a person to the knowledge of the existence of God, but something more is needed (CCC 35). Human beings are in need of God's revelation (CCC 38).

5. How Can We Speak About God?

Although we acknowledge God, and profess our belief in God as the most fundamental affirmation of our faith (CCC 199), we also acknowledge that as human beings our knowledge of God is limited, as is our ability to speak about God (CCC 40). The language that we use to talk about God is limited and imperfect, "our human words always fall short of the mystery of God" (CCC 42). Nevertheless, we continue to try to express the inexpressible, comprehend the incomprehensible, see that which cannot be seen, and grasp that which cannot be grasped (CCC 42).

As creatures it should not come as a surprise that we have such limitations, especially if we understand that our limitations are exactly those differences that define the Creator and the creature. The human person learns to accept the fact that most of our language about God, and most of the images that we use to describe God, express that which God is *not* rather than what God *is* (CCC 43).

Coming to an understanding and acceptance of this fundamental limitation helps us to understand the strengths and weaknesses of Christian theology, and the struggle that the Christian community experienced in coming to an agreement about the proper formulation for Christian creeds and dogmas (CCC 884; 890). It is also helpful in understanding the Bible, and is useful in appreciating the literary forms (poem, myth, parable, proverb, for example), that the Bible uses to express the story of salvation.

6. How Is God's Word Revealed to Humanity?

Although it is possible for the human person to know God by natural reason and through experience of the created world (CCC 50), there are obvious limitations to this awareness and knowledge. Because of the limitations of the creature (human person) to know the Creator (God), the Creator "through an utterly free decision" has chosen to reveal himself to us. This revelation has been a gradual process, with God revealing the divine plan in different stages, culminating in the person and the mission of Jesus Christ (CCC 53).

From the Christian perspective, the stages of divine revelation can be understood and appreciated in five distinct "movements" or "encounters" with God:

- The act of creation
- The covenant with Noah
- The call of Abraham
- The Chosen People of Israel
- Jesus Christ, the fullness of all revelation

The act of creation: God can be observed in the created realities of the world in which we live, including light (Gen 1:14), the oceans (Gen 1:20), cattle and wild animals (Gen 1:24), and of course, the human person (Gen 1:27). It was to the created human person that

God, from the very beginning, manifested himself and invited them to an intimate and lasting relationship with him. This relationship was broken by the sin of humanity's "first parents"; still God did not abandon humanity but promised redemption and salvation (CCC 54–58).

The covenant with Noah: The intended unity of the human race was shattered by sin, and the division of humanity through polytheism and idolatry further threatened the divine plan of salvation. The promise by God never to destroy the earth or sinful humanity again (Gen 9:9–17) remained in force, until the universal proclamation of the Gospel (CCC 56–58; Rom 1:18–25).

***The call of Abraham*:** Humanity was scattered and divided. In order to begin the process of once again gathering together the human family, God calls on Abraham, the father of a multitude of nations (Gen 12:1–2). In the person of Abraham, and in his descendants, the unity of the human family would again be established. As "trustees" of the promise, the Chosen People would wait until called again by God to be formed into the unity of the Church (CCC 59–61).

***The Chosen People of Israel*:** God formed the descendants of Abraham, as promised, and through Moses established a covenant with them on Mount Sinai. This covenant formed the people into the "priestly people of God," the first to hear the word of God preached to them (CCC 62–64).

***Jesus Christ, the fullness of all revelation*:** Until the coming of Jesus, God "spoke to our ancestors...by the prophets" (Heb 1:1). But with the coming of Jesus, we have experienced the "one, perfect, and unsurpassable Word" (CCC 65).

Christians believe that with the coming of Jesus, and the establishment of the new and definitive covenant, there will be no further revelation from God, until the glorious "manifestation of our Lord Jesus Christ" (1 Tim 6:14; CCC 66).

Undoubtedly, God continues to speak to his people, but there is nothing more that can be revealed, nothing more that could possibly "improve or complete" the revelation given to us by Jesus (CCC 67).

7. The Apostolic Tradition

Within the Christian tradition the role of the apostles has always been held in the highest esteem. Christians accept the fact that it was the apostles who had actually witnessed the Lord, both during his earthly mission and after his Resurrection. In addition to the twelve apostles named in the gospels (Lk 6:12–16), the Christian tradition has also accepted the claim of Saint Paul (Acts 22:15; Rom 1:1) and have affirmed that he too is an apostle.

Within the Christian tradition it was the role of an apostle to preach and to teach, proclaiming the gospel to all people (CCC 75). There is no disagreement among the various Christian traditions with this role description. However, within the Catholic tradition, the "apostolic authority" to preach and teach did not end with the death of the last apostle, but rather continues on in a "continuous line of succession until the end of time" (CCC 77). This "living transmission" of the apostolic authority is found in the bishops, who are the successors to the apostles and who are entrusted to transmit and communicate the message of the Gospel and the Tradition of the Church (doctrine, life, and worship) (CCC 78).

In other words, the bishops as the successors of the apostles are entrusted with the ministry of preaching and teaching "the mystery of Christ" (CCC 80). It is the ministry of the bishops, just as it once was the ministry of the apostles, to preserve, expound, and to spread the Gospel, guaranteed by the Holy Spirit (CCC 81). This transmission and interpretation of divine Revelation, entrusted to the Church, "must be accepted and honored" with devotion and reverence (CCC 82).

That being said, the ministry of the preaching and teaching authority of the Church (the magisterium) is not to be seen as superior to the Word of God. It is the Catholic understanding of the role of apostolic authority that the bishops, in union with the pope, provide only an "authentic interpretation of the Word of God" (CCC 85) and teach "only what has been handed on" (CCC 86). In this sense, then, the Catholic faithful can respond with confidence to the apostolic authority of the Church, for "he who hears you, hears me" (Lk 10:16; CCC 87).

Another essential component to the Catholic understanding of the meaning of apostolic authority and the Tradition of the Church can be discovered in the concept of *sensus fidei* (Latin, "sense of the faithful"). In this understanding of the role of the laity in the faithful passing on of the Tradition of the Church is the belief that the faithful "cannot err in matters of belief" (CCC 92). In other words, the Church, from the "last of the faithful," all the way to the Bishop of Rome, in cooperation with the workings of the Holy Spirit, cannot but be faithful to the truth that has been handed on to them (CCC 92–93).

An old catechetical formula that is often used to explain this concept of the *sensus fidei* is: "The people believe it, the bishops teach it, the pope pronounces it, and the Holy Spirit guarantees it."

8. Sacred Scripture

Within the Catholic tradition, as it is in all Christian traditions, sacred Scripture is always understood as "the word of God" (CCC 104). It is also an essential component of the Catholic tradition to accept the Scriptures as the Word of God, "written down under the inspiration of the Holy Spirit." With this understanding Catholics believe, along with their brothers and sisters in Christ, that *"God is the author of Sacred Scripture"* (CCC 105).

Catholics also believe that the Bible teaches the truth, that which is necessary for salvation is presented within the sacred text (CCC 107). However, and this is where the Catholic tradition and other Christian traditions are not in agreement, Catholics are not solely people "of the book." Catholics do not believe, as we have already noted (see the Apostolic Tradition), that Scripture is the only place where we can discover the Word of God (CCC 108).

More often than not this belief provides a singular point of contrast between the Catholic tradition and other Christian traditions. This point of contrast can be easily illustrated by recalling conversations when friends and family of other Christian traditions engage in spirited conversations about faith and religion with a Catholic. People raised in the Protestant tradition frequently quote the Bible, and seem to be able to easily provide a specific text and reference in order to claim the "authority" that they need to bolster their argument. Catholics, on the other hand, are often frustrated by their inability to quote a particular scriptural reference as they recall the necessary "authoritative resource" to support their argument; more often than not it is not a scriptural reference but rather a particular dogma or teaching that more easily comes to mind.

This inability does not have to be a negative experience nor does it mean that Catholics do not value or accept the biblical Word of God as essential. Rather, it illustrates the point made by Saint Bernard of Clairvaux (1091–1153) when he wrote that the Word of God is "not a written and mute word, but incarnate and living" (CCC 108). The Catholic tradition celebrates God's living and incarnate word, in the sacred Scripture, in the Apostolic Tradition, in the sacred liturgy, and in the teachings of the magisterium (CCC 11). It should come as no surprise to a Catholic that their response to a particular question or challenge will not necessarily be limited to a biblical quotation or reference.

9. Sacred Scripture in the Life of the Church

Faith is a personal act, it is the response of the individual person to the call of the Lord in their life (CCC 166). However, even if faith does begin as a personal act and response to God, it is not an isolated act and it does not remain on the level of the personal. A person who is given the necessary grace to believe "in Jesus Christ and the One who sent him" (Mk 16:16; Jn 3:36; CCC 161) is also called to live the life of faith that has been given to the community of believers. It is in this way that the individual person becomes "a link in the great chain of believers" (CCC 166).

One of the most powerful sources that Christians have available to them to support and nourish their faith and to thrive in holiness is Scripture (CCC 132). The Church encourages the faithful to frequently read the Scriptures (Phil 3:8) for "ignorance of the Scriptures is ignorance of Christ" (CCC 133). As beautiful and as reassuring as it is to read these words of encouragement in the catechism, it is necessary to note that this exhortation reflects the opinion of a church formed in our time and place (the late twentieth century). It has not always been the case.

An honest appraisal of Catholic pastoral history and practice would acknowledge that the Church did not always encourage all of the faithful to read the Scripture. One of the reasons for this lack of encouragement was simply because books, no matter what the subject, were not widely circulated. Another reason would be that most people, with the exception of the nobility and the educated classes, were illiterate, and therefore unable to read even if the opportunity was presented. Another reason was that the Scriptures were usually in Latin or Greek and not in the vernacular, or the common, language of the people. However, as practical and as convincing as these observations might be, they do not tell the entire story.

When a new method of printing was invented by Johannes Gutenberg (1400–1468), a method that used reusable type and encouraged the mass production of books, one of the very first books that was printed was the Bible. The Gutenberg Bible (1455) was a Latin version of the Bible, but it immediately enjoyed wide distribution. For the first time a book was available for anyone who might be interested in reading it, and on a subject that was not academic but rather of great interest to many people. The Gutenberg Bible was followed by Martin Luther's *September Bible* in German (1522) and the *King James Version* of the Bible in English (1611).

Almost immediately, instead of there being great enthusiasm for this development, there were instead words of dire warning and consequences. If the Bible could be read by anyone, that also meant that the Bible could be interpreted by anyone, or in the words of the Dominican theologian John Tetzel (1465–1519), "everyone will interpret Scripture as takes his fancy." Tetzel was, of course, correct in his observation, and as history played itself out, it can be honestly asserted that the "engine" of the Protestant Reformation (sixteenth century and beyond) was the "personal interpretation of Scripture."

As a result of the Protestant Reformation, and as a result of the Council of Trent (1545–1563), which can be viewed as the Catholic response to the reformers, a kind of polarization took place. Protestants became people of the Bible and Catholics were not (or at least this seems to be a generalized and "popular" viewpoint). It was not until the beginning of the twentieth century, and not at first in the general Catholic population but rather among academics (Catholic Scripture scholars), that Catholics "rediscovered" sacred Scripture. The encyclical *Divino Afflante Spiritu,* issued by Pope Pius XII in 1943, provided the necessary permission and encouragement which created the atmosphere for Scripture study throughout the Catholic

Church. It started slow, but eventually picked up momentum, a momentum that was obvious with the deliberations of the Second Vatican Council some twenty years after the encyclical.

There has been a revitalization of Scripture study and prayer evident in the Church since the Second Vatican Council. In the Dogmatic Constitution on Divine Revelation, also known as *Dei Verbum,* the members of the Council encouraged the reading, studying, and praying of the Scriptures by all the faithful. However, mindful of the problems and the concerns that had plagued the Church for hundreds of years earlier, the Council was concerned that the person who approached the Scriptures would do so "in the light of the same Spirit by whom it was written" (CCC 111). *Dei Verbum* provides three criteria that must be applied to the Scriptures if they are to be interpreted with a Catholic sensibility and understanding.

- Pay attention to the content and the unity of the whole Scripture (CCC 112).
- Read the Scripture within the living Tradition of the whole Church (CCC 113).
- Pay attention to the analogy of faith (CCC 114).

Pay attention to the content and the unity of the whole Scripture: Read the Scripture from the perspective of the "big picture." God's revelation has been completed in the person of Jesus Christ and the Scripture must be read and understood with direct reference to the Lord. In other words, read the Scripture and see in the Scripture the fullness of the revelation of God. Realize as you read the Scripture that Jesus completed the revelation, and in a very real sense, "filled in the blanks."

Read the Scripture within the living Tradition of the whole Church: Read the Scripture from a Catholic perspective, again from the perspective of the "big picture." Recall that just as the apostles applied and interpreted the teaching of Jesus in their own time and place, the Church continues to do the same, relying on the living apostolic authority that is present in the magisterium. If something is not clear, or if something seems not to be complete or even missing, look to the Tradition and the practice of the Church.

***Pay attention to the analogy of faith*:** An analogy is a "partial agreement or similarity" and in reference to the reading of Scripture it is another reminder to let the "big picture" emerge. The sacred truth that is portrayed in the Scriptures was slowly revealed over time. It is necessary to consider the time and the circumstance, the situation in which the people find themselves, and the reasonable possibility of what could be accomplished or understood. A person does a great disservice to both the interpretation and intention of the Word of God if they take a small portion of sacred Scripture (a single word or phrase) out of context. In the Catholic understanding of Scripture, to "splinter" the Word without reference to the lived experience of the Incarnate Word and the community of believers, and then to claim that the ensuing application or teaching is an "authoritative interpretation," would be unacceptable.

This emphasis on the "big picture" is an essential component in the Catholic understanding and interpretation of the sacred Scripture. In a very real sense it is a uniquely Catholic contribution to the understanding of the purpose of revelation and has obviously played a pivotal role in the formation of the Catholic faith tradition. (Part Three: "How to Read the Bible" continues the explanation of the Catholic perspective.)

PART TWO

The Bible

Basic Information Before Leaving Earth

An old preacher's gimmick to try and capture his audiences attention for the evening sermon is to hold up a copy of the Bible and ask the people, "What does 'bible' mean?" After soliciting a few responses the preacher would say, "**B**asic **I**nformation **B**efore **L**eaving **E**arth," a clever acrostic and certainly something with at least elements of the truth in it. But is that really the Christian understanding and meaning of the book that we call the Bible?

It is true that the Bible contains basic information, and it is also true that each human person will eventually depart this life, but perhaps that is where the benefits of such a definition begin and end.

Presenting the Bible as a kind of "how to" book, something that dropped out of the sky, or perhaps from this perspective more appropriately "deliberately dropped out of the heavens to us," has some value, but the value is limited. On the other hand, to come to an understanding of how the Bible has been formed and how it has come to the point where it is "the book" for literally millions and millions of people is a worthwhile effort.

1. Ancient Ways of Writing And Recording What Was Written

In our day and age, books are no big deal. If anything, in this age of digital technology and information, books seem to be slowly coming to a point where they might even be no longer considered as either useful or important. But that eventuality has not always been the case. At a time in the history of the development of the human person, there was a time in which there were no books; in fact, no writing of any kind because there was not yet even an alphabet which would have enabled the process. That world, the world before books, was a very different world from the world in which we live.

It is generally accepted that writing was "invented" by the Sumerians of Mesopotamia somewhere before 3000 B.C., and the Egyptians around the same time. Other cultures, such as the Chinese (1300 B.C.) and by the Indians native to Mexico (600 B.C.) developed the skill much later.

The invention of writing, and the agreement among those who actually knew how to write and who understood how the "words" were to be arranged, such as in columns, or left to right, reflected a major effort of creativity and discipline. Not only the invention of writing but also the use of clay tablets on which the writing could be preserved and stored took years and years of trial and error before it was firmly rooted and accepted as an essential means of communication.

Once it was determined that writing was both useful and important, there was a parallel determination of what was actually important and useful enough to be written down. Obviously, some of the first things that were carved into the clay tablets were business transactions and records of government regulations. You do not discover great novels, poetry, or even something as simple as a letter recorded on the clay tablets of Sumeria. But eventually, the use of writing evolved beyond the simple recordkeeping of business and government.

The next stage in the development of the "useful and the important" is what many scholars identify as the "propaganda and myths" stage. Certain cultures moved beyond simple recordkeeping and began to record information that included the birth dates of kings and nobles and the cosmic and astronomical observations and conclusions of their priests. However, it was probably the Greeks (around the year 750 B.C.) that contributed the most dramatic change to the human determination of the "useful and important."

Although the great Greek dramatic poems the *Iliad* and the *Odyssey* existed in the memorized and remembered traditions of the poetic bards of the time, they were eventually committed to writing and preserved. Not only were these great literary masterpieces preserved but many other examples of Greek poetry, humor, and philosophy were also committed to writing. Other cultures and civilizations followed suit and writing expanded from the narrowly defined uses of business and government to a much wider audience.

By the time of the Greeks, clay tablets had been replaced by two other writing surfaces that proved to be much more effective, papyrus and parchment.

Papyrus, the root of our word *paper*, grew on the banks of the river Nile in Egypt. Papyrus grows in long stems, as high as fifteen to eighteen feet, and it would be harvested, cut into the appropriate sizes, and then glued together to make a single sheet. Although one side of the papyrus (the side with horizontal sheets) provided the best writing surface, it was not at all unusual for both sides of a papyrus sheet to be used.

The other usable writing surface available to the people was parchment. Parchment is made from animal skins, specifically the skins of sheep and cows. The hair is removed and the skins are washed and repeatedly rubbed with pumice glass (a volcanic stone) until the desired surface is attained. With parchment, the side of the animal skin that was the "flesh side" (without the hair) provided the best overall writing surface.

Once it was determined if either papyrus or parchment was to be used, the second determination was if the writing was to be preserved in a roll or in a codex. These two forms of "books" were the only two choices available. If the determination was that the book was to be in the form of a roll, the writing material chosen would be sewn together into one continuous sheet, and then rolled around a wooden rod for safekeeping. A rolled book was called a volume (Latin, *volumen*). If it was determined that the book was to be in codex form, the writing material would be folded in the middle, providing four sides on which to write. The pages would then be bound together, and then covered with a protective covering, usually made of wood.

The Latin word for the trunk of a tree is *caudex,* which provides the name that is given to this type of book.

For a modern reader who would examine either a scroll or a book from ancient times, the first thing that would be noticeable is that there is very little spacing between the words. Writing material was very scarce and every inch of the material would be used. Upon closer examination the modern reader would also notice that whenever possible an abbreviation would be used, which can sometimes be very confusing, especially when the handwriting is hard to read.

One other component of ancient writings and books should be noted. Often the parchment or the papyrus would be reused, since writing material was so very expensive. Instead of starting a new project with a fresh writing surface, the ancient writer would simply clean a piece or parchment or papyrus and then write whatever it was that needed to be recorded. Also, in the binding process, it is not unusual to find pieces of parchment used that have nothing to do with the book that is being bound: it is just simply cheaper and more practical to use whatever is at hand. This was not a problem at the time, but it can be a significant problem hundreds of years later when you are trying to decipher something and you are not sure which piece of parchment goes where.

All of these components come into consideration when we consider the development of the Bible and the recording of the Word of God. The Bible emerges as a book, a book that is sacred and inspirational, but nevertheless it is a book. Each of the developments in the history of writing influence the development of the book that we identify as the Bible. As we will see, some developments are very influential, while others do not play as important of a role.

2. What Is the Bible?

The Bible that we hold in our hands today, whether it is a finely bound and leather encased copy or a simple paperback, should not be viewed in the same way that we might look at other books of the same type. The most obvious reason for this assertion would be that the Bible is not the same as other books. Christians recognize and accept the Bible as the Word of God, and therefore sacred (CCC 104). For this reason the Bible is normally placed in a position of honor, often carried in religious processions, incensed, and lifted high before the gathered assembly which then joins their voice in song, "Alleluia, Alleluia," as the assembly prepares to listen to the proclamation of the Word.

The catechism teaches that the "human words" that are collected for us in the Scriptures are the "words of God, expressed in the words of men" (CCC 101). These words are the "divinely revealed realities" (CCC 105), and as such Christians understand "God is the author of sacred Scripture."

There is really no need to go beyond this assertion, but if we were so inclined to do so, another reason that we should not look at a Bible in the same way as we might look at a similar book can be demonstrated. When we hold a Bible in our hands we are not holding a book with many chapters, rather we are holding a book that is the collection of many other "books."

The Bible is a collection of books that have been written over a long period of time. This collection includes not only many different books but also many different kinds of writing. There is poetry, history, stories, and myths. The Bible preserves for us different letters, parables, fragments of proverbs, hymns and songs, and a variety of many other different literary forms. No matter what form the "human words" may take, each word is an expression of the Word of God for us, but it is also helpful to remember, so that we can truly appreciate and understand what we read, that each literary form can offer a different perspective.

For example, it is quite helpful to learn to recognize the difference between a proverb and a parable, because each form has a different purpose. There is also a difference between a letter and a song, or a fragment of historical writing and the retelling of a popular myth. The biblical word becomes even more vibrant for the reader when we take the time to appreciate the literary form in which the Word of God is presented.

What brings all of these different literary forms together into the collection that we identify today as the Bible is the belief that each of the books in the collection testify to the faith, history, and spiritual journey of people whom we identify as our "ancestors in faith." In their stories, in their songs, in their proverbs, and in many other different forms of literature, we recognize our own spiritual journey and path. Another way of looking at the process is to recognize in the process the hand of God, who used all of these different forms of writing, and the talents of many different people, to lovingly "meet his children" and talk with them (CCC 104).

It is also extremely helpful to understand that before there were books that would be gathered together into the Bible, and before God could inspire them to be written down (CCC 105), there were other stages in the development of passing on the "story of faith." Some of these steps preceded the actual writing down of the stories because they occurred before writing was invented and some of the steps occurred after writing became an essential form of communication.

As historians, archaeologists, and Scripture scholars use their God-given talents to study the Word of God and unravel the meaning of the Word for us, a process slowly begins to emerge. Today, as a result of the work of many men and women of faith, we recognize that the first step in the process was the actual event itself, followed by the oral tradition (the recalling of the event for other people to hear and appreciate).

3. The Oral Tradition

We begin with the actual event itself. It is important to remember that the stories, the myths, and the various other forms of expression, all of which are attempts to "pass the story on," are triggered by some kind of event or circumstance. We should assume that whatever "triggers" the need to remember the event must have been important or significant or we could reasonably ask, "Why would anyone bother with it?" This is just an honest evaluation and acceptance of the fact that not everything that happens in our lives as human beings is significant or important, but some specific events, usually not as numerous or dramatic, seem to be well worth remembering.

If the event is important or significant enough the memory of the event is usually shared with other people; if the event is not that important or significant we usually do not share it with others. The way a person normally shares something is through the telling of a story, which means one person orally tells the story, while other people listen to what is being told. When this process happens, another process begins as a result of the storytelling. The people who are listening to the story must also determine if the story is worth remembering. Is it important enough and significant enough, is it humorous, is it sad, does it trigger something within me?

If the story succeeds in being well accepted, for whatever reason, that means that the likelihood of the story being told again increases. It may become a story that the group asks the individual person to repeat again, at some future time—"tell us the story of you being chased by the bear"—because it was humorous and entertaining. Or, it might be a story that is repeated again because it teaches the group something important, or challenges them to think about something, or perhaps is a story that helps them understand something that they believe is important to understand.

Some stories, for example personal stories about a particular person or family, eventually come to a point where they are shared for the last time. When the storyteller dies, the story goes with them. But other stories, especially stories that are more universal in their appeal, or stories that seem to be important or necessary, do not stop being proclaimed and shared when the storyteller dies. These stories emerge into the "collective memory" of the group.

Another way of talking about the "collective memory" of the group is to talk about what historians and scholars have identified as the "oral tradition."

The Bible, since it emerges out of the lived experience of actual people and events, contains within the books of the Bible, stories of faith, that originally were preserved in the "oral tradition" of our faith ancestors. The events that triggered the stories, the decision that the story was important and significant, and the effort that was devoted by the community to remember these stories, all play a significant part in the development of the Bible.

Stories that were originally part of the "oral tradition" would include the stories of Noah and the Ark (Gen 6:9—9:28), the call of Abraham (Gen 12), Jacob wrestling with God (Gen 32:23–33), and all the stories about Moses, the Exodus event, and other such Old Testament references.

One concern that people often experience when they first realize that many of the stories in the Old Testament come from the oral tradition is "Are the stories true?" This reaction is completely understandable because people who are living today, at least people in the well-developed countries of the "First World," do not have the experience of an oral tradition. We are more comfortable with the written word or the word that comes to us through television or radio. Another reaction that we might have to the concept of oral tradition is "How could people remember all of the details, or at least remember them accurately?"

Unfortunately there is no satisfactory means available to us to forcefully demonstrate that the oral tradition is accurate and reliable. Every attempt to do so leads to frustration because the oral tradition is so "foreign" to our experience of life. We have become so dependent on the written word that we find it difficult to even imagine what it might have been like to have lived in a time or place where the written word was not an option.

That being the situation, we are nevertheless left with the fact that the Bible does emerge from the oral tradition. And so what does this mean to us?

The Catholic perspective would suggest that it is not necessarily the details of the oral tradition that are important, but rather it is the overwhelming testimony of God's action on our behalf that is crucial. Again we are reminded that it is the "big picture" that is most important (CCC 1112–114). As people of faith we believe in the realities that are expressed in the stories of the Bible, "which faith allows us to touch" (CCC 170). This faith is then handed on, celebrated in community, and lived.

The testimony of the stories of the Old Testament inform us about what it means to believe in one God, and to love our God with our entire being. The Old Testament stories, indeed all of Scripture, tell us what it means

- to come to know God's greatness and majesty
- to live a life of thankful praise with God
- to know the unity and true dignity of the human person
- to make good use of all created things
- to trust God in every circumstance (CCC 222–227)

It would seem that these values and beliefs are the essential components that have been preserved for us and faithfully handed on.

4. The Written Tradition

As the Bible developed, the oral tradition continued to play an essential role, but another important component also emerged. Again, not so much for any specific theological reason but rather as a result of the development of civilization and the skills and talents available, many of the stories of the oral tradition were written down. More often than not the event that "triggered" the stories to be written down was the result of a crisis.

There were many kinds of crises that were experienced by our ancestors in faith. The most obvious kind of crisis that would provoke the attempt to preserve that which was important to the community would be the experience of war. War is devastating to any community, but in the period of the Old Testament, war often meant that the entire community, and everything valued by the community, was at stake. The ancient concept of "putting to the sword," or the "curse of destruction" (Josh 6:21) meant that the losing side was completely destroyed and, if at all possible, every memory or reference to them obliterated. If they were not destroyed, another option was to send the entire conquered people into exile, far away from their lands, family, and friends (2 Chr 36:17–21). Faced with this kind of threat, it is completely understandable why every attempt to preserve that which was important to the community would be made.

There is an example in the Bible when the efforts of the people to preserve their sacred traditions paid off. In the book of Nehemiah (Neh 8:1–18), we can read about the people who return to Jerusalem after the exile in Babylon, and who discover a scroll of the "Book of the Law." The Word of God, as it is contained in the book, is proclaimed to all of the people, and they reclaim what had been lost during the time of the exile.

There were of course other reasons why the oral tradition was eventually written down. One reason, as writing became more and more essential to civilization, scribes and others began the process of recording important poems, stories, riddles, proverbs, and anything else that was considered important. However, from a perspective of faith, another reason for the effort emerges. As the catechism teaches:

> "To compose the sacred books, God chose certain men who, all the while he employed them in this task, made full use of their own faculties and powers so that, though he acted in them and by them, it was as true authors that they consigned to writing whatever he wanted written, and no more" (CCC 106).

Eventually what occurred, as a result of both human progress and the inspiration of God, was that the written material became quite substantial. After years and years of people collecting and preserving, writing down that which was important, someone, either an individual person or even a group of people, came along and attempted to organize the collection. This next step in the development is referred to as the "edited tradition."

5. The Edited Tradition

Although a casual reader of the Bible might assume that the Bible flows effortlessly from the creation of the world in Genesis, chapter one, through the story of the "end of time" in the book of Revelation, this is not the case. The Bible does not present us with the story of salvation history in a natural progression, with one story building upon another story. The stories of the Bible have been arranged, and the arrangement of the stories is a process that has been agreed upon by rabbis, teachers, and saints over a long period of time. The fact that we can read the Bible and that it captures our attention and imagination in a gripping way is evidence not only of the power of the Word of God, but also evidence of the skill of the editors.

Since the Bible in the format that we have today is representative of hundred of years of development, it should come as no surprise to assert that the Bible had many different editors. We have no idea how many different editors contributed their talent and their skills to the project, but there are telltale signs of many different hands.

In the editorial process the individual editor has specific texts available for their use. For example, the editor might have the individual and collected stories that emerged from the oral tradition, along with songs, poems, riddles and proverbs, and all sorts of other material that they may have collected. As the editor attempts to weave all of these different sources together they must make a decision about what is to be included, and what is not to be included. The decision-making process is usually reflective of the intent and purpose of the editor, or another way of looking at it, "Why is the editor attempting to organize the collected material?"

There are some obvious reasons an editor might begin such a task, and there are other reasons that might not be so obvious. An obvious reason might be that the editor has been assigned the task by a king or some other person in authority. Another reason could be that the editor might simply desire to gather all of the different material that he has on a particular subject into an organized presentation. These are examples of the obvious reasons why someone might devote their talents and efforts to the task of editing.

There are other reasons, some of which that are not so obvious, for editing a text—or even a collection of stories—into the final form that we have before us today. Something as simple as a listing of the "kings of Israel and Judah" might be included, not because the names are important but rather the editor might want to make a particular point or emphasize something that is important. In 1 Kings 12:1—22:53, for example, the final copy points out that the kings of Israel and Judah had not been faithful to the covenant, and suggests that their unfaithfulness is one explanation for the turmoil that they are experiencing.

Another example might be that the people are suffering persecution, and so the editor finds stories in the oral tradition that speak of persecution and suffering: the story of Job is one such example as is Genesis 2:5—3:24 (which is sometimes referred to as the "second creation story"). Once the editor determines which stories will be used, and which stories will not be included, he arranges them in such a way so that the people who read them are provided with hope that their suffering will end, or that their suffering has a wider purpose. The final edited and carefully arranged story clearly makes the point so that no one can doubt the lesson that needs to be learned.

Of course, just because one story or one book has been edited does not necessarily mean that the process is completed. Hundreds of years come and go, and as the years go on and on one piece of edited work eventually might be included in another collection of stories, sometimes being edited again and sometimes included exactly as it was originally edited. When this occurs we are sometimes left with biblical stories that seem to contradict one another (for example Gen 21:22–31 and 26:26–33), but perhaps another way of looking at it is to recognize that it is simply reflective of the editorial process.

6. The New Testament

Up to this point most of our emphasis on the development of the Bible has referenced the Old Testament. A valid question at this point could be to wonder if the New Testament was formed in the same approximate way as the Old Testament. The answer to the question would have to be "Yes." Although the New Testament was formed in a much more compacted period of time than the Old Testament, years as opposed to centuries, the process was nevertheless similar.

The early Christian community believed that the return of Jesus was imminent and so in the first years after the Resurrection there were no written resources available. If someone wanted to know something about Jesus, all that was necessary was to inquire among one of the apostles, who were readily available. However, as time went on and Jesus did not return and the apostles began to die, the primary witnesses to the Resurrection and the teaching of Jesus could no longer be consulted.

The first written references that concerned Jesus, and which would eventually make their way into the Bible, were the letters of the apostle Paul. Eventually, in addition to these letters, the stories, the remembrances, the parables, and other teachings of Jesus, which had been orally passed on and in some instances written down and recorded, were also collected. Eventually many of these collections were included in what today we identify as the gospels. Finally, certain letters and other works, such as the Acts of the Apostles, and the letters of Peter and John, completed the testament.

Just like the Old Testament, the New Testament begins with the oral tradition, progresses to a written tradition stage, and then finally enters into a final edited tradition, which produces the Bible that we know today. The catechism clearly acknowledges and outlines the stages in the formation of the gospels:

- The life and teaching of Jesus
- The oral tradition
- The written gospels

The life and teaching of Jesus: the gospels faithfully present the life and the teachings of Jesus, "until the day when he was taken up" (Ascension).

The oral tradition: the apostles, after the ascension of Jesus into heaven, passed on to the people what they had seen and what they had been instructed and did so with the knowledge given to them as the result of being filled with the Holy Spirit (Pentecost).

The written gospels: the evangelists selected certain elements and instruction from the life of Jesus that would be helpful for the local churches, "but always in such a fashion that they have told us the honest truth about Jesus" (CCC 126).

7. How Did the Bible Become "the Book"?

The process of writing, collecting, and editing over an extensive period of time eventually produced many different books that were viewed as important and sacred, but the concept of gathering such writings into a single collection, the Bible, took many years to develop. A particular community, for example, may have possessed and referenced a scroll that contained the words of the prophet Isaiah, and they may well have been completely unaware of other books or collections. Still other communities may have possessed a more extensive collection of sacred writings, but they would not have viewed the collection as a single unified whole.

Eventually, however, people grew more and more in awareness of other writings and collections, and they also recognized the importance of what had been preserved and collected. This awareness was focused around the year 621 B.C. when the book we identify today as the book of Deuteronomy was discovered and attributed to Moses. Since Moses was recognized as the great prophet and leader of the people (the only prophet to speak to God "face to face," Ex 33:11), the words attributed to Moses were of the utmost importance. This occurrence may also have been the first time that any written word was publicly acknowledged and accepted as the "Word of God."

In the years that followed the discovery of the book of Deuteronomy, other writings that were also attributed to Moses were discovered and reverenced. Eventually, somewhere before the fourth century B.C., the five books of Moses, which today we identify as the Pentateuch and which the Jewish people identify as the Torah, were collected, preserved, and reverenced.

The process, of course, did not end with the development and acceptance of the Pentateuch. Other sacred writings were also identified and slowly became accepted as other examples of the "Word of God." By the first century B.C. a second collection known as the "Prophets" was also routinely acknowledged as the "Word of God." This second collection did not have as much authority as the Pentateuch, but it was nevertheless considered important by most Jewish people, with the exception of the Samaritans and possibly the Sadducees. Finally, probably somewhere around A.D. 66–70, certain rabbis, acknowledged as leaders in the Jewish community, made a final determination of what books would be included and accepted as the Word of God and which books would be excluded.

The process of the formation of the New Testament followed a similar development. The early Christian community in the first century A.D. accepted the "Old Testament" but had not yet determined if any of the Christian writings then circulating were sacred. Because the first century Christian community was eagerly anticipating the return of the Lord there was no sense of urgency to determine such things. However, by the second century, when the community had adjusted its view and realized that the Second Coming was going to be delayed, it was determined that certain Christian writings deserved to be honored and accepted, and therefore used in liturgy and worship as the Word of God. The process was further enabled by the growing influence of the Gentile Christian communities and the lessening influence of the Jewish Christian communities, especially after the destruction of the Temple.

The first person to attempt to organize the Christian writings was a man named Marcion (100–160). He was by most accounts a capable theologian and at times very persuasive, but today he is remembered not as a saint or as one of the Fathers of the Church but rather as a heretic. The reason is because he rejected the Old Testament and insisted that the Christian community accept as their "sacred Scripture" only the Gospel of Luke (without the Infancy Narratives) and approximately ten letters attributed to the apostle Paul. The early community recognized that they could not simply ignore God's action on their behalf before the coming of Jesus, and so they rejected his teaching. However, as a result of Marcion's efforts, it became important for the Church to come to some kind of agreement on what would be included and what would not be included in what we call the New Testament.

In some ways it can be asserted that the New Testament was determined around the year 367, or at least the primary books that make up the testament. However, it can also be asserted that the process was not completed then, because other books were added after 367 (for example Hebrews and the book of Revelation) and still other books were removed as a result of the Protestant Reformation in the sixteenth century.

From the Catholic viewpoint, however, the development of the Bible has been determined and completed. The catechism teaches that the Old Testament is composed of forty-six books (forty-five if Jeremiah and Lamentations are counted as one book) and twenty-seven books for the New Testament (CCC 120). The listing of each of the books of both the Old and the New Testament follow this section.

Although it is true that the Bible becomes "the book" because of the agreement of rabbis, bishops, and others who were entrusted with the task of determining that which was accepted and that which was not, this point might well not fill in all the blanks and provide us with an accurate picture. The Bible became the Bible, and the books of the Bible that were included in the Bible were ultimately included, not only because of an authoritative mandate but perhaps even more importantly because they were used by people of faith. In addition to being used, the books were recognized as authentic (orthodox) presentations of God's Word, which resonated with those who listened to the proclamation of the Word.

As we will see when we briefly review some of the non-biblical writings and texts that were available to people, some of which were considered for inclusion in the Bible but were eventually rejected, there are many different approaches to and interpretations of the relationship between God and his people.

8. The Books of the Old Testament

The listing that follows are the books of the Old Testament, the Hebrew Scriptures, as they are presented in the Roman Catholic Tradition (CCC 120). Books marked with an asterisk (*) would be considered as the Deuterocanonical Books/Apocrypha in Protestant Bibles and would normally not be listed as part of the Old Testament Canon. In Protestant Bibles these designated books would either not be printed in the Bible or printed in a separate section of the Bible clearly identified as Apocrypha.

In addition to the listing of the books of the Old Testament, the standard abbreviation that is used to designate the appropriate book is also provided.

Genesis (Gen)
Exodus (Ex)
Leviticus (Lev)
Numbers (Num)
Deuteronomy (Deut)
The Book of Joshua (Josh)
The Book of Judges (Judg)
The Book of Ruth (Ruth)
The Books of Samuel (1 Sam; 2 Sam)
The Books of Kings (1 Kings; 2 Kings)
The Books of Chronicles (1 Chr; 2 Chr)
The Book of Ezra (Ezra)
The Book of Nehemiah (Neh)

*Tobit (Tob)
*Judith (Jdt)
*Esther (Esth)
*The Books of Maccabees (1 Macc; 2 Macc)
Job (Job)
The Psalms (Ps)
The Proverbs (Prov)
Ecclesiastes (Eccl)/Qoheleth (Qo)
The Song of Songs (Song)
*Wisdom of Solomon (Wis)
*Ecclesiasticus/Ben Sira (Sir)
Isaiah (Isa)
Jeremiah (Jer)
Lamentations (Lam)
*Baruch (Bar)
Ezekiel (Ezek)
Daniel (Dan)
Hosea (Hos)
Joel (Joel)
Amos (Am)
Obadiah (Ob)
Jonah (Jon)
Micah (Mic)
Nahum (Nah)
Habakkuk (Hab)
Zephaniah (Zeph)
Haggai (Hag)
Zechariah (Zech)
Malachi (Mal)

It should also be noted that the Bible of the Greek Orthodox community would include additional books of the approved Old Testament Canon not included in the above listing. The additional texts would include 1 Esdras, the Prayer of Manasseh, Psalm 151, and 3 and 4 Maccabees.

9. The Books of the New Testament

The canonical books of the New Testament (CCC 120) are accepted by all Christian traditions and include the following:

The Gospel According to Matthew (Mt)
The Gospel According to Mark (Mk)
The Gospel According to Luke (Lk)
The Gospel According to John (Jn)
The Acts of the Apostles (Acts)
The Letter of Paul to the Romans (Rom)
The First Letter of Paul to the Corinthians (1 Cor)
The Second Letter of Paul to the Corinthians (2 Cor)
The Letter of Paul to the Galatians (Gal)
The Letter of Paul to the Ephesians (Eph)
The Letter of Paul to the Philippians (Phil)
The Letter of Paul to the Colossians (Col)
The First Letter of Paul to the Thessalonians (1 Thess)
The Second Letter of Paul to the Thessalonians (2 Thess)
The First Letter of Paul to Timothy (1 Tim)
The Second Letter of Paul to Timothy (2 Tim)
The Letter of Paul to the Titus (Titus)
The Letter of Paul to the Philemon (Philem)
The Letter to the Hebrews (Heb)
The Letter of James (Jas)
The First Letter of Peter (1 Pet)
The Second Letter of Peter (2 Pet)
The First Letter of John (1 Jn)
The Second Letter of John (2 Jn)

The Third Letter of John (3 Jn)
The Letter of Jude (Jude)
The Revelation to John (Rev)

10. Non-Biblical Writings and Texts

Not every editorial effort or collection of stories that circulated among the Jewish community or the Christian community made it into the Bible. There are literally dozens of examples of books that seem to present biblical material and deal with subject matter that we might recognize that were not accepted as the inspired Word of God. Each of these books mimics the "look" and the "feel" of the biblical literary form, but they are lacking in a critical component: they are not orthodox in their presentation or they contradict something that the community has identified as important. In still other instances the work was not included in the biblical canon because it fundamentally did not make a significant contribution to the revelation of the relationship between God and his people.

Scripture scholars and other researchers use non-biblical texts and writings in their study of the Bible. For the average reader of the Bible, the person who studies and prays the Bible as the Word of God for their own spiritual growth and development, non-biblical texts and writings are a curiosity. Mention, however, is made in this book because occasional reference to such materials can be unsettling and catch a person by surprise, especially when a reference is made to a non-biblical text in a sensational way. More often that not this kind of sensational reference is made in a news story or documentary which can leave a person with the impression that "something important has been discovered." Occasionally this is true, but more often than not it is essentially misleading.

An example of a discovery of non-biblical texts, along with a treasure trove of biblical writings, that provided quite the sensation and which in fact was important, was the discovery of the Dead Sea Scrolls in 1947. In that year two Bedouin teenagers were tending to their flock of sheep and goats and at the same time were playing around. They were throwing rocks into the many little caves and crevices that pockmark the area around the sea. One of the boys threw a rock into a cave and heard the sound of pottery breaking. The boys then climbed into the cave and discovered not just one ancient piece of pottery but eight very large containers, each of which contained numerous scrolls. The boys had accidentally discovered what turned out to be the ancient library of the Jewish Essene community of Qumran. The Essenes had evidently hidden the library in the caves in order to protect the scrolls from the invading Roman army (approximately A.D. 70). Once this first cave was discovered still others were uncovered, revealing literally thousands and thousands of scrolls and fragments.

The discovery of what is now known as the Dead Sea Scrolls revealed ancient writings that went as far back as the year 300 B.C. This was important because until the Dead Sea Scrolls were discovered the oldest biblical texts were all from around A.D. 1000 and biblical scholars wondered how accurate the copies might be. They discovered, much to their amazement, that the texts from the Middle Ages were remarkably accurate which indicated the great care and concern that had been dedicated to the copying process.

Examples of biblical texts that were discovered in Qumran included the oldest known scroll of the book of Isaiah and extensive parts of most of the books of the Old Testament. Non-biblical texts that were discovered included the Qumran community's *The War of the Sons of Light and the Sons of Darkness* and a book of psalmlike material entitled *Hymns of Thanksgiving.*

Examples of non-biblical writings that a person might occasionally find referenced, writings that emerged from the time of the Old Testament, would include the following:

The Book of Enoch (150–200 B.C.)
The Book of Jubilees (150–125 B.C.)
Testaments of the Twelve Patriarchs (200 B.C.)
Psalms of Solomon (50 B.C.)
Assumption of Moses (A.D. 30–45)
Martyrdom of Isaiah (A.D. 100)
Sibylline Oracles (A.D. 150)

Non-biblical writings and texts are not limited to the period of the Old Testament. There are numerous examples of texts that were used by some members of the early Christian community that were not accepted by the wider community and included in the New Testament.

A good example of such a text is the text known as the *Gospel of Peter.* According to a story attributed to the bishop of Antioch, Eusebius of Serapion (A.D. 190) discovered a Christian community using this gospel. At first he was not concerned, although he was unfamiliar with the gospel, but upon closer examination his concern was quickly manifested, and he forbid the community to use this gospel. What Eusebius discovered was that the *Gospel of Peter,* although it looked like a gospel and read like a gospel, portrayed Jesus as not truly a human person (a heresy today known as Docetism). Of course, this portrayal was in direct contrast to the Christian understanding of Jesus as both truly God and truly man (CCC 520–521).

Other examples of non-biblical texts that circulated among the early Christian community were texts that attempted to "fill in the blanks" concerning the life of Jesus that the four gospels do not inform us about. This lack of information is often referred to as the "hidden life of Jesus" or the "mysteries of Christ's life" (CCC 512–513). It should come as no surprise that some members of the Christian community wanted the mystery to be "solved," and as a result of their curiosity, some attempts were made to do so. Perhaps the most famous of this kind of writing is known as the *Protevangelium of James* (A.D. 150). This "infancy gospel," although it was not included in the canon of the New Testament, nevertheless influenced the popular imagination, particularly many of the popular stories about the Blessed Virgin. In the *Protevangelium* we find the source of the stories about her birth and dedication in the temple, the name of her parents, and also the story about Saint Joseph and how he was chosen to become the husband of Mary and the stepfather of Jesus.

Examples of non-biblical writings that a person might occasionally find referenced, writings that emerged from the time of the New Testament, would include the following:

The Gospel of Thomas (A.D. 150)
The Gospel of the Hebrews (second century)
Acts of Paul (A.D. 160)
Acts of Peter (A.D. 200)
Letter of Barnabas (A.D. 130)
Apocalypse of Peter (A.D. 130)

Probably what is most important to remember is that what is written and preserved for us in the New Testament was set down there "so that you may come to believe that Jesus is the Messiah, the Son of God, and that through believing you may have life in his name" (Jn 20:31; CCC 514). An equally important point to keep in mind when we refer to non-biblical texts is this: if it is not in the Bible it may well be somewhat enlightening, and at times even entertaining, but if it is not within the Old Testament and New Testament canon it is not essential and it is not the inspired Word of God (CCC 120).

PART THREE

How to Read the Bible

Long ago the psalmist prayed, "your word is a lamp to my feet and a light to my path" (Ps 119:105), and perhaps it is in that same spirit that a modern reader of the Scriptures should approach the Bible. In other words, the Word of God that is presented to us within the pages of the Bible can be for each person who spends time "breaking open the Word" an experience of grace. In the communication between God and his people, which emerges from the pages of Scripture, a person can learn to recognize the characteristics and components that are necessary for a personal relationship with the Lord. However, as in all relationships, there is a need to comprehend the "rules" of the communication. To enter into a relationship without some sort of preparation would not be wise, and will often lead to disappointment and frustration.

So it is with the experience of the Word of God. It may sound a little strange at first, but "breaking open the Word" can best be appreciated if the person clarifies their particular purpose and hopes before they read a single word of Scripture.

For example, as you approach the Scriptures, are you intent on simply reading the words on the page, slowly working your way through the Bible one chapter and one book at a time? Or, another example that comes to mind, have you opened the Scriptures because you are intent on studying what they might teach about a particular subject? Or perhaps, your goal is not simply to read the Scriptures or search the Scriptures for counsel and advice, but rather you desire to pray with the words of Scripture and are content to simply let whatever might happen, happen. Hopefully these simple examples illustrate the difference between reading the Scriptures, studying the Scriptures, and praying the Scriptures.

Reading the Scriptures: If your intention is to read Scripture, it is recommended, especially if the Scriptures are unfamiliar to you, not to start with the book of Genesis and work your way through the

Bible, page by page. Unfortunately, a common experience of readers who try this method is that they will soon become bogged down, and often as a result, simply give up. At the same time, don't start with the last book of the Bible either. So very often people begin with the book of Revelation because it seems to be the most "exciting" but they soon get mired in symbols and questions about what they are reading. A good suggestion is to begin with one of the gospels, perhaps the Gospel of Mark, and then perhaps Matthew or Luke. After you spend time in the New Testament and become familiar with the "ebb and flow" of the Scriptures, perhaps you might pick a book from the Old Testament that you find particularly appealing.

Another helpful clue that will enhance the experience is to determine to read one entire section at a time. Most Bibles clearly group the verses into easily manageable sections that are thematic, and are easily identified with bold headings. Don't move on to another section until you are sure that you understand the main point of what you have just read.

Studying the Scriptures: Many times after people devote themselves to a regular practice of reading the Scriptures, soon they discover they want to know and understand more. More often than not this experience may lead them to some sort of Bible-study group or some other kind of educational experience. In such a circumstance there is usually a trained leader that guides the group and enables the learning process.

For Catholics who desire to study the Bible and who desire to study the Bible from a Catholic perspective, it is very important that they join a Catholic Bible-study group. It may be appealing to go with a friend or a neighbor to a Bible-study group that they may already be part of, but it may not be what you expected. It is not that non-Catholic Bible-study groups are something to be feared, but rather it is because of the perspective and the approach to the Scriptures that might be used. (A review of Part One of this handbook might be helpful in clarifying this point.)

For a person who desires to study the Bible and who prefers not to join a Bible-study group, there are many different ways that this goal can be accomplished. For personal study it is very important to choose a Bible that provides a good introduction for each of the books of the Bible, extensive footnotes within the text, and helpful cross-references. (Refer to the section that follows "Different Translations" for help in making a choice that best fulfills your needs.)

In addition to the Bible that is chosen, another helpful tool that enhances Bible study is a *concordance* of the Bible. A Bible concordance provides the reader with an alphabetical listing of all of the words that are used in the Bible. You simply look up the word that you are interested in and the concordance provides you with the appropriate Bible reference(s). In this day and age concordances come in all different shapes and sizes and various price ranges, including helpful electronic formats that speed up the process (see Publishers of Catholic Biblical Resources, Part Ten, for appropriate recommendations).

Praying the Scriptures: Part Seven of this handbook provides a complete description of a method of praying with Scripture that might prove helpful. Readers are referred to this section.

Regardless of whether you are reading the Scriptures, studying the Scriptures, or praying the Scriptures, there are certain additional helpful points that will enhance your experience. The section that follows explains the importance of understanding the historical and literal genre and context of what you are reading, the choice and use of the many different translations of the Bible that are available, and helpful insights into interpreting the Word of God from a Catholic perspective.

1. Keep in Mind the Historical Context

Although it is true that the Bible is chock full of historical references, and at times even reads like a history lesson, in the strictest sense the Bible is not really a historical document. The people who were the instruments of God in compiling and editing the words of the Scripture did so for reasons of revelation and inspiration, not necessarily because they desired to compile a historical record. This is an important perspective to understand (CCC 109–110).

A historical document, at least in our contemporary understanding of history, is representative of the faithful recording of particular facts, dates, people, and events of a particular moment in time. As we read a historical document, we expect that the person who recorded all of the pertinent information is interested in providing the most accurate record possible. In the process of compiling the historical document, other documents that can support the information that is being compiled are often included as part of the historical record, for example, memos, certificates, maps, and anything else that might be useful. Of particular importance are the eyewitness accounts of people who were actually present for the particular event.

The historical record-keeping process and historical documentation of a particular event demands that the collection process takes place simultaneously with the event or in a time period very close to the event. Each day, in fact each moment in time that occurs between the event and the historical documentation process, "clouds" the historical record because of a variety of different reasons. Essential documentation is lost, people begin to forget all of the details, and other such completely normal and expected things occur, all of which makes the process of documentation very difficult.

Admittedly, within the historical process, there is a certain amount of interpretation that is part of the process. For example, the compiler must make certain judgments about the material that is available to them, determining what might be important, and what might be of lesser importance. But again, in our contemporary understanding of the historical process, we assume that this interpretative judgment is based on the facts, at least reflective of the best possible effort that can be devoted to the project.

In a nutshell, that is a brief description of the historical documentation process, a process that a modern-day person "takes for granted" and assumes when they open up a history book and read what is before them. Obviously, when a person reflects on the process, it quickly emerges that this was not the process used in compiling the Bible. The historical documentation tools and processes that we expect were simply not available to the people of biblical times, primarily because they did not have the essential tools of writing, collaborative documentation, eyewitness report procedures, and other such things available to them. The other reason, however, goes beyond the fact that modern historical record-keeping was not an option, and might be even more important. The people of biblical times had other tools that they valued and used, that were available to them, and which reflected their needs and concerns. Or another way of putting it, the people of the Bible do not have the same needs that we have, or even the same understandings that we might have. Something else was at work.

The tools that were available to the people of biblical times, and which they were very comfortable using and understanding, might surprise us, because in our scientific and "just the facts" society, we are unfamiliar with them. However, that being the case, they are nevertheless the tools that were used in telling the biblical story, so we must at least try to understand and appreciate them, so that we can understand and fully appreciate the Scriptures. Tools used by the authors of the biblical story include myth, legend, fiction, allegory, and parables, to name just a few. The next section, "Keep in Mind the Literary Genre and Context," examines some of the tools that were used and that we might not be completely comfortable or familiar with.

A second point that is helpful to understand and to keep in perspective when we try to read the Bible is to remember that a biblical story often has a "history" of its own. In addition to the oral tradition that is an essential component of the transmission process, most of the biblical stories were not just written once, and then passed on intact over time. Instead, what happened more often than not is that in each generation the story was finely tuned and developed. The editor or the compiler of the story, as they read the story in front of them, might suddenly recall a point that was missing or that could now be clarified as a result of his particular perspective, so it would be included.

These additions, or points of clarification, or in some instances a reworking of the story in order to change the emphasis, were not included in order to deceive. Rather, they are reflective of the fact that for many, many years before the Bible became the final "book" that we have before us today, the biblical stories and biblical record was a "living document." It was only after an extended period of time that a particular book of the Bible was considered to be in its final and permanent form.

Again, this attitude and approach to a written document or record is not reflective of "how we do things today." Today, with our modern sensibilities we would not even think of taking a story and sitting down and "rewriting" it, adding and deleting what we understood to be important. However, that is not the way that it has always been, and that is not the perception or attitude of a person of biblical times.

The same perspective and understanding was at work when it came to the question of "who is the author" of a particular book. Again, in our time and place the author of a work is clearly identified but in biblical times it was not at all uncommon to attribute a work to a famous person, sometimes alive and sometimes a person who had been deceased for a very long time. Again, this was not seen as deception but rather it was seen as a way of "honoring" a person or even, on occasion, as a way of claiming their "authority" in order to help the readers understand the importance of what they were reading. Sometimes it was not the named author of the book that was actually the person who wrote it, but rather a trusted friend or a scribe (for example, Baruch, the trusted friend and scribe of Jeremiah). In still other instances the book would be attributed to the person that established, animated, or inspired the community from which the book emerged (the Johannine communities of the New Testament).

Finally, it is important, from the historical perspective, to understand and to appreciate the particular audience for whom the book may have been originally intended. In most instances, because God works through everyday human events and experiences in order to accomplish his will, the author did not know that what they were recording would one day be understood as the revealed and inspired Word of God by millions and millions of people. In each instance, the author was writing with a particular group of people in mind. (Frankly, it was probably better that they did not know, how would they have been able to lift a quill with that kind of responsibility on their mind?)

Knowing the main concerns of the people for whom the biblical word was originally intended helps us appreciate even more what has been written. For example, there is a difference in the invitation to become people of the covenant to the people who were fleeing from Pharaoh's army and the people who were returning from the Babylonian Exile. The people that Moses spoke to were just beginning to understand what Yahweh was capable of doing on their behalf. On the other hand, the people returning from exile needed to be reminded that things could be different for them if they would return to the practices of the Law that they had abandoned. In each instance the Word that is spoken and recorded for us is the Word of God, but the audience who first hears that Word is very different. In addition, by the time we read the Word, thousands of years after the original event, we too are very different people from the people of the Exodus and the people of the Exile, and so therefore we hear and understand the Word in a completely different way.

Keeping in mind the historical context of the Bible is extremely important. An appreciation of how the Word of God has been developed over time increases our understanding and appreciation of the human person's relationship with the Lord. Realizing that God manifests his power and his will powerfully within the limits of human reason and experience, even using our weaknesses and our limitations to accomplish his purpose, is reassuring and lifegiving. The more we understand the process and grow in our appreciation of how God has revealed himself to us, the more powerful the Word of God becomes for us and the more we can trust the Word's witness and testimony.

2. Keep in Mind the Literary Genre and Context

Although it has been stated on more than one occasion in the pages of this handbook, when we open the Bible to read, study, or pray we should recall that it is not a single book, even though it is "packaged" to look like one. The Bible is a collection of many different "books," written and compiled over an extended period of time. The Bible is also a collection of many different genres of writing, some of which are obvious (such as a proverb and a letter) and some of which are not (such as an allegory or a metaphor). With these beginning points in mind we can approach the Bible with the expectation that comes from the knowledge that we have acquired and with an expectation that our experience will be grace-filled.

As we turn the pages of the Bible, we expect to discover and appreciate ancient myths and legends. We learn to recognize and appreciate the inclusion of a proverb or a riddle. We pause to appreciate the words of a song, perhaps permitting ourselves the time to imagine what it might have been like to sing the song for the first time, many years ago.

Understanding the literal genre of what we are reading is very important. In fact, it is a skill that we use every time we sit down to read, even though we might not be consciously aware of the fact that we have developed and used this skill on numerous other occasions, not just when we are reading, studying, or praying the Bible.

For example, when we read the morning newspaper, we do so with a developed sense of the literary genre we identify as "newspaper." We expect and recognize the difference between the literary form known as a news story, a feature article, an editorial piece, and a political cartoon. When we read the newspaper we effortlessly switch from one literary form to another, because we have developed the skill to do so. If someone who does not have the skill to recognize the literary form of what he or she is reading would sit down and read a newspaper without the proper preparation and awareness, he or she would come away from the experience with an entirely different point of view.

The challenge we are faced with when we read the Bible is that we may not have been educated to expect that we are going to have to develop a particular skill in order to fully appreciate and understand what we are reading. Because the expectation is not there, we might be a little surprised to learn that we need to develop a particular skill, but once we know what is expected of us, then we can take the necessary steps to learn what we need to learn.

It might be helpful to recall that this assertion that we need to develop a particular skill in order to read the Bible is very much part of the Roman Catholic tradition. The catechism teaches us that God speaks to humanity in a human way and so the human person must be attentive to what God is revealing to us (CCC 109). However, in order to understand and discover what God is revealing to us, we must "take into account the conditions of their time...and the modes of feeling, speaking, and narrating then current" (CCC 110). In other words, we must learn to recognize and appreciate the literary genres and context of what we are reading.

A second related point is not only to be able to recognize the literary genre that is being used by the author but also to be able to understand the literary context. By literary context we mean learning to ask ourselves the question, "What is the point?" We might ask ourselves why the author chose a particular genre to explain this particular point or try to imagine why the point was made at this junction in the story. Sometimes the particular way the author makes the point might not be that important, but at other times it could be significant. For example, in the Gospel of Matthew (20:1–16) is it significant that the owner of the vineyard instructs his steward to pay all workers one denarius, regardless of how many hours they worked? (A denarius was the standard payment for a full day's work.) How would the story be different if the amount of money paid was not included? Would the main point of the story be the same or different?

For most of us, we do not need to develop a finely tuned or expert understanding of the literary genres that are used in the Bible. It is enough to simply be aware of the fact that different literary genre are used and to be able to recognize a particular type of genre when we see it. Scripture scholars, on the other hand, will often spend a lifetime submerged in the details of literary genre and context (CCC 119). Regardless, in each instance, whether as general reader or Scripture scholar, the time that we spend with the Word of God is a particular gift and a unique experience of the activity of the Spirit of God (CCC 111).

Some of the distinct literary genres that are used in the Bible include myth, legends, etiologies, gospels, parables, and letters. We will briefly look at the difference between each of these literary formats and see what they can teach us.

3. Myths

The first reaction of a contemporary person when they hear the word "myth" is usually to categorize it as "fiction." More than likely this is the result of the fact that we live in a scientific and industrial world and our only real encounters with the mythic component of the human experience is perhaps something that appears on the big screen at the movie theater. As a result of this beginning and deeply rooted bias, the contemporary person has to make a real effort if they desire to discover a different perception.

In ancient times myths—stories that used concrete expressions and a concrete plot, or in other words, expressions, plot, and characterization that were recognizable to the audience—were the primary way people could talk about events and experiences that were important to them but beyond their comprehension. Today we might use psychological theory, theorems of quantum physics, or philosophical musings to express the same kind of concerns and wonderment, not necessarily because they are more accurate or satisfying, but rather because we simply have more options available to us.

With this in mind, perhaps the best way to learn about the importance of myth and how it is used in the Bible to express an important theological point is to briefly look at one of the oldest myths in the Bible, the story of creation (Gen 1:1—2:4). It is generally accepted that this myth examines the question, "How did all of this (the earth, people, animals, and so on) come about?"

The first point that we might recognize about the myth of creation, as we read it, is that the description of the earth is a description that does not accurately reflect what we now understand to be true. We know, because we have been able to observe it as a result of scientific progress: the earth is not flat, but rather round. Again, because of our ability to actually observe the earth, we know that the world does not rest on four pillars and we know that there is no dome in the sky, holding back the "waters that were above the dome" (Gen 1:6–7). Knowing all of this to be true, does that mean that the story in the Bible is not true? (CCC 285).

Another obvious example that comes to mind as we read the story is the literary framework that is used regarding "seven days and seven nights." We know that a day is composed of twenty-four hours. At times the sun is shining, and we designate that period as the "day"; the period when the sun is not shining as the "night." However, it is not until the "fourth day" of creation (Gen 1:16) that the sun and the moon are created, and so how could there possibly be a morning and a night? Does this mean that the story in the Bible is not true?

What happens, of course, is that a person can go through all kinds of gyrations and all kinds of complicated and confusing explanations to try and explain these discrepancies (and there are Christians who attempt to do so), or you can simply accept the story for what it is. The point of the myth of creation is not to provide us with a step-by-step explanation of the process of creation, but rather to inform us that all of what we see and experience has been created. The human person is not the creator, but rather the creator is God. The myth teaches us what is important and essential to know, and it does so in a delightful and a memorable way (CCC 290).

4. Legends

Another literary genre that is used in the Scriptures and that we often associate with "fiction" are legends. Legends have mythic components to them but they differ significantly from myths because legends usually have a concrete historical reference point. In other words, legends usually come from the lived experience of a particular person, or group of people, and often from a particular historical event, such as a great battle or some kind of natural disaster.

Legends usually begin with some sort of oral history, the retelling of the event or the description of the qualities of the individual person. At first, when the story is told, the people who listen to the story are usually people who have some kind of proximate or close relationship with the person or the event itself. However, as time goes on and the story is retold again and again, the audience changes, and the storyteller also changes.

It might be helpful to recall at this point, examples from your own experience of life. For instance, recall listening to the eulogy of a person who has just passed away. More often than not the eulogy stresses only the good things about a person, because none of us really want to be reminded of those things that we did not like or appreciate. If the person who has been eulogized is a person of some significance, certain components of the eulogy are repeated, again and again, upon request at certain memorable times, for example, on the anniversary of their death, or perhaps at the time of a family holiday or celebration.

Eventually, over many years, if there is still an interest in hearing about the person, the oral tradition of the story becomes significantly changed. There are recognizable components in the story, but there are also examples of exaggeration ("he always had a smile on his face, never had a bad day"). In addition to exaggeration, a specific theme or interpretation might emerge ("we always knew that he had some great purpose in life"). And then, depending on the culture and the context in which the story is told, other ingredients that could be considered magical or supernatural could even be added ("he was there, standing in front of me one moment, and the next moment he had just disappeared").

As the story is retold, again and again, especially if the story appeals to the community for which it has been a significant event or experience, it can easily become an example of what we identify as a legend.

Stories that appear in the Bible that might be identified as stories that have legendary components would include the story of the tower of Babel (Gen 11:1–9), Noah and the Ark (Gen 6—9), Joseph in Egypt (Gen 37:2—50:26), Samson and Deliah (Jdgs 13—16), and Jonah and the big fish (Jon 2), to name just a few.

5. Etiologies

Another example of a literary genre that we can routinely discover in the Bible are stories that attempt to explain the origin of something that is familiar and well known. Usually, it is a familiar town, a well, or some kind of geographical marking that is well known, but most people are unaware of how it came into existence or why it might be considered important. Such stories are categorized as etiologies, from the Latin, *aetiologia* ("determining the cause"). A very vivid example of this kind of etiology can be found in the story of the destruction of Sodom and Gomorrah (Gen 19:1–29).

To the people of the period, the ruins of the cities of Sodom and Gomorrah could be plainly seen. Undoubtedly, in their nomadic travels, all sorts of people were aware of the fact that the ruins that they now traveled past were the ruins of a place that they once experienced as vibrant and alive, and which now were scattered and destroyed by the power of an earthquake. "Why," the people asked, "did this evil and destruction fall upon these people?" The biblical story attempts an explanation, an explanation that still resonates with us today: "because the people sinned."

The story of Sodom and Gomorrah contains another example of an etiology within the story itself. In this example there was an unusual rock formation, some distance away from the ruins of the cities, but still providing a clear vantage point from which point the cities could be observed. Again the question was asked, "How did this rock formation originate?" and again, the biblical story provides an answer: "But Lot's wife...looked back, and she became a pillar of salt" (Gen 19:26).

6. Gospels

After a discussion of myth, legends, and etiologies, it might be surprising that we now move on to a literary genre identified as "gospel," but in the simplest definition, a gospel is defined as "a form of writing." However, we must also say that a gospel is a unique form of writing that seems to be peculiar to the Christian community. There is no such thing as a gospel that tells the story of Caesar Augustus, for example, or a gospel that tells us about Plato or Aristotle. There are other forms of ancient writing that inform us about the lives of famous Greek and Roman men, for example, works written by Plutarch and Suetonius, but they are not written in the style of a gospel.

What makes a gospel unique is perhaps best explained by the evangelist John who informs us that the purpose of a gospel is "that you may come to believe that Jesus is the Messiah, the Son of God, and that through believing you may have life in his name" (Jn 20:31) (CCC 124). John's definition also helps us to understand and appreciate the root word for gospel, which comes from the Greek *euaggelion,* which means "good news," or "good announcement."

Because the purpose of the gospel is to announce the good news about Jesus Christ, the evangelists included only those events, circumstances, and details about Jesus that contributed to their stated purpose "so that you may believe." This purpose is distinctly different than the reason why an author might write a biography or a historian might compile a historical record. We might wish that the gospels contained more details and answered more of our questions about Jesus but they do not (CCC 126).

Because the gospels are intended to help us believe "that Jesus is the Son of God," they are not intended to provide us with many details about the life of Jesus (or for that matter about the Blessed Mother, Saint Joseph, and the apostles). An important point that we must understand about the gospels is that they are primarily theological. As theology, the gospels are not literal records of the life and ministry of Jesus, and therefore we will discover that there are some disagreements in the gospels about details. However, the disagreements about the details do not mean that there are disagreements among the evangelists about who Jesus is and what his significance is for each of us. On this point the gospels are in total agreement: Jesus is the Christ, God's Incarnate Son, and the power of God is for the salvation of all people of faith (CCC 124).

Although the gospels are in agreement about Jesus, one of the most obvious differences that we discover about the gospels is that three of the gospels—Mark, Matthew, and Luke—seem to be very similar in style and content (thus the designation "synoptic Gospels"). On the other hand, the fourth gospel, the Gospel of John, seems to stand apart from the earlier synoptic Gospels. This becomes very observable when we compare and contrast them. For example, of the 661 verses that make up the Gospel of Mark, 606 of those same verses appear in the Gospel of Matthew, while 380 appear in the Gospel of Luke. This helps explain the familiar feeling a reader might experience as they read, study, or pray one of the synoptic Gospels.

The Gospel of John, on the other hand, or as it is sometimes named "The Fourth Gospel," is distinctly different. In John's Gospel, the ministry of Jesus takes place almost completely in and around Jerusalem and not predominantly in Galilee. There are no parables in John's Gospel, but there are long theological discourses. John tells us about only a few of the miracles of Jesus, but admittedly each of them are unique. It is John who relates to us the story of Jesus changing water into wine at Cana (Jn 2:1–12), the story of the man born blind (Jn

9:1–38), and the story of raising Lazarus from the dead (Jn 11:1–44). All of these points contribute to the beauty of the gospel, but also set it apart from Mark, Matthew, and Luke.

7. Parables

One of the most powerful literary forms that are present in the synoptic Gospels, a format that is used by Jesus to teach, is the parable. Jesus did not invent parables and there are examples of parables in the Old Testament (2 Sam 12:1–4), but Jesus did use the format effectively and they are certainly identified with him.

A parable can best be defined as a story that is told in order to reveal the truth. Understood in this way there are certain components that are necessary for a parable to be effective. The necessary components would include a comparison, a specific audience, and a challenge.

Comparison: a parable always presents a single, understandable comparison. For example, the kingdom of heaven can be compared to a "farmer who goes out to sow his seed" or to a "mustard seed." Or the "weeds" are compared to the "wheat."

Specific audience: a parable is always related to a specific group of people who are gathered together at a particular place and time, and who can be identified as "the poor," or the "scribes and the Pharisees," or the "tax collectors at Matthew's house."

Challenge: a parable always challenges the audience to do something that is specific, such as a new way of understanding reality (the prodigal son) or a new way of thinking about the power of faith (the mustard seed).

If you read the parables that are found in the synoptic Gospels, and you keep these three components in mind, you will learn to appreciate the power of parables and the effectiveness of the teaching of Jesus. You will also grow in your understanding of why some people acknowledged Jesus as a great teacher, while others simply walked away in frustration and disappointment.

When reading the parables of Jesus another component is often at work. Parables can also be understood in an allegorical sense. In other words, not only is there the message that Jesus intended for the specific audience, there is also a deeper message, or if you prefer, "a second level of meaning," in the parable. For example, read the story of the parable of the sower and the seed in Mark's Gospel (4:3–9). This is the original parable, as told by Jesus. Now read the allegorical interpretation of the parable, also found in the Gospel of Mark (4:13–20), where the second level of meaning, perhaps the "spiritual" meaning of the parable, is revealed.

8. Letters

The final literary genre or form that we will review, but by no circumstances does this mean that we have looked at each and every literary genre that is represented in the Bible, is what we call a "letter." Perhaps of all the different literary genres that we have discussed up to this point, it might be fair to state that most of us are probably comfortable with the format of a letter. Not only have we received letters, but we have also written letters, and as a result have a basic knowledge of the genre.

The letters that are found in the Bible, most of which are attributed to the apostle Paul, for the most part follow the basic outline of a typical Roman and Jewish letter. There is an opening, thanksgiving, message, and conclusion.

Opening: The opening of the typical Roman and Jewish letter identifies the name of the person who sends the letter ("From Paul," Rom 1:1), the person to whom the letter is intended ("God's beloved in Rome," Rom 1:7), and then finally, a greeting ("Grace and peace..." (Rom 1:7b).

Thanksgiving: After the greetings it was customary to give thanks, usually for some kind of specific reason, for that which the author is particularly grateful, for example, "because your faith is proclaimed throughout the world" (Rom 1:8).

Message: The message that follows is that which makes up the main content and subject matter of the letter. In the example of the Letter to the Romans, it is quite an extensive message (Rom 1:16–16) or in the Letter to Philemon, quite brief (Philem vs. 8–22).

Conclusion: The conclusion of the letter usually contains some sort of additional greetings and blessings: "I commend to you our sister Phoebe" (Rom 16:1); and often a wish for good health. Paul would often end the letter with a prayer (Rom 16:25–27).

The format and the discipline of the letter genre permitted the writer to take the necessary time that they needed to develop their thoughts. There is a certain pace to the writing of a letter that encourages a more thoughtful approach, and also the ability to review what has been written and determine if that is what you really intend to say. For this reason a letter can often be much more thought-provoking and detailed, constructed to teach, explain, exhort, or encourage.

Of course, and at this point it comes as no surprise, not all of the writings in the New Testament that are identified as a letter are truly letters, and not all of the letters identified with the apostle Paul, or

James, or John, were in fact written by the apostles named. For example, although the Letter to the Hebrews is identified as a letter, upon closer examination we realize that it is not. It doesn't really have the "feel" or the "sense" of a letter. Many Scripture scholars believe that it is probably better categorized as a "homily" or a "sermon." In other words, the Letter to the Hebrews has its roots not in the discipline of a letter but rather in the distinctly different style and presentation of a rhetorical and carefully constructed sermon that was first preached and then recorded.

Scripture scholars are in general agreement that the letters of the apostle Paul, listed here in the order that they were written, include: 1 Thessalonians, Galatians, Philippians, 1 Corinthians, 2 Corinthians, Romans, and Philemon. The letters that are attributed to the apostle Paul, but which were most likely written by a close associate or disciple, include: 2 Thessalonians, Ephesians, Colossians, 1 and 2 Timothy, and Titus.

9. Different Translations

Unless you are reading the Scriptures in Latin or Greek, what you are reading is a translation. Actually, if you are reading the Bible in English, for example, you are in fact reading a translation of a translation. The original language of the biblical story was Ugaritic, Aramaic, Hebrew, Greek, and other languages, long before the stories were collected into the Hebrew Bible, the Greek Septuagint, or the Latin translation of the Greek text.

Translations, although they permit the reader to read the text in the vernacular, no matter how good they might be, seldom succeed in actually capturing completely the original and full meaning of the text. A good way to illustrate this is to recall those occasions when you might watch a captioned foreign film. As you read the captions, dutifully appearing at the bottom of the screen, "translating what is being said," you soon sense that "you are missing out on the real story." Even if you have the words, it is difficult to accurately match the words with the feelings and the emotions that are being expressed. You leave such a captioned film with an appreciation for what you have just seen, but also with the knowledge that you didn't enjoy the full nuanced presentation. As it is with films, so it can be with Bibles.

Since most of us are never going to read the Scripture in the original language, we are always going to be dependent on the translation, and as a result, the choice of the translation that we use is of the utmost importance. In a sense, when we choose a translation, what we are doing is affirming the skills, the perspective, the dedication, and the purpose of the people who were entrusted with the translation process. For this reason it is helpful to learn at least a few pertinent facts about the different translations of the Bible that are available.

For many people the choice of a translation unfortunately will be made not based on the text, but rather based on the packaging. For example, they want a "pocket bible," or a "bride's bible," or a "family bible," in order to meet a particular need or circumstance. If a choice of a Bible is based on the packaging, then the translation really becomes secondary. Still others will chose a Bible because it is advertised as the "Catholic edition" or because it has an imprimatur. Again, in this instance, the choice of the translation is secondary. However, if you are actually going to read, study, or pray the Bible, it might be worthwhile to take a few extra steps in the selection process, and choose a Bible that you find appealing, and that you know that you will actually read.

Revised Standard Version: The RSV, published by Oxford University Press (1952/1962), along with the NRSV (the New Revised Standard Version, 1989), is a popular choice. The reason the RSV is identified as the "revised" version is that it is a revision of the King James Version (KJV, 1611) of the Bible which has been the standard "Protestant" version of the Bible since the time of the Reformation. The RSV has a familiar "feel" and "tone" to it, although at times it can be a little jarring to modern readers because of some of the antiquated words and expressions that are used. The NRSV is very sensitive to gender-specific language, sometimes referred to as "inclusive" language.

New International Version: The NIV, published by the International Bible Society (1978/1984) is a popular ecumenical edition of the Bible. It is somewhat more traditional that the RSV, probably reflective of the fact that it was produced by a group of biblical scholars, reacting to the "less than enthusiastic" reception that the RSV edition received from conservative Protestant individuals and congregations who feared that the RSV might have strayed too far from the original KJV.

New American Bible: This edition of the Bible, published by the Confraternity of Christian Doctrine (1970), is most familiar to Catholics. The Lectionary that is used in the Liturgy of the Word at Mass often uses the NAB translation, and so this is the translation that we hear proclaimed from the pulpit. The New Testament and the psalms have been revised (1991), and the Old Testament is currently under revision. The NAB is sensitive to gender-inclusive language, whenever the reference is to a human person, but retains the traditional language and expressions used in reference to God.

The New Jerusalem Bible: A favorite of students of the Bible because of its extensive footnotes and references, and of those who use the Bible for prayer because of its poetic language. The NJB is a translation of the French edition of *La Sainte Bible* (1966). The NJB is published by Doubleday (1985).

Christian Community Bible: This Bible is the first-ever Bible translation from the developing world and is well known in Latin America, Asia, Africa, and Oceania. The text introduces the reader to the language, the expressions, and the feelings of the poor and the oppressed. The extensive margin notes and introductions to each of the books of the Bible provide a clear and insightful historical context for the Word of God. Published by Claretian Publications (Philippines) and Liguori Publications (United States), 1995.

One other translation of the Bible should be noted here, more for a historical perspective than anything else. Just as many Protestants viewed the King James Version of the Bible as the "authorized text" of the Bible, Catholics often viewed the DousayRheims-Challoner as the "authorized text." This version of the Bible was based on the Latin Vulgate as required by the Council of Trent. However, in 1943, with the encyclical by Pope Pius XII, *Divino Afflante Spiritu,* which encouraged translations of the Bible from the original language, this particular translation was slowly replaced with translations that were more in line with the directives of the encyclical.

In addition to particular translations of the Bible there are other resources available to the general reader which are more appropriately identified as a paraphrase of the biblical text. These resources attempt to present the Bible in a more popular style, a style that might be more appealing to the reader. Since they are not translations of the text, these "bibles" are seldom used for worship or for biblical study. They include *The Living Bible* and the *Reader's Digest Bible,* to name just two.

10. Interpreting God's Word Today

You have chosen your Bible and you have determined if your primary purpose is to read, study, or pray the Bible. You have familiarized yourself with the basics of Bible exegesis (determining the literary genre, historical context, and so on) so you know what to expect. You have taken all of the preparatory steps that are necessary and recommended. Now what?

The next step in your spiritual journey, in your relationship with God, is to "break open the Word." In the words of the catechism, "the Father who is in heaven [now] comes lovingly to meet his children, and talks with them" (CCC 104). But as you break open the Word, and as you reflect on the Word of the Lord, you will also enter into a process that is called "interpretation." In other words, the Scriptures are meant to communicate God's will, teaching, direction, and encouragement to his people, and God's people are asked to "apply" what they have heard. This process of "applying what we have heard" means that we will interpret the Word for our time and place, our need and circumstance. It is also the experience of what the catechism identifies as "the incarnate and living" Word of God (CCC 108).

As we have previously noted, interpretation of the Word of God is really "where the action is," and because of this "action" there is potential not only for growth but also perhaps for other experiences that might not be so helpful. The Church is concerned about interpretation of the Scriptures because of the experience of the Church in history. One specific historical concern is that the interpretation of the Word of God should not be too narrow or confining (review Part One of this handbook, particularly "Sacred Scripture in the Life of the Church"). On the other hand, the Church does not desire to constrict or limit, as it once did, the experience of the People of God being nourished by the Word, for as the catechism teaches, "ignorance of the Scriptures is ignorance of Christ" (CCC 133).

There are four main areas where the interpretation of Scripture seems to produce the most "headlines" and where all Catholics should as least pay close attention. They include the interpretation of Scripture as it applies to issues of Church dogma and tradition, the interpretation of Scripture as it applies to issues of the moral life (lifestyle), and issues that are routinely grouped under the heading of "inclusive language." The fourth area of concern is the subject we refer to as "fundamentalism," which merits an entire section of its own (which follows this section). These four main areas are not the only areas of concern, but they do seem to attract the most attention and the most enthusiastic debate.

Dogma and Tradition: A quick review of Church history reveals that there are changing and constantly shifting questions about Church dogma and tradition. A quick journey back to the Council of Trent (sixteenth century) reveals that much of the discussion centered around certain dogmatic teachings and sacraments of the Church (the Council defined seven sacraments), and related issues of authority and jurisdiction. Today, however, the main dogmatic issues that seem to preoccupy people, and which have many people turning the pages of the Scriptures, have to do with questions more reflective of the concerns of the twenty-first century, or at least concerns of the twenty-first century in the developed world. Perhaps the dominant dogmatic question concerns the place and role of woman in the Church, specifically the question about the ordination of women. "What does the Bible say, and what is God's will for us in this matter?"

As we know this in not an issue that is limited only to the Catholic Church; it has been debated, prayed about, and interpreted by other Christian traditions in a variety of different ways.

Obviously the questions about the role of woman in the Church and of the ordination of women are well beyond the scope of this book, but it is a wonderful debate and concern for all Christians. However, what is within the subject matter of this handbook, and which can be useful and perhaps even enlightening for Catholics, is that this debate clearly illustrates an important Catholic position:

we are not only people of the Word, but we are also people of the Tradition (CCC 95). In other words, the question itself reveals at least a partial answer and insight into the particular perceptions and interpretations of the community itself.

Moral life and lifestyle: Seemingly modern questions about morality that send people once again to the pages of Scripture for some sort of enlightenment and direction include all the issues about the sacredness of human life (abortion, euthanasia, the death penalty). Other issues that our society might identify as "lifestyle issues," such as the question of homosexuality, and other "hot-button" issues, also send people to the Bible for clarification. Some of these issues will have some kind of biblical reference, while others are not mentioned. Still others seem to be referenced, but there is often fierce debate about the context and the meaning of the words of Scripture.

As individual Catholic readers of Scripture search the pages of the Bible for answers and insights, and as they wrestle with the interpretation of the Word of God, they are also reminded of the role of the magisterium, the teaching authority of the Church in these matters. Catholics look to the pope and to their bishops when seeking interpretation and understanding of "truths contained in divine Revelation or having a necessary connection with [it]" (CCC 88). Very modern problems and concerns bring us face to face with long held convictions and realities.

Inclusive language: Not to infer that the issues named above are not important, but it seems that the topic that provokes quite a bit of animated conversation is the issue that concerns the use of language in the sacred text. It seems that almost everyone has an opinion about their particular viewpoint of how language is used, of what is important and what might be less of a concern.

For example, for centuries people heard or read the words of Paul's

Second Letter to the Thessalonians, "We must always give thanks to God for you, brothers" (2 Thess 1:3), without thinking twice about it. Today, however, those same words can provoke all kinds of responses, depending on the audience. For some, "brothers" is easily translated into a concept that includes both male and female, while for others, it is a gender-specific designation that eliminates all females. In this instance, the Scripture must be adjusted to read, "we must always thank God for you, brothers and sisters."

Not only is the use of inclusive language something that demands the addition of "brothers and sisters," but some go even farther and argue for the elimination of male-dominated language used in reference to God. As example of this change would be the change in wording of the traditional doxology, "Father, Son, and Holy Spirit," to "Creator, Redeemer, and Sanctifier."

This discussion of the use of language generates far more energy than the discussion that followed the elimination of the "thees and thous" and the change from "Holy Ghost" to "Holy Spirit" that occurred several years ago, soon after the liturgical reforms of the Second Vatican Council.

Again, a discussion of the use of inclusive language goes far beyond this handbook, but again it does help to underline the importance and the role of interpretation, as it applies to the Word of God and the sacred text.

11. God Said It, I Believe It: Fundamentalism

Throughout the pages of this handbook the Catholic perspective of the sacred Scriptures has been outlined. Again and again we have referred to the role of Scripture and Tradition in the Catholic understanding of God's revelation. We have repeated the teaching of the catechism that urges all Christians to be "attentive to the content and unity of the whole Scripture" and the necessity of reading the Scripture within "the living Tradition of the whole Church" (CCC

112–113). Finally, we have presented well-accepted conclusions and interpretations of the Scriptures, based on commonly agreed upon tools of exegesis, all with the intention of presenting a balanced and integrated handbook for the studying, reading, and praying of the Word of God.

There is, however, another approach to the Bible that is distinctly different from what we have presented.

Biblical fundamentalism teaches that the Bible is *inerrant*, or in other words, contains no errors whatsoever—scientific, historical, or spiritual. Biblical fundamentalism teaches that the Bible, because it is God's Word, must be viewed as literally true in all things.

From this perspective, a biblical fundamentalist would accept as literally true the creation story in the book of Genesis. A biblical fundamentalist would insist that the world as we know it was created in seven days, exactly as the Bible teaches. As a result of this conviction, a biblical fundamentalist would reject, or at least hold in great suspicion, such commonly accepted viewpoints of modernity, such as the theory of evolution, as being incompatible with the Word of God.

Although it would be quite easy, and perhaps even somewhat enlightening, to provide other examples that would illustrate the subject, it would seem that this one, single reference might suffice.

In order for a viewpoint such as biblical fundamentalism to be held, despite all evidence to the contrary, there must be something in the viewpoint that is appealing, or at least reassuring. Some people suggest that fundamentalists simply prefer that the world be "black and white" or "well-ordered and managed," and if you cannot find that viewpoint in the Bible, the Word of God, where else would you look for an answer?

Perhaps biblical fundamentalism is reflective of the desire for clarity, or perhaps it is reflective of some other strongly held conviction. Or perhaps it is simply the perspective and the viewpoint that a person has been taught and experienced their entire life, and there is no compelling reason to change. Human beings often seem to resist change, and to seek an entirely different system of perception and interpretation would be a significant change.

We could leave this subject at this point, and do so with some sense of understanding. However, to do so would to be less than forthright, for there is another side to the fundamentalist perspective.

As we have stated, Catholics on the whole are not biblical fundamentalists. Our official teachings, as outlined in the catechism and which we have examined here, consistently present a viewpoint that would welcome exegesis and support further study and scholarship. However, that does not mean that Catholics are not fundamentalists in other "non-biblical" viewpoints, or people that hold for the inerrancy of the Word of God manifested in some other way.

Catholics, in fact most religious traditions, hold some kind of fundamental position that they consider to be inerrant, unshakable, and unchanging. For Catholics, the place to discover fundamentalism is not the Scriptures, but it can be found in the Tradition, specifically in what the catechism identifies as the "charism of infallibility" (CCC 890). Catholics believe that the certainty of truth can be discovered in the teaching authority of the pope in union with the bishops in what is called the magisterium of the Church (CCC 888–892).

Many of our non-Catholic brothers and sisters, who do not understand or appreciate the Catholic understanding of authority, shake their heads in wonder and disbelief when the pope speaks and the community accepts his teaching. Their reaction is not unlike our reaction when we shake our heads in wonder and disbelief when a biblical fundamentalist faith community makes an authoritative decision or judgment from their faith tradition.

PART FOUR

Salvation History

The scriptural story of salvation history begins with the book of Genesis and the creation of the world and concludes with the book of Revelation, also known as the Apocalypse (CCC 120). In the pages between these two books are the stories, the history, the successes, and the failures, but most of all the ordinary and sometimes extraordinary people whose spiritual journey is presented to us for our inspiration and guidance. Not every story and not every encounter with God has been recorded but certainly many of those encounters that have been generally accepted as important and significant have been preserved in the pages of Scripture.

If a person is so inclined to do so, and many people have certainly been so inclined, it is possible to read the Bible from the very first story of Genesis all the way through to the end. As a person reads the words of Scripture, their personal sense of the communication between God and humanity as it is played out in the events and experiences of the biblical story becomes more and more clear. Certain powerful themes emerge, such as the faithfulness of God, in spite of human sinfulness and the significance and the power of the Christ event personified in the person of Jesus, the Son of God. It is possible to discover in the words of Scripture hope, to experience an understanding of your personal relationship with the Lord, and to understand in context the particular teachings of the Lord.

What follows is a thematic overview of what can be understood as the history of salvation (the biblical story of the relationship between God and humanity). This thematic overview is presented as a capsulated introduction and overview of salvation history and perhaps as a helpful aid to Bible study and appreciation. In the overview not only is the biblical story presented but also, where appropriate and necessary, references to the Scriptures, including cross references, and references to the catechism are provided in the hopes that this additional information might enhance the review.

Although we use the term "salvation history," it is helpful to recall that when we read the Bible we are reading about historical events and experiences presented from a "faith perspective." The people who passed on the stories of the Bible were not necessarily interested in preserving a historical record but were primarily motivated to pass on a theological reflection and interpretation of the historical events. If some particular event or experience or even something as simple and unassuming as a particular number or descriptor would contribute to the theological "punch" of the story it would be included; if it did not contribute it would not necessarily be included. For this reason, as we read the stories, we might sometimes be struck by what seems to be an obvious exaggeration, for example, the whole span of Abraham's life was "one hundred seventy-five years" (Gen 25:7). From a historical perspective we would expect that some birth record or other document would support this assertion; from a faith perspective we understand that this means that Abraham lived a long and a blessed life because of his relationship with God.

Another way of appreciating this truth is explained in the catechism, in a section entitled "The senses of Scripture" (CCC 115–117). In this section the catechism teaches that there are two senses of Scripture, the literal sense and the spiritual sense. The literal sense is understood as "the meaning conveyed by the words of Scripture," dependent on what we know from our study of the Bible and the complimentary sciences, such as archeology, cosmology, history, sociology, and other related areas of expertise. The spiritual sense can be understood in three ways: allegorical, moral, and anagogical.

The allegorical sense of Scripture means that we can read a particular scriptural story and recognize within the story the significance of the Christ event. For example, the crossing of the Red Sea can be understood as an allegory of Christian baptism (Ex 14:15–31).

The moral sense of Scripture means that we can refer to a particular Scripture reference and discern from the directive, "how to act justly," as Saint Paul teaches us (1 Cor 10:11). An example of the moral sense of Scripture can be found in the teaching of Jesus concerning divorce (Mk 10:1–12).

The anagogical sense of Scripture means that we can refer to a particular Scripture reference "in terms of their eternal significance." For example we can think of the Church on earth as a sign of the heavenly Jerusalem, the kingdom that is to come (Rev 21:1—22:5).

1. Introduction to the Law (Torah)

The first five books of the Bible are collectively referred to as the Torah (in Hebrew, "instruction") or as the Pentateuch (in Greek, "five"). No matter how these first five books are identified they should be viewed as perhaps the most important books of the Old Testament since they inform the reader what it means to be chosen by God and how a person should live as a member of God's family.

Traditionally the first five books of the Bible are attributed to the authorship of Moses, perhaps because he is the dominant human personality. However, to hold that Moses wrote these books introduces all sorts of problems, the most obvious of which is that there is often disagreement over the order of events and circumstances, disagreements that probably would not occur if the story was being seamlessly told by one person. The other reason that argues against the authorship of Moses is that occasionally something is included that Moses could not have written, for example the description of his own death (Deut 34:5–12).

Modern-day scholarship is in agreement that there were probably four distinct authors, each providing their own insight and expertise, as they listened to the Word of God active in their lives. The four authors are routinely described as J (material associated with the name of Yahweh); E (material referring to God, in Hebrew "Elohim"); D (material found only in the book of Deuteronomy); and P (material having to do with the Law or with priests, by far the largest portion of the text).

PRE-HISTORY
(Gen 1—11)

The Bible begins with the book of Genesis (Hebrew, "in the beginning") and with the well-known stories of the Bible that most people can easily recall. It is in the first eleven chapters of the Bible that we hear the stories about the creation of the world, the story of Adam and Eve and their fall into sin. We hear about Cain and Abel, Noah and the flood, the tower of Babel, and other such interesting and engaging tales. As we read these stories, full of drama and unexpected plot twists, we are left with the overall impression of the creative power of God and the relationship between the Creator and his favorite creation: the human person. That is exactly the point of the stories and that is the theological perspective that the Bible offers us.

A helpful perspective in reading the first eleven chapters of Genesis is to remember that what is being presented is religious mythology. By asserting that these stories are mythological does not mean that they are not true; in fact they are profoundly true, presenting theological truths of great importance. What is important is to remember, and what the Bible is teaching us, is not that God created the world in seven days (a literal interpretation), but rather that God created the world (a theological truth). In addition the first eleven chapters teach us about human life, death, sin, faithfulness, and other important subjects.

The catechism offers a helpful perspective and teaching that clarifies the Catholic understanding of sacred Scripture and seems especially important to understand the context of the first twelve chapters of the book of Genesis.

> In order to discover *the sacred authors' intention*, the reader must take into account the conditions of their time and culture, the literary genres in use at that time, and the modes of feeling,

speaking, and narrating then current. "For the fact is that truth is differently presented and expressed in the various types of historical writing, in prophetical and poetical texts, and in other forms of literary expression" (CCC 110).

THE STORY OF THE PATRIARCHS
(Gen 12:1—50:26)

The stories of Abraham, Isaac, and Jacob (Israel), along with the stories of the strong and faithful women who were their companions—Sarah, Rebecca, and Rachel—introduce us to semi-nomadic Bedouins to whom the call of God was given. These people of the Old Testament (tenth–sixth centuries B.C.) were men and women who lived in a land where there were distinct and fiercely proud tribes, cultures, and the many and varied household gods to whom these people related. It was in this atmosphere that we are told of the call of Yahweh given to Abraham, the response of Abraham and his kinsmen to this call, and the covenant that was sealed. As a result of different expressions of the power of God, for example, making Sara, the wife of Abraham, who had been infertile pregnant with a child, these people slowly embraced the notion of what today we identify as monotheism, the belief in one God.

Again the stories are full of action, complete with the details of a lifestyle that is mostly unknown to us in the modern world. The stories speak of values, and the struggles and sacrifices necessary to secure these values, in a manner that we can understand, because the people are people with whom we feel a common bond. Our lives are not the lives of Bedouins, but are lives of struggle, desiring to follow the will of God as we understand it and as it is revealed to us.

Chapter 22:1–19, for example, tells the story of Abraham and Isaac. From archeological discoveries we have learned that it was not uncommon among the people of that time and place to sacrifice to their god their firstborn son as a sign of their total devotion. Abraham perceived that this was something that was required of him, and he was prepared to demonstrate his commitment to Yahweh by sacrificing Isaac. The story does not unfold in the manner that the people who first heard it might have expected, for Yahweh is not a God who will demand such a sacrifice. The relationship between Abraham, his descendants, and Yahweh (including the price of the covenant and the promise) will not include human sacrifice. The story concludes that Abraham learns something important about Yahweh, and Yahweh "learns" something important about Abraham. As a result of this action, and the experience as it unfolds, we too learn something about our relationship with God.

The book of Genesis presents four significant points that the catechism underlines as important foundation stones for the spiritual journey. The first point is that God has revealed himself to us and that revelation has not been destroyed by sin (CCC 54–55). The second point that God established a covenant with Noah, a covenant that was in force until the proclamation of the Gospel by Jesus (CCC 56–58). The third and fourth points are that God chose Abraham (CCC 59–61), and it is through Abraham that God began the formation of his people, Israel (CCC 62–64).

THE EXODUS EVENT

(Ex 1—40)

The book of Exodus (Hebrew, "names"; Greek, "journey") is essentially a story about Yahweh, the people who are oppressed, and the victory that God will give to those who suffer oppression. In the forty chapters of Exodus we read about events that took place around 1250 B.C. We learn that the people of Israel are oppressed in Egypt. We are introduced to the great lawgiver of the Old Testament in the person of Moses. We read of the struggle with Pharaoh and the departure from Egypt, and finally the experience in the wilderness and at the mountain of God. Each of these events are described with the details of God's action on behalf of the people, including the familiar stories of Moses and the burning bush (3:1–6), the ten plagues inflicted on Pharaoh and Egypt (7:14—10:29; 12:29–30), the first celebration of the Passover (12:1–28), the crossing of the Red Sea (14:21–31), and the presentation of the Ten Commandments to the people (20:1–17).

The allegorical symbols of the book of Exodus are numerous and it is all but impossible for a Catholic to consider the Exodus events without reference to the sacramental life of the Church. Saint Paul, in 1 Corinthians 10:1–11, speaks about the Exodus event as a type of baptism, with all of the people eating the same spiritual food, and drinking the same spiritual drink, references to manna (Ex 16:21–23) and to the water that flows from the rock at Meribah (Ex 17:6). Jesus also makes a direct reference in his teaching to the manna in the desert when he exclaims, "my Father...gives you the true bread from heaven...I am the bread of life" (Jn 6:31–35).

However, for Christians, the most important event recorded in the pages of the book of Exodus is the night of the first Passover. Christians believe that the commemoration of the Passover feast, celebrated each year in anticipation and expectant longing, has been made perfect in the Passover of Jesus. It is in the Passover of Jesus, foreshadowed by the Passover of the Jewish people so long ago, that God's saving plan "was accomplished 'once for all' by the redemptive death" of Jesus Christ (CCC 571).

LAWS FOR HOLINESS
(Lev 1–27)

The book of Leviticus, the shortest book of the Pentateuch, presents a collection of laws that refer to the festivals, celebrations, and sacrifices of the ancient people of Israel. The main concern of the book is to promote and ensure holiness. The Holiness Code (Lev 17:1—26:46) is the core of the book, providing the reader with one understanding of holiness from an Old Testament perspective, that is "to be set apart." Determinations of "clean" and "unclean," "pure" and "impure," are very important considerations in this book.

IN THE WILDERNESS

(Num 1—36)

The book of Numbers is about the wanderings in the desert after the liberation from Egypt and before the entrance into the Promised Land. The book does contain quite a few numbers, specifically the concerns for the "numbering of the members of each tribe," or a census as we might determine it today. But the dominant theme of the book is the description of many of the events and circumstances of the forty years of wandering experienced by the people. As the story unfolds we are left with a real appreciation of the hardships that were endured by the people as they journeyed: the desert becomes a real symbol of what it means to be tested and tried in faith.

A powerful Christian symbol can be found in the story of the bronze serpent (Num 21:4–9). In Saint John's Gospel this story (Jn 3:14) is presented as a foreshadowing of the power of the cross of Christ, "as Moses lifted up the serpent in the wilderness, so must the Son of Man be lifted up." In addition to this story, a powerful and poignant blessing can be discovered in chapter 6:24–26.

THE LAW GIVEN AT MOUNT SINAI

(Deut 1—34)

The book of Deuteronomy presents itself as the record of the instructions given by Moses to the people of Israel on the plains of Moab before they enter the Promised Land. The book recalls how the Lord powerfully acted on behalf of the people by helping them defeat different kings, challenges the people to follow the Law as it has been presented to them, clearly making the point that there is only one way to please God, and finally, urges the people to remain committed to the covenant, which will lead to life and to reject those ways that lead to death. The book concludes with the appointment of Joshua as the successor of Moses while at the same time beautifully summing up the contribution of Moses with the declaration: "Never since has there arisen a prophet in Israel like Moses, whom the LORD knew face to face" (34:10).

For Christian readers, the sacred prayer of the Jewish people, the Sh'ma Israel (6:4–9), "Hear O Israel: The LORD is our God, the LORD alone" and the explanation of why the people had been chosen by God (7:7–8), "because the LORD loved you," are two important scriptural truths.

2. Introduction to the Historical Books

The designation of the books of the Bible that we identify as "historical" is a Christian designation; the Jewish tradition would identify these books with the prophets. They are designated as historical books because they deal predominantly with the history of the Chosen People from their settlement in the Promised Land, through the time of the Judges up until the establishment of the monarchy, and into the destruction and division that followed the reign of King David and Solomon. The story continues about the divided kingdoms and the struggle to remain faithful to Yahweh, the period of the exile into Babylon, and then the return to Judah and Jerusalem and the rebuilding of the Temple and the renewal of the covenant.

An expectation might be that the historical presentation would continue uninterrupted, perhaps up until the time of Jesus, but that is not the case. Immediately after the story of Queen Esther, as the books are presented, and historically after the return from the Babylonian Exile, there is a break in the story for a period of approximately three hundred years. This time can best be described as the period in which Israel is occupied by various foreign powers, whatever country was the dominant power of the time. This domination is broken for a very short time by the period that is known as the Maccabean Revolt (approximately 180–132 B.C.), the period from which the last two historical books of the Old Testament emerge.

JOSHUA, THE SUCCESSOR OF MOSES
(Josh 1—24)

The book of Joshua tells the story of how the people, under the leadership of Joshua, take possession of the land of Israel, including the well-known story of the battle for the city of Jericho (6:1–21). Joshua is portrayed as a great military leader, but even more importantly, as a man who follows the will of God to perfection. Because Joshua is faithful, the people are successful.

Modern readers might struggle with some of the realities of the ancient world, including the understanding of the people of the time for a concept that we might identify as "holy war." Modern sensibilities do not easily accept a notion that God would demand the wholesale slaughter of human beings (6:21), but for the people of that time and place it was a reality and an expectation. Catholics will contrast the biblical notion with the teaching of the Church as it is found in the catechism, recognizing in the contrast the slow development and appreciation of the Word of God as it is understood and accepted:

> "Every act of war directed to the indiscriminate destruction of whole cities or vast areas with their inhabitants is a crime against God and man, which merits firm and unequivocal condemnation" (CCC 2314).

FROM JOSHUA TO THE MONARCHY
(Judg 1—21)

The "judges" of Israel, whose stories are collected in the book of Judges, are not government officials as the name might suggest, but rather charismatic men and women who were acclaimed for their wisdom and leadership. These men and women would be "raised up by God" when the occasion warranted it, such as when the people strayed away from the covenant or when they were faced with an outside threat. The twelve judges include people who are not well known, such as Othniel and Shamgar, and others whose stories are very well known, such as Samson (13–16) and Gideon (6:11—8:32). The judges were active in Israel between the death of Joshua and the establishment of the monarchy, roughly from the period of 1100–1000 B.C.

For Christian readers, the book emphasizes how easy it is for people to forget the presence of God in their lives and to be distracted by other events and circumstances. The people of Israel, even though God has so powerfully acted on their behalf, nevertheless constantly struggled with the temptation to turn away from Yahweh and to turn to some other God, or to place their trust in some other way. Even though it is a story of events and circumstances of thousands of years ago, the truth of the temptation and the struggle to remain faithful to God can be appreciated by modern readers.

A ROMANTIC INTERLUDE
(Ruth 1—4)

This short story, following the book of Judges and preceding the books of Samuel, presents the love story of Ruth and Boaz, the parents of Obed, who becomes the father of Jesse, who is the father of King David. Since the Davidic monarchy is so important in the history of Israel and also in the Davidic lineage of Jesus (Mt 1:5), the establishment of the genealogy of David is also important. More than a love story, however, the book of Ruth also presents an important biblical truth: salvation is offered to all people who are willing to accept it (Ruth was not an Israelite but a Moabite; she abandons her country and her beliefs and embraces the covenant). The presentation of this biblical truth, combined with the importance of the Davidic roots of the story, helps us to understand why the book of Ruth is included at this point in the history of salvation.

Old Testament literature is filled with examples of the widow as a symbol of powerlessness within Israel's patriarchal culture. In this story, three women become widows: Naomi, the wife of Elimelech and the mother of two sons, Mahlon and Kilion, and their wives, Or'pah and Ruth. After the deaths of husband and sons, the story of the widows unpacks the important theme of covenant fidelity *(hesed)*. The women symbolically echo Israel's covenant with Yahweh. That is, faithfulness among Naomi, Or'pah, and Ruth, despite the deaths of their husbands, is evidence that Yahweh will be faithful to his covenant people no matter what happens. Ruth, in particular, childless and widowed, honors her fidelity by caring for her mother-in-law and taking Boaz, a close relative of her dead husband, to be her future spouse. In so doing, she ensured propagation of the bloodline of her husband and remained faithful to levirate law.

SAMUEL, SAUL, AND DAVID
(1 Sam 1—31)

This story of royal intrigue begins with the story of the judge and prophet Samuel and his service to the people during the struggle with the Philistines. Despite the respect that the people had for Samuel and for the other judges that preceded him, there was a growing desire in Israel for a king. Samuel warns the people of Israel about their desire to be ruled by a king (8:11–18), but they insist that this is what they need and desire. Finally, Samuel gives in and anoints Saul as the first king of Israel (10:1), but very quickly regrets that he has done so (15:11). Samuel regrets his choice because Saul is reluctant to "put to the sword" or destroy all that he had captured in battle while he invoked the name of Yahweh; he kept most of the best for himself. In a very real sense Saul does exactly what Samuel had feared when he resisted making a king for Israel at the start, knowing that the kings would take for themselves what had traditionally been given only to Yahweh. As a result of Saul's action, Samuel chooses David as king, in response to the word of Yahweh which Samuel understood as rejecting Saul (16:1–2). With the anointing of David as king, the fierce rivalry between Saul and David begins, a rivalry that ends only with the suicide death of Saul at Mount Gilboa in a battle with the Philistines.

Despite the very human struggles that are part of this book, and the very human personalities that are also presented, an overriding theme of the book is the recognition of the "finger of God" at work on behalf of the people. It may well have been necessary in the development of the people of Israel to have a monarchy in order to organize and progress, but the monarchy was acceptable only if it was dependent on Yahweh. The role of the prophet as the interpreter of the Word of God and as the person who "guarantees" that Yahweh will be heard is present at the very beginning. A successful and a blessed king listens and acts on the Word of God, while a king who insists on ignoring God's word will only fail, and will also bring disaster to those who follow him.

THE STORY OF KING DAVID
(2 Sam 1–24)

The story of King David dominates this book (1000–962 B.C.) and although it is named after Samuel, he never is mentioned. Rather, what we read about is the story of a man who is passionately in love with Yahweh, but who is also passionate about many other things. The great strengths of King David are presented, but there is no attempt to cover up his weaknesses. As we read about his brilliant tactical decisions, such as choosing Jerusalem for his capital—a city ideally located between the northern and the southern reaches of his kingdom—we also read about poorly made moral decisions. The adulterous and murderous story of Bathsheba (the mother of King Solomon) reveals the depths of David's lust (11:1—12:15), while the story of his rebellious son Absalom reveals the depth of his love and also his loss (19:1–8).

For the Christian, the passionate story of David is a wonderful story of faith and the constancy of the love of God. The story related to King David by the prophet Nathan (12:1–7) about the poor man and his one little lamb is a popular penitential meditation. However, the story of the Davidic covenant (7) is the most important reference found in the pages of this book because it is from this story that the hopes for a promised messiah that is to come finds its origin and inspiration.

UNITY AND DISUNITY
(1 Kings 1—22)

This first book of Kings covers the time period of roughly 960–850 B.C., a time in which Israel disintegrates from a single united kingdom into two kingdoms in the north and in the south. The book begins with the last days of King David and then describes the ascendancy of Solomon and many of the achievements of his forty-year reign, emphasizing his reputation for wisdom (3:16–28) and his role in the building of the magnificent Temple in Jerusalem. However, soon after his death, his son Rehoboam is unable to keep the united kingdom together and Jeroboam is appointed king in what is now Israel (the northern kingdom) while Rehoboam remains king of Judah (the southern kingdom). The rest of the book recounts the comings and goings of the kings of both kingdoms, pronouncing judgment on each of them. According to the author, with the exception of only two kings of the southern kingdom of Judah (Hezekiah and Josiah), none of the kings were truly acceptable or good.

One other major personality emerges in the book and he is not a king but rather a prophet. Elijah makes his appearance in chapter 17 and the stories of this great prophet are easily recognizable to the Christian reader, probably because of the role that Elijah plays in the Messianic expectations we are familiar with in the New Testament. Of special importance are the miracles that are associated with Elijah and later attributed also to Jesus, especially the miracle of the widow's son raised to life in 1 Kings 17:17–24 (Elijah) and in Luke 7:11–17 (Jesus).

COLLAPSE OF THE KINGDOMS
(2 Kings 1—25)

The second book covers the time period of 850–587 B.C. In this period of time the northern kingdom of Israel collapses in the year 722 B.C. as a result of the victory of the Assyrians over the armies of Israel (17:5–6). To make matters worse, just a short one hundred thirty-five years later, the southern kingdom of Judah collapses with the defeat of their armies by the king of Babylon, the famous King Nebuchadnezzar (25:8–12).

The second book of Kings presents us with a listing of the kings of both Judah and Israel, and in each case judges them. With few exceptions each king, despite the warnings of the prophets Elijah, Elisha, and Isaiah (all of whom play a role in the turmoil that is experienced), comes up short. Instead of relying on Yahweh, the kings attempt to make different political alliances, all of which fail miserably, and lead to even more suffering and destruction. The judgment of the author of the book is that all of this occurred to the people "because the people of Israel had sinned against the Lord" (17:7).

For Christian readers perhaps the most important reference is found in the first chapters of the book, specifically the story of the prophet Elijah being taken up to heaven in a fiery chariot (2:11–12).

This reference is important because in the time of Jesus many people expected that Elijah would return, much in the same way that he departed, and on his return announce the beginning of the Messianic time (Mt 17:10; Mk 9:13).

WHAT ABOUT THE PROMISE?
(1 and 2 Chr)

At first glance it would seem that the two books of the Chronicles tell much of the same story that has been presented to us in the books of First and Second Kings. Admittedly, Chronicles is a little more far reaching, beginning with Adam and detailing as much as possible the people and the significant events to the end of the monarchy, but there is much more here then just additional historical material that might not have been included in the earlier work. The authors of the books of the Chronicles are consumed with answering the question that seemed to preoccupy the people of their time, "How could Yahweh abandon us, especially after the promise he made to David that he and his successors would rule forever?" (2 Sam 7:12–13).

The answer to the question is found in the understanding of the perspective of the historical review provided: the people, and especially their kings with very few exceptions, failed to remain faithful to the terms of the covenant. "I will be your God and you will be my people" (Gen 17:1–9) was not uppermost in their minds and in their hearts, and so they suffered the punishment and the disasters that happen when Yahweh is abandoned.

If the failures of the kings and their people are outlined, there is also a portrait presented and a judgment made of both a faithful king and a faithful people. It should not be a surprise that the judgment is made that the king who was faithful to Yahweh, despite his many sins and weaknesses, was King David. His deathbed prayer (1 Chr 29:10–19) sums up what is expected, but sorely lacking, in both king and people.

For Christian readers, perhaps the most surprising but, at the same time, the most gratifying reference is found at the very end of the Chronicles. The person that becomes Yahweh's tool in the restoration of the people is a very unlikely choice. It is Cyrus, King of Persia, a Gentile, who orders in the name of Yahweh the restoration of the Temple in Jerusalem and the return of the people to Judah (2 Chr 36:22–23). Yahweh is such a powerful God that even those people who have not been chosen to serve him are nevertheless "pressed into service" and compelled to do God's will. If that is the case for a Gentile, how much more so should it be for God's Chosen People?

RETURN FROM CAPTIVITY
(Ezra 1–10)

Ezra (in Hebrew, "help") was a scribe, a religious man who had returned from exile in Babylon to Jerusalem. His main concern was to restore the Temple in Jerusalem, and by restoring the Temple to restore a healthy and a vibrant Jewish life and worship in Jerusalem. Although this was his main concern, his effort was not universally accepted. In particular the resident Samaritans, who had not gone into exile, at first offered to help in the rebuilding of the Temple but were rebuffed in their efforts to contribute (4:1–23). As a result of their offer to help being refused they then stood in opposition to the rebuilding, delaying it until the period of 520–515 B.C. In addition to the problems with the Samaritans, another challenge was the fact that so many Jewish men had married non-Jewish spouses, causing other problems, particularly the worship of gods other than Yahweh. In response to this problem, the marriages were dissolved (10:2–3) and all foreign wives and children were sent away.

For Christian readers, the presence of the Samaritans and the tensions between the Samaritans and the Jewish people, five hundred years before the coming of Christ, is helpful in understanding the New Testament references to Samaritans. Understanding the animosity, and also the roots of the animosity, helps make the story of the woman at the well (Jn 4:9) and the parable of the Good Samaritan (Lk 10:33) in the life of Jesus even more vibrant and moving.

RENEWING THE COVENANT
(Neh 1—13)

Nehemiah was a contemporary of Ezra and served as the governor of the newly restored province of Judah. His concerns were many of the same concerns of Ezra; not only did he desire to rebuild the Temple, he also wanted to rebuild the walls of Jerusalem for protection, something a governor would appropriately be concerned about. The book of Nehemiah tells us of these efforts but also tells us of the renewal of the covenant (8:1—10:39) under the direction of Ezra. In this renewal ceremony, the people confess their sins, and renew their commitment to the Temple and to the Jewish traditions that had been forgotten and not fully practiced during the time of the exile in Babylon.

RECOGNIZING THE PIOUS JEW
(Tob 1—14)

The book of Tobit is placed in the listing of the historical books but it should be viewed more as a commentary, presented in the form of a story, illustrating the qualities of piety and devotion. Written around two hundred years before Christ, the story is intended for those Jews who found themselves outside of Israel, living in the Diaspora among the Gentiles. The book is about the power of prayer and the role of faith, powerfully portraying the need to remain faithful to God, no matter what the difficulties of life might be.

Christians might find the story of the relationship between Tobias, the son of Tobit, and the (arch)angel Raphael of particular interest (4:1—6:18), as well as the powerful prayer of Tobit (13:1—17), which recalls the faithfulness of God.

IT TAKES A WOMAN
(Jdt 1—16)

Even the most casual reader of the Old Testament will observe that the pages of the Old Testament reflect a patriarchical, or male-dominated, culture and society. With very few exceptions most of the powerful figures of the Old Testament are men, so on those few occasions when a woman dominates the scene we sit up and take notice. The story of Judith (and the story of Esther that follows) is one such occurrence.

Judith is placed among the historical books because it purports to be a story from the time of the Assyrian conquest in the eighth century B.C. (see 2 Kings). However, the story was probably not recorded until around the same time as the book of Tobit, and it emerges from the same theological and cultural mind-set: a concern about maintaining Jewish identity and culture.

In the story, Judith is a Jewish widow who saves her town by beheading the Assyrian general Holofernes, a scene captured in many powerful works of art especially in the famous artwork by Girolamo Mocetto (1454–1531) from the sixteenth century. Judith's heroism proclaims to the oppressed people that God will not abandon them and will use whatever and whomever he chooses in order to ensure that his will is accomplished.

QUEEN ESTHER AND KING XERXES I
(Esth 1—10)

This is a great story, filled with examples of bravery and heroism, and also a story that provides an incredibly evil villain. The hero of the story is Esther, a Jewish girl who becomes the queen of the Persian King Xerxes (in the story he is identified as Ahasureus), and the villain is Haman, who is an advisor to the king and who has a plan to exterminate the Jews in the kingdom. The struggle between Esther and Haman, with Esther emerging as the winner and Haman hanging on the giblet he had intended for others, provides great drama and is simply fun to read. The story provides the rationale for the Jewish feast of Purim (9:18–28).

JUDAS MACCABEUS—THE HAMMER
(1 Macc 1—16)

The historical details that prompted the revolt that was led first by Mattathias, and then later by his son Judas, are starkly exposed in the first chapters of the book. Mattathias and other faithful Jews recognized the changes that were being imposed upon them, specifically Hellenistic pagan values, would destroy Judaism and Jewish culture and heritage (1:14). The most intolerable change was the addition of pagan altars for worship throughout Israel, including the rebuilt Temple in Jerusalem. This action provoked the fierce and unrelentless rebellion, and for a short time even the independence of Israel, until their eventual absorption into the Roman Empire.

For the Christian reader, the historical details may be of some interest, but the most important contribution may well be the "background" information it provides for an understanding of the culture and mentality of Israel, even during the time of Jesus. Nations that conquered Israel realized that they could not treat the people of the conquered territory in the same way that they may have treated other lands. In short, the Jewish people, fiercely loyal to Jewish customs and traditions and to the ritual and practices of the Temple in Jerusalem, would not compromise. This attitude provided fertile ground for the hope of the people for a messiah (Mt 12:23; Lk 1:32), and it provided the necessary fuel to energize the Zealots (Lk 6:15; Gal 1:14), and even to give pause to the ruling authority when a decision was to be implemented (Mt 27:24).

MARTYRDOM OF THE JUST

(2 Macc 1—15)

Although this book provides us with even more details about the time of the Maccabees, perhaps the stories of the martyrdom of the old man Eleazar (6:18–31) and the story of the martyrdom of the seven brothers and their mother (7:1–42) stand out. Although the stories are gruesome, what is particularly of importance, especially to the Christian reader, is the introduction of a theological point that was just emerging in Jewish thought. The idea of an eternal reward (7:9) and a resurrection to new life (7:14) motivates each of the seven brothers and inspires them to the witness that they provide, ultimately frustrating their persecutors and giving glory and honor to God.

3. Introduction to the Writings

The first five books of the Bible as we have seen are designated as the Torah or the Pentateuch. The historical books are so designated because they outline the history of the Chosen People. The prophetic books (which follow this section) are easily grouped together because each book is identified with a particular prophet. These designations leave us with the books of the Bible that do not fit neatly into any other category; for organizational purposes these books are collected together and identified simply as the "writings."

Another way of thinking about the writings is to identify the books as "wisdom literature." Wisdom literature, which is really a collection of practical and inspirational teachings about how life can and should be lived, certainly began with the oral tradition of passing on practical advice to children and family members. Eventually, these traditions were collected and organized, sometimes as proverbs, sometimes as the written reflections of a person known and accepted as wise, sometimes as poetry, and also in other forms of literature that slowly developed over time.

In the writings that follow some will be very poetic, some will be inspirational and religious, and some might even come across as quite secular and even cynical.

Certainly a distinct part of the writings is the book of Psalms. The psalms, many of which are attributed to King David, grew out of the ritual and the cultic practices of the spiritual life of the people. Most of the psalms can be directly associated with the worship practices in the Temple in Jerusalem. Today, of course, the psalms are a very popular form of prayer.

THE STORY OF JOB
(Job 1—42)

The story of Job is an attempt to answer a question that remained unanswered even in the time of Jesus: "What is the cause of suffering and pain?" or as the question is put in the story of the man born blind, "Which parent sinned?" (see Jn 9:2). Job attempts to answer this question and other related questions about suffering, but none of the answers provided truly satisfies. Finally, God arrives on the scene (38:1—42:6) and his response to Job's questioning puts Job right back to where he was at the very beginning: "Naked I came from my mother's womb, and naked shall I return there; the LORD gave, and the LORD has taken away; blessed be the name of the LORD" (1:21).

THE BOOK OF PSALMS
(Ps 1—150)

Psalms are hymns, songs, and prayers, many of which were intended to be sung or at least accompanied by music. It is impossible to summarize the many different themes or the many different emotions expressed in the psalms in a short summary. Certainly most people have at least one psalm that they have chosen as a favorite, including Jesus who prayed a portion of Psalm 22 ("My God, my God, why have you forsaken me?") while hanging on the cross (Mt 27:46). Some of the most popular psalms include Psalm 23 ("The Lord is my shepherd"), Psalm 51 ("Have mercy on me, O God"), and Psalm 88 ("O Lord, God of my salvation").

PROVERBS

(Prov 1—31)

King Solomon, who had a reputation for wisdom (1 Kings 3:16–28), has been traditionally credited with writing and collecting the proverbs that make up this book. However, the extent of the collection is beyond the ability of one person, and some of the Proverbs seem to come from other cultures and even other wisdom collections. The book of Proverbs is not intended to be read from beginning to end, but lends itself more to browsing, taking time to prayerfully consider and meditate on what has been written. Like the psalms, many people have a favorite proverb. Some of those that are often quoted include: "The fear of the Lord is the beginning of wisdom" (9:10) and "Anxiety weighs down the human heart, / but a good word cheers it up" (12:25).

ECCLESIASTES/QOHELETH

(Eccl 1—12)

This book is the personal reflection of a wise man on his experience of life. It is a very unusual book because it is not very hope-filled, at times seeming to be rather skeptical. All and all, however, it is brimming with wonderful advice and an often quoted meditation, "There is a season and a time for everything under heaven" (3:1–8).

THE SONG OF SONGS

(Song 1–8)

Also known in some texts as the Canticle of Canticles, this book presents us with one of the clearest examples of the different possibilities for the interpretation of Scripture. On the one hand, a literal interpretation of the book might lead the unprepared reader to blush, since it is a celebration of human sexuality and beauty. On the other hand, interpreting the book allegorically, the Song of Songs has been viewed in the Jewish tradition as a symbol of God's love for Israel, and from the Christian perspective, as a symbol of Christ's love for the Church. Regardless of the perspective that the reader may choose, the book also presents other challenges to the modern reader. Since so many poetic images are provided, including examples that come directly from the ancient world that are unknown to us, there is sometimes a difficulty understanding the point the author is trying to make. Patience and a good Bible dictionary become a necessity.

THE BOOK OF WISDOM

(Wis 1—19)

Although this book purports to have been written by King Solomon, it is actually a composition from a much later date, very close to the time of Jesus (100–28 B.C.). As such, the book reflects later Jewish theological development, specifically the reflections about immortality which can be found in the first five chapters. In addition to the reflections on eternal life (3:1–9), Christian readers will also recognize the powerful image of Wisdom that is presented as a feminine presence, present throughout all of salvation history (7:22—8:1).

ECCLESIASTICUS/THE WISDOM OF BEN SIRACH
(Sir 1—51)

We know the author of Ecclesiasticus to be Jesus Ben Sirach, because it is provided in the prologue by his grandson. We know that he was a sage, living in Jerusalem around the year 180 B.C., and we know that his grandson translated the book into Greek about fifty years later. The fact that the book was translated into Greek is important, because it was an attempt to offer practical Jewish advice and values to young Jewish men and women who were not living in Israel and who were heavily influenced by the Hellenism of the day. Sirach was concerned, as are many parents today, that the traditional values were being eroded and not practiced, and this book is an attempt to provide a different perspective. Sirach's assertion that "to fear the Lord is the beginning of wisdom" (1:14) is a familiar sentiment to most Christians.

4. Introduction to the Prophets

Of the forty-six books of the Old Testament, eighteen books, or almost one-half of the books, are designated as "prophetic." This designation does not mean that these books "foretell the future," as many people assume was the main function of a prophet. Although it is true that a prophet on occasion warned the people about a future event that would occur (very soon, and not hundreds or even thousands of years into the future), especially if they did not repent and change their ways, the primary role of a prophet was to "speak for God" (the Greek root of the word, prophet) (CCC 64; 218). As such, prophets understood that they were called by God to proclaim God's word, and most of the prophets understood that this call was going to be difficult, and not universally acclaimed (Amos 7:12–17; Jer 20:7–18, for example).

Prophets not only called people to repentance and judgment,

prophets also announced good news, "salvation." True enough, they wanted people to remain faithful to the Lord and to the covenant, but they also wanted to remind people that God was willing to repair that which was destroyed and begin again with a new relationship (Jer 31:31–34).

One of the concerns faced by the prophets, and by the people of the time, was the question, "How can you know if a prophet is really sent by God?" On more than one occasion different messages were preached, both in the name of the Lord, and each message called the people to a different response (Jer 28:1–17). In the format in which we have the prophetic message preserved, we know that the message was true because the message has been preserved for us today and the conflicting message has been forgotten, but it was not always so clear for the people of the Old Testament. The Bible recognizes this quandary and offers a solution: only the test of time will determine that which is true and that which is not (Deut 18:21–22).

Finally, three of the prophetic books are not only understood as prophetic, they are also understood as apocalyptic. Apocalyptic (from the Greek meaning "revelation," or "unveiling") literature always emerges from a time of persecution and suffering. In each instance apocalyptic literature insists that despite what seems to be happening, God will in fact prevail, and not only prevail, but will prevail in glorious victory. The apocalyptic books are Lamentations, Baruch, and Daniel. In addition parts of Isaiah (24–27), Ezekiel (38–39), and Zechariah (12–14) are also understood as examples of apocalyptic literature. In the New Testament, the book of Revelation is apocalyptic.

THE THREE ISAIAHS

(Isa 1—66)

The first fact that the reader should know about this book is that it is a collection of the words of not one but three distinct prophets, all living at a different time and each facing a different kind of concern. The prophet Isaiah, for whom this book is named, was a married man who prophesied around Jerusalem for forty years (circa 740 B.C.). The words of this first prophet Isaiah are found in the first thirty-nine chapters. The second prophet Isaiah came about two hundred years later. He, too, prophesied around Jerusalem, but he prophesied in a much different world than the original Isaiah; his words are recorded in chapters forty through fifty-five. The third prophet Isaiah is unknown to us but we do know that his words are collected in chapters fifty-five through sixty-six.

Isaiah, presented to us in the unified form of a biblical book, is probably quoted more than any other book in the Bible. New Testament writers seem to be particularly fond of the prophet. Specific themes that are important to the Christian tradition would include the Emmanuel prophecy that is used as a reference to the birth of Jesus (Isa 7:14 and Mt 1:23) and the numerous references to the "suffering servant," in which Christian readers recognize the life and ministry of Jesus (42:1–4; 49:1–7).

JEREMIAH

(Jer 1—52)

The prophet Jeremiah is seen as a prophet who vividly illustrates the personal cost, in terms of suffering and disappointment, that is often the price that must be paid in order to preach the Word of God. Jeremiah's message was often not well received and the prophet endured all sorts of punishment and abuse because he remained faithful to the Word of God as he understood it. Readers identify with his call (1:4–10), his suffering at the hands of his enemies (37:11—38:6), and with his confidence in the Lord (31:31–34).

LAMENTATIONS
(Lam 1—5)

This short collection of prayers (laments) follows the book of Jeremiah because tradition attributes the collection to him. When we read the prayers we are able to recognize the depth of feeling and passion that these prayers reflect. The people are dismayed by the destruction of Jerusalem and their exile into a foreign land, but despite their suffering and even their complaints, they are still a people of faith and they believe that somehow they will be delivered.

BARUCH
(Bar 1–6)

This book is attributed to Baruch, the secretary or scribe of the prophet Jeremiah, and for this reason the book is positioned here. Modern scholarship has determined that the book was not written by Baruch and was probably composed sometime during 200–60 B.C., which would place it during the time of the Maccabeans.

EZEKIEL
(Ezek 1—48)

This is an unusual book and is often difficult to read because unlike other books in the Bible that record the *words* of the prophet, this book records the *visions* of the prophet (37:1–14). The visions are filled with heavenly creatures, strong images, sights, and sounds, and even dramatic gestures, such as eating the scroll on which the Word of God is written (3:1–3).

Christians will recognize that Ezekiel is often referred to as "son of man" (mortal, or human being), a title that over time was accepted as messianic and one that is often used by Jesus (Mt 8:20; 9:6).

DANIEL AND THE LIONS' DEN
(Dan 1—14)

This book, understood not as a prophetic book but rather as apocalyptic literature, follows Ezekiel, perhaps because of its tone and message. It is a book filled with wonderful and inspiring stories, some of which are well known, for example, Daniel in the lions' den (14:31–42) and the perils of Shadrach, Meshach, and Abednego (3:8–30). The stories are not without purpose, as they demonstrate the need for courage and perseverance in faith under persecution, which will be rewarded by God.

In Protestant bibles the book of Daniel is considered as part of the apocrypha, with chapters thirteen and fourteen identified as Susanna (13:1–64) and Bel and the Dragon (14:1–42).

AN UNUSUAL LOVE STORY: HOSEA AND GOMER
(Hos 1—14)

The prophet Hosea was a contemporary of the prophets Micah, Amos, and Isaiah. Living during this rich period of the revelation of the Word of God (750–735 B.C.), Hosea dramatically and vividly illustrated the state of the relationship between Yahweh and his people. The dramatic portrayal occurs when Hosea marries Gomer, a prostitute, and with her produces three children, each of whom symbolize the relationship of the people with the Lord when they do not remain faithful to the covenant. In short they will be defeated (1:4–5), and in their defeat they will not be pitied (1:6–7) and will no longer be identified as the people of God (1:8–9). Unfortunately, as was often the case, the people did not pay attention to Hosea and they soon suffered the consequences of their unfaithfulness.

JOEL

(Joel 1—4)

Not much is known about the prophet Joel or even with any certainty about the time when he lived and prophesied. It seems that the work emerges from the time after the exile and the return of the people from Babylon, so most scholars place the book somewhere between 500–350 B.C. Again, the concerns of the prophet are familiar to us, but in this instance there is a little harder edge and sense of urgency to his message. Joel calls the people to an awareness of what needs to be accomplished during the difficult period in which they live, but he wants them to act forcefully now, and not some time in the future.

Two references in the book of Joel are familiar to Christian readers. The first, a call to repentance, fasting, and prayer is often heard on Ash Wednesday (2:12–18). The second is an unusual twist, probably reflective of his time, when Joel turns around the famous prophecy of Isaiah (Isa 2:4); in Joel the exhortation reads, "beat your plowshares into swords, and your pruning hooks into spears" (3:10).

THE CRY OF THE POOR

(Am 1—9)

The prophet Amos was a shepherd who spoke passionately about the sharp divisions that occurred between the "haves" and the "have nots" of his day and age (750 B.C.). In this stark division between the rich and the poor, Amos makes it clear that although the Lord is aware of sins of all of the nations, the Lord is particularly saddened by the sins of his Chosen People (3:2). Although the law of God is to be followed by all people, those who profess to be the sons and daughters of God have a particular responsibility to care for God's people. This responsibility cannot be dismissed or replaced by pious practices or devotions (5:21–25) but must be reflected in justice.

THE SHORTEST BOOK IN THE OLD TESTAMENT

(Ob vs. 1–21)

The book of Obadiah is the shortest book in the Old Testament, consisting of one chapter and only twenty-one verses. The main concern of the book is to pronounce God's judgment on Edom, a neighboring country that was south of Judah. Scholars situate the book around the destruction of Jerusalem in 587 B.C. and speculate that Edom may have helped the Babylonians in the destruction of the city; for this reason they will be severely punished.

A WHALE OF A STORY?

(Jon 1—4)

Two strong themes emerge from the book of Jonah. The first theme that emerges is that you cannot escape, despite your best efforts, from the call of God. When God wants something to happen it happens, and whatever it takes to make it happen God will use (2:1). The second theme is a theme about the universal mercy of God. When people listen to the voice of God and follow his word, even those who are not the Chosen People (such as the people of Nineveh), God will be generous to them (3:10). Christians are certainly familiar with this story and will also recognize the powerful prayer of Jonah, which is often used today (2:2–9).

MICAH

(Mic 1—7)

The prophet Micah was a contemporary of Isaiah and Amos, and he was also known to the prophet Jeremiah (Jer 26:18). Like the prophet Amos, Micah is distressed by the separation between the rich and the poor (2:1–2; 6:11–12), and like the prophet Isaiah he recognizes that the people will suffer for their sins, but also reassures them that they will be again raised up (2:12–13).

For the Christian reader, two references in Micah stand out. The first reference is a reference that speaks of a ruler of Israel that will emerge from Bethlehem (5:2), later repeated by Matthew in his Gospel (Mt 2:5–6) in reference to the birth of Jesus. The second is a familiar refrain, used during the season of Lent to call the community to prayer: "O my people, what have I done to you? / In what have I wearied you? / Answer me!" (6:3).

NAHUM
(Nah 1—3)

If a person wants to know what it means to be "on message," the prophet Nahum provides a perfect example. Nahum has one overriding concern: he is looking forward to the destruction of the Assyrians, the enemy of Judah and Israel (a destruction that occurs in 612 B.C. when the Babylonians defeat them). His focused message to the people seems to be, "Be patient, God will take care of them" (1:2–3).

HABAKKUK
(Hab 1—3)

We know that Habakkuk is a prophet because he is identified twice as a prophet (1:1; 3:1), but beyond this we know little of who he was. He seems to be mostly concerned with the age-old question, "Why does God allow bad things to happen to good people and not do something about it, especially when they ask for help?" (1:2). His answer to the question, an answer that may have inspired the apostle Paul (Rom 1:17), is to simply surrender to God and accept that you do not always know or understand why "faith as a whole constitutes the answer" (CCC 309).

ZEPHANIAH
(Zeph 1—3)

The prophet Amos introduced the concept (Am 5:18–20), but it is the prophet Zephaniah who takes up the message and makes it his own: the Day of Yahweh is the dominant theme of this book. Zephaniah understands that the Day of Yahweh will be a day when Yahweh will punish those who have opposed his will and who have not been faithful to his commandments. For this reason it will be a day of judgment. The concept is taken up in the New Testament and understood as the "Day of the Lord" and also as the Second Coming of Christ (2 Thess 2:2; 2 Pet 3:10; Phil 1:6) (CCC 681–682).

AUGUST—DECEMBER, 520 B.C.
(Hag 1—2)

Usually we cannot identify the exact dates when a particular prophet lived, let alone identify the exact dates of his prophetic activity, but in the case of the prophet Haggai we are able to do so. Our pinpoint accuracy is provided by the prophet in the first verses of the book, collaborated by historical research.

Eighteen years have come and gone since the people have returned from exile and they no longer have the enthusiasm to work on the Temple. Haggai exhorts the people to work, even though, because of their circumstances, the Temple will not be as grand as it once was, one day it can be all that they hoped it would be (2:3–8).

ZECHARIAH
(Zech 1—14)

Just as the book of Isaiah presents us with the prophetic words and activity of three distinct prophets, the book of Zechariah presents us with two prophets. The first eight chapters, written primarily in a prosaic style, are reflective of the work of the actual prophet Zechariah.

He is concerned with the return of the people from exile in Babylon and with the restoration of the Temple. The next chapters, primarily poetic, are the work of the anonymous prophet. His main concern is to reassure the people that God will continue to protect them and will not abandon them.

Christian readers will identify with the prophecy of the protective shepherd (11:14–17), who cares lovingly for the flock, and also with the reference to the "thirty pieces of silver," which is reminiscent of the price that is paid to Judas for betraying Jesus (11:13b; Mt 27:3).

MALACHI
(Mal 1—4)

The last book in the Old Testament, Malachi (in Hebrew, "my messenger") is difficult to date. References within the text indicate that it is probably sometime after the return from exile and sometime after the Temple has been rebuilt and is in use, but it is difficult to determine for certain. The words of the prophet are very familiar, reminding the people that they have not been faithful and warning them that God will judge them.

For Christian readers, it is interesting to note that the last words of the Old Testament (4:5–6) are words that prophesy the return of the prophet Elijah, which will usher in the Messianic age. Of course, the New Testament takes up this theme in the person of John the Baptist, who is understood in the Christian tradition to be the person who fulfills this prophecy and announces the coming of Jesus Christ (Mt 11:14).

BETWEEN THE TESTAMENTS

The Old Testament covers a historical period of approximately nineteen hundred years, from the time of the first encounter of Abraham with Yahweh through the return of the people to Jerusalem from exile in Babylon. During this time frame we have seen how the Chosen People moved through a series of changes, not only in their relationship with God but also in their relationship with the world in which they lived and experienced God. A summation of this progression (all dates are approximate) would include the Patriarchal period (2000–1700), the Egyptian sojourn (1700–1300), the Exodus and wilderness experience (1300–1250), followed by the period of the conquest of the promised land and the Judges (1250–1000). The progression continues with the establishment of the monarchy (1000–900), followed by the divided monarchy (900–750), the kingdom of Judah (750–600), the Babylonian Exile (600–538), followed by the return from exile and the restoration of Jerusalem and the Temple, which was the primary concern of many of the prophets.

From a general historical perspective, with the beginning of the domination of the geographical area of the area that we identify today as the Holy Land by the Persians in 550 B.C., the Jews never again became a significant political force. The Persians were followed by the Greeks and Alexander the Great in the period known as the Hellenistic period (350–75 B.C.), and then finally by the Roman occupation of Palestine beginning in 63 B.C. There was the period of the Maccabees (167–63 B.C.), but even during this period of independence it was only a matter of time before the significant political and military power of the day enforced its will.

The Bible presents us with a pretty clear picture of the important events and circumstances, at least from a faith perspective, from the time of the patriarchs through the return from the Babylonian Exile. However, the Bible does not present us with the same kind of details and perspective for the approximate five-hundred-year period between the return from the exile to the coming of Jesus. This is important to note because it helps us understand that the purpose of the Bible is not to present us with the story of our history, but rather the interpretation of our theology, the story of our relationship with God.

From a theological perspective, which slowly developed over time, the people's perspective and understanding of their relationship with God moved from an expectation of an anointed, politically powerful and astute king such as King David, to the expectation of an anointed, but spiritually powerful messiah. Of course, Christians identify this anointed one as Jesus, the Messiah; the people of the Old Testament tradition do not accept this designation. The New Testament begins with the introduction of the person who has fulfilled this expectation, identified in the first words of the Gospel of Matthew as "Jesus the Messiah, the son of David, the son of Abraham" (Mt 1:1).

5. Introduction to the Gospels

For hundreds of years biblical readers assumed that the gospels were a biographical presentation of the life and ministry of Jesus Christ. Although it is true that most of the biographical information that we have about Jesus comes from the four gospels, the gospels were not intended to be biographical statements about Jesus. The gospels are theology, each gospel distinctly presenting to the reader a specific portrait of Jesus which emerged from a particular Christian community based on their understanding of the Word of God and their experience of the Lord (CCC 126).

When we examine the four gospels we note that three of the gospels—Matthew, Mark, and Luke—seem to be very similar, while the fourth gospel, the Gospel of John, seems to be distinctly different. Although it is true that Matthew, Mark, and Luke (referred to collectively as the "synoptic Gospels," from the Greek meaning, "to be viewed with one eye") are similar, each gospel is also unique. The most obvious difference is that in the Gospel of Mark there is no Infancy Narrative (the story about the birth of Jesus), while in the gospels of Matthew and Luke the Infancy Narrative is prominent.

The Gospel of John, on the other hand, is distinctly different from the synoptic Gospels. The Gospel of John seems to be much more symbolic, even poetic at times, and the portrait that it presents of Jesus differs considerably. Even the biographical details presented in the Gospel of John are not always the same as the details that are presented in the synoptic Gospels. For example, in the synoptic Gospels the ministry of Jesus appears to be for a period of one year, while in the Gospel of John it is for three years. Another significant difference is that in the synoptic Gospels, Jesus speaks in parables, while in the Gospel of John, he never speaks in parables but rather in long, theological discourses.

The differences between the synoptic Gospels and the Gospel of John should not be a cause of concern. Although it is true that through the centuries many people have attempted to "merge" the four gospels into one single, historical, and biographical portrait (and have not succeeded in doing so), the more acceptable position is to permit the gospels to witness to Jesus as they were originally intended. The gospels are portraits of faith and belief, inviting the reader to be inspired by the Word of God and to apply that Word to their own life (CCC 124).

The catechism teaches that just as it is important to understand the senses of Scripture when we read the words of the Old Testament (CCC 115–118), the gospels demand a different skill. In particular we approach the gospels with an understanding and appreciation of the fact that the gospels emerged through a three-step process (CCC 126):

- ***The life and teaching of Jesus:*** the gospels present to us the historical person of Jesus, what he did, what he taught us, and what he has called us to do.
- ***The oral tradition***: the apostles, after the Ascension of Jesus into heaven, passed on to us, based on their own experience and enlightened by the power of the Holy Spirit, the truth of what they experienced.
- ***The written gospels***: The writers of the gospels selected cer-

tain elements that came to them from the oral tradition and other elements that had been written down, and passed on to us the honest truth about Jesus Christ.

THE GOSPEL OF MATTHEW
(Mt 1–28)

The Gospel of Matthew appears as the first gospel in the Bible because for centuries it was assumed that this was the oldest gospel, the Gospel of Matthew the tax collector (9:9; Mk 2:14; Lk 5:27). However, modern biblical scholarship places the gospel somewhere between A.D. 80–90, written not by Matthew, but probably by an anonymous Jewish Christian, perhaps writing somewhere in Antioch (present-day Syria). The gospel is longer than the Gospel of Mark and contains approximately 80 percent of Mark's content. The addition of the Infancy Narrative, two miracle stories, the cure of the centurion's servant (8:5–13), and the cure of the mute demoniac (12:22–23) account for most of the difference.

As a Jewish Christian, Matthew makes it a point to identify Jesus as the fulfillment of all of the prophecies and promises made in the Old Testament. Jesus is the Son of David, he is the fulfillment of the promise that a messiah will come, but most important of all, he is the one who remained faithful to the Word of God, unlike the people of the Old Testament.

Central to the Gospel of Matthew is the Sermon on the Mount, chapters 5—7, in which Jesus demonstrates that he is the Word of God. The Sermon on the Mount is one of five discourses that are contained in the gospel, the others include the cost of discipleship (chapter 10); the parables of the Kingdom of Heaven (chapter 13); what it means to be a Christian (chapter 18); and teachings about the life that is to come (chapters 23—25).

THE GOSPEL OF MARK
(Mk 1—16)

Today it is generally accepted that the Gospel of Mark is the oldest of the gospels, probably written somewhere between A.D. 66–70, perhaps in the city of Rome. Tradition has it that the author of the gospel is the companion of Saint Peter, the John Mark that is referred to in the Acts of the Apostles (Acts 15:37). The shortest of the four gospels, it is generally agreed that this gospel is one of the resources used for both the Gospel of Matthew and the Gospel of Luke.

Mark's Gospel does not begin with an explanation of the birth of Jesus but rather with his baptism in the Jordan River by John the Baptist. Mark presents Jesus as the fulfillment of the prophets (1:3; Isa 40:3), and as Jesus emerges from the waters of baptism, as God's beloved son (Mk 1:11; Ps 2:7; Isa 42:1).

As the story of Jesus unfolds in the gospel, there is a certain sense of urgency in the telling. Mark does not seem to spend too much time on any one particular event or experience, but rather seems to present one piece of evidence after another as he approaches the climax of his story. His intent seems to be to reveal the true identity of Jesus, which the people do not understand (4:41), but which the demons certainly comprehend (1:24; 3:11). This sense of urgency continues throughout the presentation. Finally, at the very end of the gospel, and perhaps appropriately proclaimed by the Gentile Roman soldier at the foot of the cross of Jesus, "Truly this man was God's Son!" (15:39), the reader is confronted with the inescapable truth. In a sense this pronouncement seems to say, "You should get it by now, and if you don't, here is the most unlikeliest of all witnesses, and he understands it!"

Of interest is the assertion by the majority of biblical scholars that the gospel originally ended with 16:8, and that the final twenty verses of the gospel (which witness to appearances of the risen Christ and the Ascension into heaven) were added later. Without a doubt, there is a different impact if the gospel ends with the supposed silence of the woman at the tomb, "for they were afraid." Because we know that the women did not remain silent for long, we are left to speculate about what might have happened to persuade them to break their silence and to tell the "rest of the story."

THE GOSPEL OF LUKE
(Lk 1–24)

The Gospel of Luke is unique because the gospel is really volume one of the story; volume two is the Acts of the Apostles, written by the same author. However, that being the case, traditionally Luke is presented separately from the Acts of the Apostles and with the gospels of Matthew and Mark.

It is generally agreed that the gospel was written around A.D. 85, probably by Luke the physician, a traveling companion of the apostle Paul. Most scholars assume that Luke was a well-educated man, probably a Gentile, who knew the Scriptures in Greek, and as such a convert to Judaism, before he became a convert to Christianity. There is no real agreement on the geographical location of where the gospel was written, although strong arguments are made for both Greece and Syria.

It is Luke's Gospel that provides us with some of the best-loved stories of Jesus, including the Annunciation (1:26–38), the Visitation (1:39-45), the parable of the Prodigal Son (15:11–32), and the walk to Emmaus (24:13–35). In addition to the stories, it is Luke who provides us with the *Magnificat* (1:46–55) and also with Zechariah's prophecy (1:68–79) and Simeon's Canticle (2:29–32). More than any other gospel, Luke's is filled with the images and the details of the life of Jesus that are so easily recalled by most Christians.

In addition to the images and the stories, a dominant theme of the Gospel of Luke (and also the Acts of the Apostles) is the presence of the Holy Spirit. Everything that unfolds does so because of the activity of the Spirit of God (1:35; 2:25; 10:21; 12:12, for example). Women also play a very prominent role in the gospel story, beginning with the Blessed Mother (1:46–55) and the prophetess Anna (2:36–38). Other references include the woman who washed the feet of Jesus (7:36–50) and the listing of the names of the women who accompanied Jesus in his ministry (8:1–3).

THE GOSPEL OF JOHN
(Jn 1–21)

The Gospel of John is traditionally attributed to the "disciple whom he loved" (19:26), the same person who stood at the foot of the cross of Jesus as an eyewitness to the crucifixion (19:35). However, as is usually the case, it now seems doubtful that the traditional author was in fact the real author; most Scripture scholars would argue that the apostle John was the "authority" behind the gospel, if not the actual writer. Regardless, it seems that the gospel emerged somewhere between A.D. 90–110, probably from the city of Ephesus (on the west coast of modern-day Turkey).

The first point that the reader notices about the Gospel of John is that it is distinctively different from the synoptic Gospels. The gospels of Matthew and Luke begin with the Infancy Narratives, the Gospel of Mark with the baptism of Jesus by John the Baptist, while the Gospel of John begins with a hymn to Jesus as the Incarnate Word of God. The Incarnate Word is the eternal Word of God, which becomes flesh and comes to dwell with the people of God. Another way of looking at it is that the synoptic Gospels begin with a localized event with a unique geography that eventually becomes universal, while the Gospel of John begins with a cosmic and universal theological assertion that becomes "flesh" in the person of Jesus at a specific time and place.

John's Gospel is presented in two main parts: the Book of Signs

(2:1—12:50) and the Book of Glory (13:1—20:31). In the Book of Signs, Jesus reveals himself to the people of God through a series of signs (healing miracles, the miracle of the loaves and fish, Jesus walks on the water). For some people, the signs convince them that Jesus is truly the Son of God, while for others the signs do not lead them to faith but rather to reject Jesus and to seek his destruction. In the Book of Glory, we learn that through the obedience of Jesus to his Father in heaven, an obedience that eventually leads him to the cross, Jesus assumes the glory that has always been his and sends the Spirit of God to those who believe.

It is in John's Gospel that some of the most powerful and recognizable witnesses to the ministry of Jesus emerge, stories that play a very prominent role during the season of Lent and the Church's preparation for the feast of Easter. The Samaritan woman at the well (4:1–42), the man born blind (9:1–41), and the raising of Lazarus from the dead (11:1–4). In addition to these stories the gospel provides us with the story of the adulterous woman (8:1–11), which does not appear in any of the other gospels.

6. The Acts of the Apostles (Acts 1—28)

As we already noted, the Acts of the Apostles is volume two of the story told by the author of the Gospel of Luke. Although it is entitled the acts of the "apostles," it could just as easily be titled the Acts of Peter and Paul, because these two apostles dominate the work. Peter is the main character in the first ten chapters, often appearing with John (Acts 2—12), while Paul is the main character in seventeen chapters (Acts 13—28), first appearing with Barnabas, and then on his own.

The story of the Acts of the Apostles begins in Jerusalem and informs us of the Ascension of Jesus into heaven and the story of the feast of Pentecost, the powerful coming of the Holy Spirit. It ends in Rome, with the arrival of the apostle Paul. Although the Acts of the

Apostles is presented as a historical presentation, we need to remind ourselves that it is not history in the strictest sense that we understand it today, but rather it is theology. The beginning and the end of the story reflect this assertion because the progression of the story is an illustration of what Jesus promised: "You will be my witnesses in Jerusalem, in all of Judea and Samaria, and to the ends of the earth" (1:8b).

This assertion that the Acts of the Apostles is not primarily historical, but rather theological, should not be upsetting. All of us realize, through our own experience of life, that the progression of the events and the experiences of our lives are not seamless, neat and tidy down to the littlest detail. So it is with the people of the New Testament, as it was with the people of the Old Testament. For this reason when we read the story that is presented to us, it is helpful to recognize that what we are reading is a summary, the perception of the individual author, making the best decisions that he can make to help us understand and appreciate the workings of the Holy Spirit and the missionary activity of the early Church (CCC 849–856). The author's intention is to explain to us what he knows and understands to be true and helpful.

7. Introduction to the Letters

The world of the New Testament emerges from a culture that was dominated by Greeks and Romans. This is an important point to understand because the dominant culture of the time influenced the people who lived and worked in the cities, towns, and villages of the day and who were also the people to whom the apostles were preaching. Normal, everyday people formed the early Christian communities, Jew or Gentile, and because they were people of their time and place, there were certain things that they were accustomed to and accepted as both routine and necessary.

Communication in the time of the New Testament, a time where there were no printing presses, no newspapers, no effective form of mass communication, a time where the vast majority of people did not read or write, was primarily oral communication. Communication occurred through word of mouth and, occasionally, if something was important enough or essential, it was written down. Archeology has unearthed literally thousands and thousands of fragments of letters that deal with ordinary things such as business or legal matters, but also some very formal letters that follow a distinctive structure, a structure provided by the Greek and Roman formulation of the day.

The letters that make up the New Testament, letters that are sometimes referred to as *epistles* (literary, intended for general circulation), would have been routinely accepted in the world of the New Testament as necessary for communication. Certainly, in the Christian communities formed by the apostle Paul, a letter would have been expected by the members of the community from the apostle as a way for the community and the apostle to maintain their relationship. There were also letters from the various Christian communities (1 Cor 7:1, for example) to the apostle, bringing him up to date and sending greetings, letters that have been lost and not available to us.

There are twenty-one letters in the New Testament, of which fourteen letters are from the apostle Paul. Not only are the number of letters important but also the time period in which the letters emerged. The earliest writings in the New Testament are not the gospels, but rather the letters, some of which were written as early as the year A.D. 50, or just twenty years after the death of Jesus. The earliest dating of the first gospel would be about fifteen years later. The primary reason for this is because the early Christian community expected Jesus to return (the Second Coming) quite soon, and there was no need to record his life or his teachings since there were many eyewitnesses available to the community. However, once it became clear to the community that the return would not happen as quickly as they once assumed and the apostles and other eyewitnesses began to pass away, there was a need to preserve the life and teachings of Jesus.

ROMANS
(Rom 1—16)

Although the Letter to the Romans appears first in the New Testament listing, it is actually the last letter that Paul wrote, probably around the year A.D. 57–58 while he was still in Corinth. The letter is a theologically challenging letter (Scripture scholars consider it to be the most comprehensive and important Pauline letter), not always easy to read or understand as it presents many essential theological and dogmatic points. Perhaps the most important theological point that is discussed in this letter is Paul's theology of "justification by faith" (3:21—4:25), which has often been a point of division between Catholics and Protestants (CCC 161).

It is also interesting to note that this letter of Paul to the Church in Rome was to a Christian community that was founded by someone other than Paul. At the time of his writing, Paul had not yet visited this community, and therefore was not as intimately involved with the members of the community as he might have been with other Christian communities. For this reason, some Scripture scholars argue that this letter was intended as a kind of letter of introduction from the apostle to the community of believers that he intended to soon visit. Of course, we do not know if this was the original purpose of the letter or not, but it does provide at least one perspective that can be helpful as we read what has been written.

FIRST CORINTHIANS
(1 Cor 1—16)

This is one of two letters that Saint Paul wrote to the Christian community in Corinth (modern-day Greece) that have been preserved for us (there is some indication that as many as seven letters may have been composed). Written around A.D. 56 while Paul was in Ephesus, this letter is very pastoral in tone, reflecting Paul's deep affection, but also concern, for this favorite Christian community.

The Corinth community was established in what we might call today a "tough town." The city was adjacent to two very busy seaports and, as a result, had a very large transient population. In addition, Corinth had a reputation as the "city of love," as sacred prostitutes to the goddess Aphrodite (Venus) were in residence. The Christian community reflected the population at large and, as such, the community, although vibrant, faced some serious factional difficulties, along with problems with sexual behavior, marriage, and the eucharistic liturgy, to name a few.

It was within this atmosphere and to this challenging community of believers that Paul developed the image of the Church as the "Body of Christ" (12:1–31) and offered the beautiful hymn to love (13:1–13).

SECOND CORINTHIANS
(2 Cor 1—13)

In this second letter, written approximately one year after the first letter to the community—but this time from Macedonia—Paul seems to be responding to certain factions within the Corinth community that have rejected his leadership. Among the many themes of the letter which seem to emerge powerfully is the apostle's assertion that "the love of Christ urges us on" (5:14). In other words, Paul continues to minister and preach despite the obstacles, and he invites the members of the community to respond in the same way because of the "love of God" and the "ministry of reconciliation" (5:11–21). Compared to the "new creation in Christ" that they all have received, the petty little arguments and disagreements don't seem to amount to much.

GALATIANS
(Gal 1—6)

This letter, written perhaps around A.D. 54, but even perhaps as much as three years later, is addressed to the Christian Community of Galatia (a large area that would include modern Turkey). In this letter Paul does not hold back and is vehement in his presentation and arguments. The primary reason for the vehemence is that certain people are questioning his authority to preach the gospel and are also questioning his presentation of the gospel as being "unorthodox." In short, these opponents are demanding that the Gentile converts must also follow the dictates of the Jewish law, including circumcision, if they want to follow Jesus. Paul insists that this matter has already been decided and that Saint Peter has agreed that it is not necessary for Gentile converts to conform to the Old Law (2:10–14). The main body of the letter spells out the implications of what it means to be freed by Christ and what is required for a person to "remain free" (5:1) (CCC 1741; 1748).

EPHESIANS
(Eph 1—6)

The vast majority of Scripture scholars believe that this letter was not written by the apostle Paul but more than likely by one of his disciples, probably around A.D. 90. It is addressed to "the saints who are in Ephesus and are faithful in Christ Jesus" (1:1), and so the writer probably assumed that it would have a wide distribution, certainly beyond the Church in Ephesus.

In the letter, appealing and recognizable Pauline themes, such as the Church as the household of God (2:19–22), the Body of Christ (4:3–6), and the bride of Christ (5:21–33), are expanded upon. In a beautiful prayer of thanksgiving which introduces the letter (1:3–14), Christ is proclaimed as the one who unites all of creation in heaven and on earth, and Christians are identified as those who are called to share in this work.

The Letter to the Ephesians has been viewed as the letter that provides us with the best insight into the heart and the mind of the apostle Paul. It is commonly accepted by Scripture scholars that the Letter to the Romans provides the reader with the contextual and complex argumentation of Saint Paul's theology, while the Letter to the Ephesians omits much of the complexity and offers instead the clarity and enthusiasm of Paul's message.

PHILIPPIANS

(Phil 1—4)

The city of Philippi was a seacoast town (modern-day Greece) which was named after the father of Alexander the Great. Saint Paul visited here around A.D. 50 and wrote this letter, from prison, about six years later.

From the very first verses of the letter, the intimacy that Paul feels for this church is obvious as he writes, "I thank my God every time I remember you" (1:3). Perhaps it is because of this intimacy that Paul reveals, without any hesitation or defensiveness, insights into his life and motivation, all of which he now "regards as loss" (3:5–15) when he considers it in light of his "faith in Christ."

Certainly one of the highlights of the letter is the Hymn to Christ (2:5–11). Another favorite reference is the familiar exhortation, "Rejoice in the Lord always, again I say, Rejoice!" (4:4–7) (CCC 2632).

COLOSSIANS

(Col 1—4)

This letter, to the Church in Colossae, was to another church that Paul did not establish; it was established by Epaphras, a companion of Paul (4:12). This is also a letter that most Scripture scholars agree was probably not written by Paul, but probably by someone else, around A.D. 80–90.

The purpose of the letter is to help the Colossians understand and fully appreciate that Christ is the one in whom all wisdom and knowledge can be discovered (2:2–3), correcting a false impression that seems to be present among them (2:8–23). The author introduces his subject by quoting a Christological hymn (1:15–20) that was probably familiar to this early Christian community, a hymn which proclaims that Christ is "the head of all creation." The author, having made his point about Christ, then moves on and exhorts the community to live in union with Christ, with "your minds on things that are above" (3:2), and to let their lives be lives lived in witness to the "new self" (3:10) this union brings.

FIRST THESSALONIANS

(1 Thess 1—5)

This letter is the earliest written document that can be found in the New Testament. Written by the apostle Paul to the Church in Thessalonica (modern Greece) in A.D. 50–51, it is not known for its great theological themes but rather for its tone of thankful praise and pastoral concern. In particular the letter addresses a particular issue of this early Christian community, their concern about the Second Coming of Christ.

Evidently this early community, eagerly anticipating the return of the Lord, had experienced some deaths among the members of the community (4:13–18). Other members of the community seemed to devote a considerable amount of energy thinking and discussing what the Second Coming might mean. Still others had decided not to discuss it or worry about it, but simply to wait, and not to do much work while they were waiting. Paul addresses all of these concerns by assuring the members of the community that everything is in God hands, including each of them (5:10), and that a much better choice is to live as "children of light" (5:4–11).

SECOND THESSALONIANS

(2 Thess 1—3)

There is little agreement about the authorship of this second letter to the Thessalonians. Some argue that Paul wrote the letter shortly after the first letter (A.D. 51–52) and still others argue that it was written by a disciple of Paul, probably somewhere in the latter part of the first century (A.D. 90–100). The letter again addresses concerns about the Second Coming of the Lord, this time in even more explicit detail then the first letter.

Although no one knows for sure what might have happened, speculation is that the reassuring tone of the first letter to the Thessalonians did not calm their fears or questioning but in fact heightened them. This second letter makes it clear that the wicked will be punished on the day of judgment (1:6–10) but also states it, in answer to a specific assertion (a false letter, supposedly from Paul), that the day of judgment had not yet arrived (2:2). Paul informs the community that there will be specific signs (2:9) that accompany and precede the day of judgment and so there will be no doubt when it actually comes. Finally, Paul is forced to return to the situation of certain members of the community who, for all practical purposes, simply stopped working in order to wait for Christ: "Anyone unwilling to work should not eat" (3:10–12) (CCC 673–675).

FIRST TIMOTHY
(1 Tim 1–6)

The Letter to Timothy is the first among the three letters that are collectively known as the "Pastoral Epistles" (also 2 Timothy and Titus). This letter emerges from the latter part of the first century, in a time when the structure of the Christian community was emerging (based on the secular models of the time) and therefore is not accepted as a letter written by Paul. The letter speaks about the different roles in the Christian community, including bishops and elders (Greek, *episkopoi* and *presbyteroi*), deacons (Greek, *diakonoi*), and other roles of service and ministry (3:1–13). In addition to the description of some of the roles within the community the author seems to be concerned primarily that all members of the community are treated with respect (5:1–2) and that each member of the community has their needs met, aided by those who can well afford to do so (6:17–19).

SECOND TIMOTHY
(2 Tim 1–4)

Although it is generally accepted that this second letter was not written by Paul to Timothy, there does seem to be at least some fragments of an original letter from Paul included. Also, even though this letter appears as the "second letter," there are some indications that this letter in fact is earlier than what we today know as the First Letter to Timothy.

The letter can be enjoyed, and provide ample opportunity for reflection, because the tone of the letter is very upbeat and reassuring. Paul is encouraging Timothy not to be discouraged by what seems to be a lack of success but to remain faithful to his call (4:1–5). He further encourages Timothy to avoid those things that are merely distractions, quarrels, and philosophical disagreements, and that accomplish nothing in the long run (2:23–26).

Of particular interest is the statement about the inspiration of Scripture (3:16–17), which has played a very important role in the Church's development and understanding of the Word of God (CCC 105–108).

TITUS

(Titus 1—3)

This letter, probably from the first century, continues many of the themes from the letters to Timothy. The letter is concerned with the tensions that are present in the community (1:10) and with the person (in this case Titus) whom Paul understands has the authority to lead the community and to address the issues (2:1). Again, Paul explains the necessity of having leadership in the community that is effective, an effectiveness that comes through the witness of a person's life (1:6-9). However, he also points out that a good life is not completely the result of personal talent or discipline, but rather is the result of grace (2:11–12), which has been given to us because of Christ (3:3–7).

PHILEMON

(Philem, only verses)

Only 335 words, this letter was written by Paul while in prison, perhaps around A.D. 55 or even later while in Rome, A.D. 61–63. At first glance the letter may look like a simple appeal for a favor, but perhaps this perception is incomplete. Although it is true that Paul is asking Philemon to treat his runaway slave Onesimus with compassion, there is more here than just the obvious.

Paul is writing as a prisoner, as a person who knows what it means not to be free. He is writing as a person who has led a difficult life, full of suffering in service of the gospel, to a man who is head of a house-church, a Christian community. He is asking Philemon to accept Onesimus back, not as a slave but as a brother. He is asking that the legal penalty not be applied, and he asks that Philemon accept

Onesimus as "you would welcome me" (17b). Finally, he is asking all of this not just as a favor, but rather so that Philemon will refresh Paul's "heart in Christ" (20b).

Although there is no historical record of Philemon's response to Paul, the fact that the letter was preserved may well indicate that he did all that Paul requested.

HEBREWS
(Heb 1–13)

Generally accepted as one of the most powerful and theologically poignant New Testament texts, at one time the text was attributed to the apostle Paul but modern Scripture scholarship does not accept this designation, unsure of whom the author might be. The date for the composition of the text is also not agreed upon: some scholars suggest A.D. 60, while still others suggest a date for composition approximately twenty years later. Finally, there is firm agreement that the letter is in fact not a letter, but perhaps a sermon, or in the words of the text itself, best understood as a "word of exhortation" (13:22).

In the introduction, Jesus Christ is portrayed as the person through whom God "has spoken to us" (1:2) and as God's son, far superior to the prophets, or angels, or anyone else. This theme continues throughout the text, culminating in the assertion that Jesus is higher than even Moses, the great giver of the Law (3:1–6). Each of these assertions are powerful statements that would have certainly captured the attention of a Jewish audience, but in Hebrews they serve only as an introduction to the central message. Hebrews introduces an image of Jesus that appears no where else in the Scriptures: Jesus is the High Priest (3:1—10:39). Not only is Jesus the High Priest, but Jesus is superior to any other high priest ever experienced by the People of God, because Jesus is the Son of God.

The text concludes with a review of major biblical personalities who were known to be people of faith. Abel (11:4), Noah (11:7),

Abraham (11:8), Sarah (11:11), Isaac, Jacob, and Esau (11:20), and many others, all of whom are a great "cloud of witnesses" (12:1) to the salvation planned by God in Jesus Christ.

JAMES

(Jas 1—5)

Attributed to James, often referred to as the "brother of the Lord" (Mk 6:3; Mt 13:55; Gal 1:19), it is actually an anonymous text, probably emerging between A.D. 90–100. Technically not really a letter, the text is unique in that it mentions Jesus Christ only twice (1:1; 2:1) and does not seem to be overly concerned with Christian theology or concerns—it could just as easily be an example of Old Testament wisdom literature (that is, Sirach, Proverbs). Another problem with the text is that it seems to contradict Saint Paul's teaching on the role of justification by faith (2:14–26), a contradiction that so discouraged Martin Luther that he labeled the letter as the "epistle of straw."

Difficulties aside, the text presents us with an opportunity for reflection, specifically a reflection on the role of faith in action (2:14–17) and the power of the tongue in speech (3:3–12). The text is also extremely important insofar as it references the practice of "anointing of the sick" (5:14–16), a sacrament of the Church (CCC 1519–1520).

FIRST PETER

(1 Pet 1—5)

Most Scripture scholars attribute this letter to a disciple of the apostle Peter, writing from Rome late in the first century (A.D. 70–90). The letter has played an important role in the development of the theology of the sacrament of baptism, explaining that baptism is being "born anew" (1:23) and introducing the concept of the baptized Christian community as "a royal priesthood" (2:9) (CCC 1268, 1546). For the reformers of the Protestant Reformation, it became an essential text, not in the development of their theology of the sacrament of baptism, but rather in their argument against the need for an ordained priesthood (also Rev 1:6, 5:10).

First Peter (5:6–9) also provides us with a familiar meditation used in the Church's celebration of night prayer (Compline).

SECOND PETER
(2 Pet 1–3)

This letter, also attributed to Peter but most certainly the work of an anonymous author writing in the second century (A.D. 130), has the distinction of being the latest book in the New Testament. A section of this letter seems to be taken from the Letter of Jude (2:1–18), and there is also a direct reference to the writings of the apostle Paul (3:15–16), in which the author speaks of the difficulty of understanding some of what Paul has written. However, that being the case, the letter nonetheless offers an important teaching on the role of the inspiration of the Holy Spirit in reference to the Scriptures (1:19–21) and further insight into the necessary disposition of a Christian who patiently waits for the return of the Lord (3:8–10).

FIRST JOHN
(1 Jn 1—5)

The text is most certainly not a letter, and not really an epistle, but perhaps can best be understood as "further instruction and guidance," a treatise from the Johannine community (A.D. 100). It takes up many of the beautiful themes that were first expressed in the Gospel of John, specifically the difference between light and darkness (1:5–7), the primacy of love (2:3–6), and the testimony of God the Father, who has revealed to us his Son, Jesus (5:9–11). The text was written as early as ten years after the completion of the gospel, in response to members of the community who were in error about their perception of Jesus. Some members of the community had even departed from the community, which was the cause of great sorrow, but also which prompted a reaffirmation of what the community knew to be true (4:1–6).

SECOND JOHN

(2 Jn, only verses)

This is most certainly a letter, and a very short letter at that. It was written around A.D. 100 by a person often identified as John the Presbyter. The purpose of the letter is twofold: to reaffirm that the commandment to love is not a new commandment (v. 6) and that Jesus Christ was truly a human being (v. 7). The need for the reaffirmation and the warning about false teachers (v. 10) indicate some of the issues that challenged the early Christian community.

THIRD JOHN

(3 Jn, only verses)

Another letter, also attributed to John the Presbyter, around the same time as the previous letter, has the distinction of being the shortest book of the New Testament. The letter illustrates that there were tensions within the Christian community, and that things did not always work out as planned. In particular, this letter tells us of two Christians, Gaius and Demetrius, who are faithful members of the community, and a certain Diotrephes, who is stirring up trouble. The letter is both a letter of praise and thanksgiving for faithfulness, and also a warning of potential trouble.

JUDE

(Jude, only verses)

This letter, attributed to Jude, the brother of James, emerges from the latter part of the first century (A.D. 95–100) and is written by an unknown author to a community that has not been identified. Again, the letter is primarily concerned with disruptive members of the community (12–13). It reassures the faithful that those who cause division within the community will be punished by the Lord. Various Old Testament personalities and images are recalled and offered as examples of what will happen to those who behave in such a manner.

8. The Book of Revelation (Rev 1—22)

The last book of the New Testament, traditionally attributed to John of Patmos (A.D. 92–96, at the end of the reign of the emperor Diocletian), is also known as the book of the Apocalypse. Scripture scholars agree that the author of Revelation is not the author of the Gospel of John.

Of all of the books of the New Testament, the book of Revelation causes the most discussion and it is the source of countless speculation. Many television evangelists present the book as prophecy, and purport to understand the chapters and verses of the book as a type of "predictor" for what has happened in our modern world and what we might look forward to. From the Catholic perspective this is, at best, unfortunate.

It may be disappointing for some to realize that the book of Revelation is not filled with coded secrets, dictated by Christ to John, but once they get over their disappointment, they might then recognize the main purpose of the text. Catholics understand the book of Revelation to be not prophetic (in the misunderstood sense of prophetic) or predictive literature, but rather apocalyptic. Catholics understand that the language and the symbols of the book of Revelation all proclaim and illustrate a single, important truth (God will ultimately prevail over evil, so do not be discouraged or dismayed), and not a multitude of hidden revelations that need to be deciphered.

The well-respected Catholic Scripture scholar, Rev. Raymond E. Brown, writing in *An Introduction to the New Testament,* offers a perspective on the book of Revelation that is quite helpful. He suggests that in the scientific world in which we live and work, the book of

Revelation stands as a witness to the power of images and symbols, helping us to understand and to appreciate a reality and a truth that cannot be measured but which is nevertheless important (p. 810).

PART FIVE

A Selection of Scripture Prayer Services

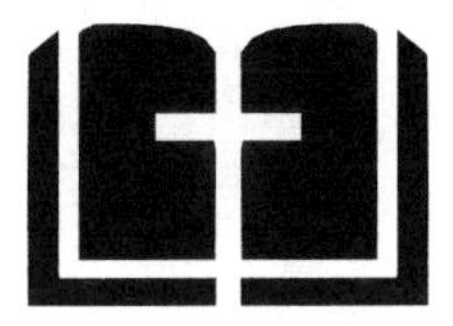

The selection of scripturally based prayer services that follow are intended as helpful prayer experiences either for the individual reader, a family, or perhaps a community of people such as a parish Bible-study group. The selection of themes are suggestive of particular events and experiences in everyday life when it may seem appropriate, and even encouraging, to "break open" the Word of God.

Although the power of the Word provides the primary experience, the praying of the Word can be enhanced through the addition of certain ritual and accouterments that are suggestive of the sacred. For example, the addition of a burning candle and an appropriate picture or religious article is sometimes very useful in setting the appropriate mood. The prominent display of the Bible that will be used for the proclamation of the Word is also helpful. Many people light incense, make use of appropriate silence and sacred gestures, such as bowing, and sing a favorite hymn.

Each of the services that follow are intended for congregational use, but may be easily adapted for private prayer and reflection.

This section also includes the traditional seven penitential psalms, each with an introduction and the full text of the psalm. These psalms are powerful through their imagery and in the emotion and the feelings they invoke. The praying of a penitential psalm is appropriate throughout the year and as part of a personal daily examination and prayer for forgiveness.

1. Preparing for Advent

Theme: Make ready the way of the Lord

Celebrant: Let us raise our hearts to the Lord. No one who hopes in the Lord will be disappointed.

All: We place our trust in you, O Lord, for our salvation belongs to you alone.

Celebrant: Lord Jesus Christ, Savior of the world. You are present with us as our God and our Redeemer. The expectation of the Old Testament, the longing of your people for the coming of God and our redemption, finds fulfillment in you.

All: Come, Lord Jesus.

Reading of the Word

Isaiah 7:10–15, followed by a period of silent reflection.

Response to the Word of God

Celebrant: For thousands of years, humanity has been looking for your coming. At the dawn of human history, when our first parents sinned, your coming was promised, for God said to the serpent:

All: "I will put enmity between you and the woman, between your seed and her seed; he shall crush your head."

Celebrant: Abraham could see your day from afar; all nations of the earth would be blessed in one of his descendants:

All: In you, O Lord; for you chose to become a man, a son of Abraham.

Celebrant: A thousand years before your coming, the promise was made to David, Israel's great king, that his line would never perish; that his Son would rule over all the people of the world.

All: You, Lord, are the Son of David, the King of the new Israel, of redeemed humanity. You are our King forever.

Celebrant: In ancient times the prophets announced your coming to the people. The picture they drew became ever clearer: Son of the virgin, friend of the poor and oppressed, Redeemer from our sins, man of sorrows, judge of the world, strong God! From generation to generation humankind waited and hoped.

All: But now you are with us. The first coming is now a reality. You have come and redeemed the world.

Second Reading

Mark 1:3–8, followed by a period of silent reflection.

Response to the Word of God

Celebrant: Lord Jesus Christ, incarnate Son of God. You are present here among us in the Holy Eucharist.

All: We kneel before you and adore you.

Celebrant: In a few weeks, we will again celebrate the great feast of your birth, the remembrance of your first coming to this earth. Make our hearts ready for these holy days, so that we may receive the overflowing fullness of that grace you merited for us by your incarnation. Sink the earnest words of the Baptist deep into our hearts: "Make ready the way of the Lord! Make straight his path."

All: Give your blessing Lord, to our prayers and our penance during this holy season of Advent.

Celebrant: Lead us to true conversion and an improvement in our lives on the holy feast of Christmas, so that we may, once again, experience the salvation that God has prepared for us in you, our Lord and our Redeemer.

All: Give us the grace to know you, the incarnate Son of God, ever more profoundly and love you more sincerely.

Celebrant: Let the heavens rejoice.

All: And the earth be glad.

Celebrant: For our God is coming and will show mercy to the poor.

All: He is our Savior.

Celebrant: Let us pray. O God, with joyful longing we look forward to the holy feast of Christmas, when we will, once again, celebrate the human birth of your son.

All: We receive him with joy as our Savior.

Celebrant: Give us full sharing in his redemption so that we may raise our faces with confidence when he comes to judge the world, he who lives and reigns with you forever and ever.

All: Amen.

Celebrant: Glory to the Father, and to the Son, and to the Holy Spirit.

All: As it was in the beginning, is now and ever shall be, world without end. Amen.

Third reading

Luke 1:26–38, followed by a period of silent reflection.

Response to the Word of God

Celebrant: Holy Mary, Mother of our Lord. We also think of you in this holy season of Advent. It is your image that stands as the first sign of redemption over the darkness of sin and death that covered all people when Adam and Eve sinned.

All: You are that woman who, in your Son, would win victory over the serpent.

Celebrant: Together with the Redeemer, you, his mother, were also announced to a waiting world through the prophet:

All: "Behold, a virgin shall conceive and give birth to a son; his name shall be Emmanuel, God-With-Us."

Celebrant: In your Immaculate Conception, holiest Virgin, the first light of a new day broke forth. You are the dawn that heralded, to the world, the rising of its true light, who is Christ the Lord! Redeemed by the power of your son, you gave, to the world, our Redeemer.

All: We praise you for your Immaculate Conception, holy Virgin Mary.

Celebrant: With the angel's message, the final hour of the great Advent dawned; the waiting of our world for the promised Redeemer found fulfillment. For all humanity, you consented to God's plan of salvation. Thus, you became a new Eve, a new mother for all the living, the mother of God's children.

All: We are grateful to you, O holy Virgin, Mother of our Lord, and our mother too.

Closing Prayer

Celebrant: Let us pray. Our Father in heaven, each year you gladden us with the expectation of the feast of our redemption. Please grant that as we joyfully receive your only begotten son as our Savior, we may also, one day, welcome him confidently as our Judge, Jesus Christ, your Son and our Lord, for he lives and reigns with you in the unity of the Holy Spirit, God forever.

All: Amen.

2. Preparing for Lent

Theme: Plant deep within us the desire to repent from our sins

Celebrant: Create in me, O God, a pure heart; give me a new and steadfast spirit.

All: Do not cast me out of your presence, nor take your Holy Spirit away from me.

Celebrant: God our Father, we come before you with open hands and an expectant faith. We believe that you desire to be with your people and that you form us, daily, in the image and the likeness of your Son. We pray that you remove, from us, this day, all that separates us from you and keeps us far from your kingdom.

All: Send out your Spirit and renew the face of the earth.

Reading of the Word

Ezekiel 36:24–28, followed by a period of silent reflection.

Response to the Word of God

Celebrant: Return to the Lord with all of your heart.

All: Leave the past in ashes and turn to God with tears and fasting, for God is slow to anger and ready to forgive.

Celebrant: Let the priests and ministers of the Lord lament before God's altar and say:

All: Spare us, Lord, spare your people. Do not let us die for we are crying out for you.

Celebrant: Lord, take away our wickedness and make us turn to you.

All: Help us, O God, our Savior, rescue us because of the honor of your name.

Celebrant: Let us pray. Direct our hearts, Lord, to your kingdom, heal us of our sin and ignorance. Grant to each of us the precious gift of time so that we may repent and be freed from all that binds us. We ask this in the powerful name of Jesus, your Son.

All: Amen.

Second Reading

Romans 6:2–6,12–14, followed by a period of silent reflection.

Response to the Word of God (The Litany of Penitence, Episcopal)

Celebrant: We have not loved you with our whole heart, mind, and strength. We have not loved our neighbors as ourselves. We have not forgiven others, and we have been forgiven.

All: Have mercy on us, Lord, have mercy.

Celebrant: We have been deaf to your call to serve, as Christ served us. We have not been true to the mind of Christ. We have grieved your Holy Spirit.

All: Have mercy on us, Lord, have mercy.

Celebrant: We confess to you, Lord, all our past unfaithfulness: the pride, hypocrisy, and impatience of our lives.

All: We confess to you, Lord.

Celebrant: Our self-indulgent appetites and ways, and our exploitation of other people.

All: We confess to you, Lord.

Celebrant: Our anger at our own frustration, and our envy of those more fortunate than ourselves.

All: We confess to you, Lord.

Celebrant: Our intemperate love of worldly goods and comforts, and our dishonesty in daily life and work.

All: We confess to you, Lord.

Celebrant: Our negligence in prayer and worship, and our failure to commend the faith that is in us.

All: We confess to you, Lord.

Third Reading

Matthew 9:1–8, followed by a period of silent reflection.

Response to the Word of God

Celebrant: Accept our repentance Lord, for the wrongs we have done: for our blindness to human need and suffering, and our indifference to injustice and cruelty.

All: Accept our repentance, Lord.

Celebrant: For all false judgments, for uncharitable thoughts toward our neighbors, and for our own prejudice and contempt toward those who are different from us.

All: Accept our repentance, Lord.

Celebrant: For our waste and pollution of your creation, and our lack of concern for those who are to come after us.

All: Accept our repentance, Lord.

Celebrant: Restore us, good Lord, and let your anger depart from us;

All: Favorably hear us, for your mercy is great.

Celebrant: Accomplish, in us, the work of your salvation.

All: So that we may demonstrate your glory to the world.

Celebrant: By the cross and passion of your Son, our Lord.

All: Bring us, with all of your saints, to the joy of the Resurrection!

Closing Prayer

Celebrant: Almighty God and Father, as we begin this holy season of Lent, fill us with a desire to repent of our sins. Grant us a generous portion of your Holy Spirit who strengthens us each day, and calls us to make a life-giving response to your love which is active in our lives. Help us see you in our brothers and sisters and have the necessary courage and fortitude to build your kingdom. We ask all of this in the name of Jesus, your son, and our brother.

All: Amen.

3. When You Need to Be Forgiven

Theme: Return to me with all of your heart

Celebrant: As Christians, we gather together, just as our brothers and sisters who have gone before us once assembled, and we do so in the name of the Father, and of the Son, and of the Holy Spirit.

All: Amen.

Celebrant: As once the Spirit of God hovered over the waters at the moment of creation, and as that same Spirit hovered over the waters of our baptism, we gather in expectant wonder and awe. We understand all that we are, and all that we hope to be, comes to us from God as a gift. We acknowledge that even though we are aware of God's grace, and accept the power of the Spirit, there are moments in our lives when we have neglected to fully participate with the activity of the Spirit of God. For this refusal to cooperate we ask pardon and forgiveness, not only of our God but also of the community gathered here. Together we pray:

All: I confess to almighty God, and to you, my brothers and sisters, that I have sinned through my own fault, in my thoughts and in my words, in what I have done, and in what I have failed to do; and I ask the blessed Mary, ever virgin, all the angels and saints, and you, my brothers and sisters, to pray for me to the Lord our God. Amen.

First Reading

Joel 2:12–18, followed by a period of silent reflection.

Psalm Response (Psalm 51, adapted)

Celebrant: Have mercy on me, O God, in your love.
In your great compassion blot out my sin.
Wash me thoroughly of my guilt; cleanse me of evil.

All: Today, help us turn away from sin and be faithful to the Gospel.

Celebrant: For I acknowledge my wrongdoings
And have my sins ever in mind.
Against you alone have I sinned;
What is evil in your sight I have done.

All: Today, help us turn away from sin and be faithful to the Gospel.

Celebrant: You are right when you pass judgment
And blameless in your sentence.
For I have been full of guilt from birth,
A sinner from the womb of my mother.

All: Today, help us turn away from sin and be faithful to the Gospel.

Celebrant: I know you desire truth in the heart,
Teach me wisdom in my innermost being.
Cleanse me with hyssop and I shall be clean,
Wash me, I shall be whiter than snow.

All: Today, help us turn away from sin and be faithful to the Gospel.

Celebrant: Fill me with joy and gladness;
Let the bones you have crushed rejoice.
Turn your face away from my sins and blot out all my offenses.

All: Today, help us turn away from sin and be faithful to the Gospel.

Second Reading

Romans 6:2–4,12–14, followed by a period of silent reflection.

Celebrant: Create in me, O God, a pure heart;
Give me a new and steadfast spirit.
Do not cast me out of your presence
Nor take your Holy Spirit away from me.

All: Stir up, within us, the cleansing power of your Holy Spirit.

Celebrant: Give me, again, the joy of your salvation
And sustain me with a willing spirit.
Then I will show wrongdoers your ways
And sinners will return to you.

All: Stir up, within us, the cleansing power of your Holy Spirit.

Celebrant: Deliver me, O God, from the guilt of blood
And of your justice, I shall sing aloud
O Lord, open my lips,
And I will declare your praise.

All: Stir up, within us, the cleansing power of your Holy Spirit.

Celebrant: You take no pleasure in sacrifice;
Were I to give a burnt offering,
You would not delight in it.

All: Stir up, within us, the cleansing power of your Holy Spirit.

Celebrant: O God, my sacrifice is a broken spirit;
A contrite heart you will not despise.
Shower Zion with your favor;
Rebuild the walls of Jerusalem.

All: Stir up, within us, the cleansing power of your Holy Spirit.

Third Reading

Matthew 9:1–8, followed by a period of silent reflection.

Celebrant: We have heard God's Word proclaimed to us and have meditated on that Word. We now approach our Father in heaven, with an open heart, confessing our sins, and asking, in faith, for mercy. As we ask for forgiveness, we are aware that forgiveness is celebrated within the community that is also gathered here. Just as our sins have wounded the Body of Christ, our forgiveness has restored the Body of Christ.

Note: If a communal celebration of reconciliation is to take place at this point, the individual confession of sins is celebrated as the sacrament of reconciliation is received. If this is not a communal or sacramental celebration, some individual form of confession of sins and acknowledgment of responsibility is appropriate at this time. After everyone has gathered together at the appropriate time, the community is invited to conclude their prayer.

Celebrant: Let us now all pray the traditional prayer of the Church, taught to us by Jesus, that expresses our beliefs and hopes.

All: Our Father, who art in heaven, hallowed be thy name; thy kingdom come; thy will be done on earth as it is in heaven. Give us this day our daily bread; and forgive us our trespasses as we forgive those who trespass against us; and lead us not into temptation, but deliver us from evil. (For the kingdom, the power, and the glory are yours, now and for ever.) Amen.

Celebrant: The Lord be with you.

All: And also with you.

Celebrant: May almighty God have mercy on us, forgive us our sins, and bring us to everlasting life.

All: Amen.

Celebrant: Your sins have been forgiven, stand up and walk. Depart from this place in peace. Share with your brothers and sisters the creative power of God and the forgiving spirit that you have received this day.

All: Thanks be to God.

4. A Prayer Service for Those Near Death

Theme: May angels lead you

It is important to walk with our loved ones, as far as we can, along their journey to death. We cannot cross over into their new home, but we can certainly accompany them as far as the door. I would encourage you to pray this prayer close to your loved one. Sit on the edge of the bed, hold his hand, touch her head, shoulders, or arm. It is a comfort to your loved one to know that you are there on the journey with the Lord to their new home.

Introductory Rites

Leader: We journey with you (name) toward your new home. We will go with you as far as the front door. We will wait and pray as you pass through this door into your new home in the kingdom of God. Let us walk together, sharing the love we have, in faith and peace.

Leader: Let the peace of the Lord rest upon you.

All: Let the peace of the Lord rest upon you.

Leader: We ask that the angels lead you to your new home.

All: Let the peace of the Lord rest upon you.

Leader: We ask Jesus, who is "the Way," to make smooth your path.

All: Let the peace of the Lord rest upon you.

Leader: We ask Jesus, who is "the Light," to make bright your path.

All: Let the peace of the Lord rest upon you.

Leader: We ask Jesus, who is your friend, to walk beside you today.

All: Let the peace of the Lord rest upon you.

Psalm Prayer: Adapted from Psalm 51

Leader: Hear our voices, Lord; we are calling.

All: Hear our voices, Lord; we are calling.

Leader: One thing we ask of the Lord, this we seek: To dwell in the Lord's house all the days of our lives, to gaze on the Lord's beauty, to visit God's temple.

All: Hear our voices, Lord; we are calling.

Leader: Do not, Lord, hide your face from us; do not cast us off; for you are our help, O God our Savior.

All: Hear our voices, Lord; we are calling.

Leader: We believe that we shall enjoy God's goodness in the land of the living. We take courage and wait for the Lord; we are stout-hearted, and we wait for the Lord.

All: Hear our voices, Lord; we are calling.

Second Reading

Reading from the Word of God: John 14:1–3

Leader: "Do not let your hearts be troubled. Believe in God, believe also in me. In my Father's house there are many dwelling places. If it were not so, would I have told you that I go to prepare a place for you? And if I go and prepare a place for you, I will come again and will take you to myself, so that where I am, there you may be also."

(A period of silence)

Individual Silent Prayer

Individually, each person present comes forward and silently places their hands on their loved one, praying quietly for a few moments.

Into Your Hands

Leader: Lord, we commend (name) into your loving hands!

All: Lord, we commend (name) into your loving hands!

Leader: We place you lovingly into the care of God our Father. We release you from anxiety and concern. We free you to leave this life and journey into the life of the Lord.

All: Lord, we commend (name) into your loving hands!

Leader: We see you as God sees you, a spiritual being, created in the image of God, embraced by God's presence and now returning home.

All: Lord, we commend (name) into your loving hands!

Leader: We will let go of our earthly hold on you. We will not bind you. We leave you in the hands of the Lord who will guard your comings and goings both now and forever.

All: Lord, we commend (name) into your loving hands!

Leader: May Jesus now flow into you. May Jesus be your food and drink. May Jesus be your passion, strength, and life. May Jesus be your shelter and keep you safe.

All: Lord, we commend (name) into your loving hands!

Leader: Let us pray the prayer that Jesus taught those who love him.

All: Our Father, who art in heaven, hallowed be thy name; thy kingdom come; thy will be done on earth as in heaven. Give us this day our daily bread; and forgive us our trespasses, as we forgive those who trespass against us; and lead us not into temptation, but deliver us from evil. (For the kingdom, the power, and the glory are yours, now and for ever). Amen.

Closing Prayer

Leader: May the Lord support you (name) all the day long. May the Lord lead you when the shadows lengthen and the evening comes.

May the Lord embrace you when the busy world is hushed, the fever of life is over, and your work is done. May the Lord bring you to a safe lodging, to a holy rest, and peace at last.

All: Amen.

Closing Blessing

Prayed by all present, as they extend their hands over their loved one.

All: May the Lord bless you (name) and keep you. May the Lord make his face shine upon you, and be gracious to you. May God look upon you with kindness, and give you peace. May almighty God bless you, the Father, and the Son, and the Holy Spirit. Amen.

Leader: May the angels of God surround you, and carry you to Paradise!

All: Amen.

Additional Prayers and Songs

The following are offered as suggestions if you wish to sing a song together or play recorded music:

"Be Not Afraid": Robert J. Dufford, S.J. (From the collection: *Earthen Vessels*).

"Take, Lord, Receive": John Foley, S.J. (From the collection: *Earthen Vessels*).

"Be With Me: Psalm 91": Marty Haugen (From the collection: *With Open Hands*).

"Lay Your Hands": Carey Landry (From the collection: *Abba! Father!*).

Suggested Scriptural Prayers and Readings

Psalm 23: The Divine Shepherd

Psalm 42: Longing for God and His Help in Distress

Psalm 121: Assurance of God's Protection

Isaiah 43:1–7: Restoration and Protection Promised

Matthew 11:28–30: Jesus Thanks His Father

John 11:17–27: Jesus the Resurrection and the Life

Romans 6:3–9: Dying and Rising With Christ

Romans 8:31–39: God's Love in Christ Jesus

5. Seeking the Spirit of Discernment

Theme: I seek to know your will, O Lord

Celebrant: O God, come to my assistance.

All: Lord, make haste to help me. Glory to the Father, and to the Son, and to the Holy Spirit. As it was in the beginning, is now and ever shall be, world without end. Amen.

Celebrant: The Scriptures have assured us that if we seek to know the will of the Lord, God's Word will reveal the path that we must follow. We gather together with expectant faith, confident of the power of the Word of God in our midst. We gather together with an open heart, straining to listen to the Spirit of the Lord in our midst.

First Reading

2 Kings 6:15–17a, followed by a period of silent reflection.

Response to the Word (Psalm 119, adapted)

Celebrant: Lord, you lay down your precepts to be carefully kept. Make our ways steady in doing your will and keep our eyes firmly fixed on your commandments.

All: Blessed are those who observe God's instructions, who seek God with all their hearts, and who do no evil but walk in God's ways.

Celebrant: With all my heart I seek you and in my heart I treasure all of your promises. Blessed are you, O God, teach me to do your will.

All: Blessed are those who observe God's instructions, who seek God with all their hearts, and who do no evil but walk in God's ways.

Celebrant: I cling to your instructions, do not disappoint me. I run the way of your commandments, for you have given me freedom of heart. Bend my heart to your instructions, not to selfish gain.

All: Blessed are those who observe God's instructions, who seek God with all their hearts, and who do no evil but walk in God's ways.

Second Reading

Ephesians 1:17–19a, followed by a period of silent reflection.

Response to the Word (Psalm 119, adapted, continues)

Celebrant: Lord, keep in mind the promises that you have given to your servant, the promises on which I have built my hope. It is my comfort in distress, and it is your Word that gives me life.

All: Blessed are those who observe God's instructions, who seek God with all their hearts, and who do no evil but walk in God's ways.

Celebrant: My task, O Lord, is to keep your Word. I have reflected on my ways and I turn my steps to your instructions. Even though I am distressed, I do not forget your law and I do not disregard your commandments.

All: Blessed are those who observe God's instructions, who seek God with all their hearts, and who do no evil but walk in God's ways.

Celebrant: How pleasant your promise to my palate, sweeter than honey is your Word in my mouth. Your Word is a lamp for my feet, a light on my path.

All: Blessed are those who observe God's instructions, who seek God with all their hearts, and who do no evil but walk in God's ways.

Celebrant: May my prayer come into your presence, rescue me as you have promised. May my lips proclaim your praise, for you teach me to do your will.

All: Blessed are those who observe God's instructions, who seek God with all their hearts, and who do no evil but walk in God's ways.

Third Reading

Luke 24:30–32, followed by a period of silent reflection.

Discernment Exercise

In the silence that follows the proclamation of the Word of God, all are invited to participate in an exercise of discernment. The choice of the experience that is to be discerned is opened to the power of the Word through a series of four questions. Each question, honestly reflected upon, leads the discerning person closer and closer to God's will for them, in this circumstance, at this particular time in their life.

The four questions are

1. What are my thoughts and feelings about this choice/experience?
2. What have other people, whom I love and trust, told me about this choice/experience?
3. When I imagine myself choosing a particular option, how do I feel about what I have chosen, and what I have not chosen?
4. Reflecting upon what has now been revealed to me, and as I lay all of what I have learned before God, what emerges as a

possible direction? Does my choice conflict with, or complement, the Word of God, as I now understand and appreciate it in my life this day?

Concluding Prayer

Celebrant: Each of us have tried, with the help of the Spirit of the Lord, to open ourselves to the will of God for us. Some of us have been able to reach a decision that we are confident is from the Lord and reflective of God's will for us. For others, the will of God has not yet emerged, so we are called to be patient, and await the clarity we seek with expectant faith. However, regardless of how we might feel at this moment, we are, nevertheless, able to join our voices together in praise and thanksgiving to God.

All: I will praise you, Lord, for your have counseled me (Ps 9:2; 145:1–2) and I will lift up my hands in the assembly of your faithful people (Ps 22:22). I will extol you at all times (Ps 34:1) and I will praise your name among all of the peoples of the earth (Ps 57:9). I will praise your name in song (Ps 69:30), I will praise you with my heart (Ps 138:1) and I will praise you while I live (Ps 146:2). My lips shout for joy for when I praise you (Ps 71:23) for you have put a new song into my mouth (Ps 40:3). I will sing and praise your might forever (Ps 21:13).

Blessed be the Lord (2 Chr 9:8).

Blessed be the name of the Lord forever (Job 1:21).

Blessed be the Lord, my rock (2 Sam 22:47).

Blessed be God, the Father of our Lord Jesus Christ (Eph 1:3).

Amen. Alleluia.

6. The Seven Penitential Psalms

The seven penitential psalms, as listed by the Vulgate enumeration, are 6, 31, 37, 50, 101, 129, and 142; modern interpretations list them as 6, 32, 38, 51, 102, 130, and 143. The penitential psalms are found in the Old Testament, or as it is sometimes identified, the Hebrew Scriptures, in the book of Psalms. They are traditionally understood to be prayers that express sentiments of repentance and sorrow for sin.

Since the sixth century, these psalms have been classified as "suitable for penance." Cassiodorus (Roman monk, 490–583) interpreted them allegorically and taught that they were indicative of seven means available for obtaining forgiveness: baptism, martyrdom, almsgiving, a forgiving spirit, conversion of the sinner, love, and penance. During the Middle Ages, at the direction of Pope Innocent III, they were commonly recited on the Fridays of Lent. Pope Saint Pius X (1903–1914) added them to the Divine Office for recitation during Lent. They are still widely used in the liturgy, especially Psalm 129 (130), the *De Profundis,* and Psalm 50 (51), the *Miserere.*

Another traditional understanding of the penitential psalms are that they are representative of the lament of Jesus in his passion and death. The traditional encouragement for the praying of the psalms is often discovered in the voices of the saints who discovered, within these psalms, the experience of the voice of Jesus praying. In Psalm 38, for example, the "voice" of the Lord seems very present: "My wounds stink and fester within me. Stooped and bowed down, I go about mourning all day" (Ps 38:5–6, adapted).

The following is a presentation of these psalms, in an adapted form, using modern-day terminology.

Psalm 6, the prayer of the afflicted, is the prayer of a sick person. It is a traditional intercessory prayer which asks for the grace to be freed from the sickness of sin, it also affirms the intention to have nothing to do with evil.

O Lord, in your anger do not reprove;
nor punish me in your fury.
Have mercy on me, O Lord, for I have no strength left.

O Lord, heal me, for my bones are in torment.
   My soul also is gently troubled.
How long, O Lord, how long?
How long will you be?
Come back to me, O Lord, save my life;
rescue me for the sake of your love.
For no one remembers you in the grave;
who will praise you in the world of the dead?
I am weary with moaning;
I weep every night, drenching my bed with tears.
My eyes have grown dim from troubles;
I have weakened because of my foes.
Away from me, you evildoers,
   for the Lord has heard my plaintive voice.
The Lord has heard my plea;
   the Lord will grant all that I pray for.
Let my enemies fall back in shame,
   all of a sudden—the whole bunch of them!

Psalm 32 is representative of the relief that is often felt after the confession of sin. Buried sin ruins the conscience. Confession is understood to be a type of liberation. A person's well being, in the truest sense of the word, depends upon the quality of their relationship with God: what sin has destroyed will only be restored by trust in God who pardons the humble and the repentant.

Blessed is the one whose sin is forgiven,
   whose iniquity is wiped away.
Blessed are those in whom the Lord sees no guilt
   and in whose spirit is found no deceit.
When I kept my sin secret,
my body wasted away,

I was moaning all day long.
Your hand day and night lay heavy upon me;
draining my strength, parching my heart
 as in the heat of a summer drought.
Then I made known to you my sin
 and uncovered before you my fault,
 saying to myself,
"To the Lord I will now confess my wrong."
And you, you forgave my sin, you removed my guilt.
So let the faithful ones pray to you in time of distress;
waters may overflow, the flood will not reach them.
You are my refuge;
you protect me from distress
 and surround me with songs of deliverance.
I will teach you, I will show you the way to follow.
I will watch over you and give you counsel.
Do not be like the horse or the mule-senseless
 and led by bit and bridle.
Many woes befall the wicked,
But the Lord's mercy enfolds those who trust in him.
"Rejoice in the Lord, and be glad, you who are upright:
 sing and shout for joy, you who are clean of heart."

Psalm 38 teaches that the greater the sin, the greater must be our trust in God. Oftentimes, people relate sickness to sinfulness. It is not unusual for people to assume that their suffering is connected to their choices and actions. Another very common reaction, perhaps because of the presence of guilt, is the assumption that "things will go wrong" because of sin. This psalm reflects such feelings and assumptions. Another traditional interpretation is that it is reflective of the agony of Jesus in his passion.

O Lord, rebuke me not in your rage,
  punish me not in your fury.
Your arrows have struck me;
your hand has come down heavily upon me.
Your anger has spared no part of my body,
my sin gives no peace to my bones.
For my transgressions overwhelm me;
they weigh me down like an unbearable load.
My wounds stink and fester within me,
  the outcome of my sinful folly.
Stooped and bowed down, I go about mourning all day.
My loins burn, my flesh is diseased,
my body, worn out and utterly crushed;
I groan in pain and anguish of heart.
All my longing O Lord is known to you;
my sighing is not hidden from you.
My heart pounds as my strength ebbs;
  even the light has deserted my eyes.
My friends avoid me because of my wounds;
my neighbors stay far off.
Those who seek my life lay snares for me;
those who wish me harm speak of my ruin
  and plot against me all day long.
But like a deaf-mute,
I neither hear nor open my mouth.
I am like one whose ears hear not and whose mouth
  has no answer.
For I put my trust in you,
O Lord; you will answer for me, Lord God.
I pray, "Don't let them gloat over me
nor take advantage of my helplessness when my foot slips."
For I am about to fall, my pain is ever with me.

I confess my transgression,
I repent of my sin.
Many are my foes;
many are those who hate me for no reason,
those who pay me evil for good and harass me
  because I seek good.
Forsake me not, O Lord, stay not far from me.
O my God, come quickly to help me, O Lord, my Savior!

Psalm 51, the *Miserere,* laments the sinful condition of humanity and admits the presence of personal sin in the life of the penitent. This psalm imagines the sinner standing humbly before the throne of God, expecting both to be forgiven and that a new heart and spirit will be freely given. The proof, offered to God, of the sinner's true repentance is the broken spirit of the penitent, freely laid before the throne of God; the expectant response is God's gift, to the sinner, of a pure heart.

Have mercy on me, O God, in your love.
In your great compassion blot out my sin.
Wash me thoroughly of my guilt; cleanse me of evil.
For I acknowledge my wrongdoings
And have my sins ever in mind.
Against you alone have I sinned;
What is evil in your sight I have done.
You are right when you pass sentence
And blameless in your judgment.
For I have been guilt-ridden from birth,
A sinner from my mother's womb.
I know you desire truth in the heart,
Teach me wisdom in my inmost being.
Cleanse me with hyssop and I shall be clean,
Wash me, I shall be whiter than snow.

Fill me with joy and gladness;
Let the bones you have crushed rejoice.
Turn your face away from my sins
and blot out all my offenses.
Create in me, O God, a pure heart;
Give me a new and steadfast spirit.
Do not cast me out of your presence
Nor take your holy spirit away from me.
Give me again the joy of your salvation
And sustain me with a willing spirit.
Then I will show wrongdoers your ways
And sinners will return to you.
Deliver me, O God, from the guilt of blood
And of your justice I shall sing aloud
O Lord, open my lips,
And I will declare your praise.
You take no pleasure in sacrifice;
Were I to give a burnt offering
You would not delight in it.
O God, my sacrifice is a broken spirit;
A contrite heart you will not despise.
Shower Zion with your favor;
Rebuild the walls of Jerusalem.
Then you will delight in fitting sacrifices,
In burnt offerings and bulls offered on your altar.

Psalm 102 is an examination of conscience, originally prayed, according to tradition, by King David. This examination leads a person to a way of life that is reflective of perfection and the desire to do only God's will, each and every day. At the same time, this psalm leaves the penitent with a question that needs to be answered by God: "When I do all of these things, then will you come to me?"

Hear my prayer, O Lord;
  let my cry come to you.
Do not hide your face from me
  in the day of my distress.
Incline your ear to me;
  answer me speedily in the day when I call.

For my days pass away like smoke,
  and my bones burn like a furnace.
My heart is stricken and withered like grass;
  I am too wasted to eat my bread.
Because of my loud groaning
  my bones cling to my skin.
I am like an owl of the wilderness,
  like a little owl of the waste places.
I lie awake;
  I am like a lonely bird on the housetop.
All day long my enemies taunt me;
  those who deride me use my name for a curse.
For I eat ashes like bread,
  and mingle tears with my drink,
because of your indignation and anger;
  for you have lifted me up and thrown me aside.
My days are like an evening shadow;
  I wither away like grass.
But you, O Lord, are enthroned forever,
  your name endures to all generations.
You will rise up and have compassion to Zion,
  for it is time to favor it;
  the appointed time has come.
For your servants hold its stones dear,
  and have pity on its dust.

The nations will fear the name of the LORD,
  and all the kings of the earth your glory.
For the LORD will build up Zion;
  he will appear in his glory.
He will regard the prayer of the destitute,
  and will not despise their prayer.

Let this be recorded for a generation to come,
  so that a people yet unborn may praise the LORD:
that he looked down from his holy height,
  from heaven the LORD looked at the earth,
to hear the groans of the prisoners,
  to set free those who were doomed to die;
so that the name of the LORD may be declared in Zion,
  and his praise in Jerusalem,
when peoples gather together,
  and kingdoms, to worship the LORD.

He has broken my strength in midcourse;
  he has shortened my days.
"O my God," I say, "do not take me away
  at the mid-point of my life,
you whose years endure
  throughout all generations."

Long ago you laid the foundation of the earth,
  and the heavens are the work of your hands.
They will perish, but you endure;
  they will all wear out like a garment.
You change them like clothing, and they pass away;
  but you are the same, and your years have no end.
The children of your servants shall live secure;
  their offspring shall be established in your presence.

Psalm 130 is a prayer about suffering. The psalmist cannot remember a time without oppression. However, despite pain and suffering, there was always expectant hope. We are to be like the watchman who, although surrounded by seemingly complete and eternal darkness, never gives up hope that soon a new day will dawn for all who await this divine redemption.

Out of the depths I cry to you, O Lord,
O Lord, hear my voice!
Let your ears pay attention
To the voice of my supplication.
If you should mark our evil,
O Lord, who could stand?
But with you is forgiveness,
And for that you are revered.
I waited for the Lord, my soul waits,
And I put my hope in his word.
My soul expects the Lord
More than watchmen the dawn.
O Israel, hope in the Lord,
For with him is unfailing love
And with him full deliverance.
He will deliver Israel from all its sins.

The last penitential psalm, Psalm 143, is a cry for mercy from a person who has been beaten down and oppressed. The psalmist pictures the penitent as a piece of farmland that has experienced drought for an extended period of time, now longing for a drop of cool and refreshing water to restore life to the earth. The psalm gives us certain hints that the penitent is weak and needs a response very quickly or they will be lost. They are not so lost and forsaken, however, that they lack the energy to pray that all of their enemies are destroyed!

O Lord, hear my prayer, listen to my cry for mercy;
Answer me, you who are righteous and faithful.
Do not bring your servant to judgment,
For no mortal is just in your sight.
The enemy has pursued me,
Crushing my life to the ground,
Sending me to darkness with those long dead.
And so my spirit fails me,
My heart is full of fear.
I remember the days of long ago;
I mediate on what you have done
  and consider the work of your hands.
I stretch out my hands to you,
And thirst for you like a parched land.
O Lord, answer me quickly:
  my spirit is faint with yearning.
Do not hide your face from me;
Save me from going down to the pit.
Let the dawn bring me word of your love,
For in you alone I put my trust.
Show me the way I should walk,
For to you I life up my soul.
Rescue me from my enemies, O Lord,
For to you I flee for refuge.
Teach me to do your will,
For you are my God,
Let your spirit lead me on a safe path.
Preserve me, O Lord, for your name's sake;
Free me from distress, in your justice.
You who are merciful,
Crush my enemies and destroy all my foes,
For I am your servant.

PART SIX

The Bible and the Sacraments

Most Catholics, or at least those who were formed and trained in catechetics before the Second Vatican Council, are routinely able to respond to the question, "What is a sacrament?" by repeating the formula they learned at a very young age: "A sacrament is a sign, instituted by Christ, to give grace." In addition to their ability to summarize sacramental theology in a definition provided by the Baltimore Catechism, they are also able to name each of the sacraments, seven in all, that the Church teaches are necessary for salvation.

A working assumption for most Catholics would be that since the sacraments are instituted by Christ, most certainly this institution of the sacraments should easily be discovered in the Scriptures. Due to this assumption many are disappointed, or somewhat frustrated, when they turn to the Scriptures and attempt to read about the institution of a particular sacrament. I suspect that they are looking for the same unambiguous clarity in the Scriptures that they have become accustomed to in their catechetical texts. In other words, they expect to find Jesus specifically making the statement: "This is a sacrament," but there are no such statements to be found in the Scriptures.

The Protestant Reformers before the Council of Trent (mid-sixteenth century) also looked for this same kind of clarity, but were unable to discover it to their satisfaction. As a result, many of the reformers were able to accept only two signs of God's grace that they were willing to designate as sacraments: baptism and the Eucharist. Admittedly, the references to baptism and the Eucharist are numerous, but the references to the other five sacraments are also present in the Scriptures and can be discovered in the ministry of Jesus, as well as in the ministerial practices of the early Christian community.

In the section that follows, the scriptural foundation for the sacraments is presented. This is neither an exhaustive presentation nor does it include every possible scriptural reference, but it does provide a firm foundation for the sacramental theology of the Church, as well as the essential elements necessary for a beginning appreciation of the Church's teaching.

1. Jesus and Baptism

One of the most vivid stories of the gospels is the story of the baptism of Jesus, by John the Baptist, in the Jordan River. Archaeologists and other scholars have told us that the ritual baptism that John was performing was not at all unusual in the Jewish culture of that time and place. Water had always played a significant role in the salvation history of the Jewish people in times of transition and change in their corporate history. The Red Sea, for example, had figured prominently in the escape from Egypt. As well, the Jordan River had come into play earlier since it was the river the people had to cross to enter the Promised Land. For this reason, the use of water as a sign and symbol to indicate a transition in a person's life and spiritual journey could be connected to the corporate journey of faith experienced by the community.

When Jesus appeared at the Jordan to be baptized by John, he was on the cusp of a significant change in the direction of his life. The traditional way of understanding this change is that Jesus was moving from his "hidden life" to his "public life." However, it is understood that the baptism of Jesus, although certainly not required as an indication of his willingness to convert, but perhaps, rather, a sign of his "self-emptying" (CCC 1224), was definitely indicative of a transition and a change. Why he chose to present himself to John at this specific moment and place is not known; what is known is that immediately after he emerged from the river, "And a voice from heaven said, 'This is my Son, the Beloved, with whom I am well pleased" (Mt 3:17).

Although it is documented that Jesus was baptized at the beginning of his ministry, it is not clear if Jesus and his disciples baptized people during the years of his public ministry; the gospels do not agree on this point. However, the gospels do agree that Jesus, after his Resurrection, instructed his disciples to use this sign and symbol of conversion and change: "Go therefore and make disciples of all nations, baptizing them in the name of the Father and of the Son and of the Holy Spirit" (Mt 28:19).

The community of the apostles took this command very seriously and, from the day of Pentecost forward, the Church administered baptism to all those who wished to take part in "*the washing of regeneration and renewal by the Holy Spirit*" (CCC 1215). The apostle Peter, preaching to the crowds who had gathered to hear the apostles, proclaimed, "Repent, and be baptized every one of you in the name of Jesus Christ so that your sins may be forgiven; and you will receive the gift of the Holy Spirit" (Acts 2:38).

2. Baptism Scripture References

Exodus 17:2, "Give us water to drink...."

Ezekiel 36:25, "I will sprinkle clean water upon you, and you shall be clean from all your uncleanlinesses...."

Ezekiel 47 states that where there is the cleansing waters, there will be life.

Romans 6:3–4, "...all of us who have been baptized into Christ Jesus were baptized into his death?...Just as Christ was raised from the dead...so we too might walk in the newness of life."

1 Corinthians 12:13, "For in the one Spirit we were all baptized into one body...."

Galatians 3:27–28, "As many of you as were baptized into Christ have clothed yourself with Christ....for all of you are one in Christ Jesus."

Ephesians 4:5, "One Lord, one faith, one baptism."

Matthew 28:19, "Go therefore and make disciples of all nations, baptizing them in the name of the Father and of the Son and of the Holy Spirit."

Mark 1:9–11 refers to the baptism of Jesus in the Jordan River.

John 4:14, "...those who drink of the water that I will give them will never be thirsty. The water that I will give will become in them a spring of water gushing up to eternal life."

John 7:38, "...let the one who believes in me drink. As the scripture has said, 'Out of the believer's heart shall flow rivers of living water.'"

3. Jesus and the Holy Spirit

Throughout his earthly ministry, Jesus acted with courage and compassion; he stretched out his hand to nourish and heal and to give new life where there was once only death. This ministerial action was an activity that Jesus identified to his followers as something that was enabled in him by the fact that he was filled with the Spirit, "The Spirit of the Lord is upon me, because he has anointed me to bring good news to the poor..." (Lk 4:18). It was only after the Resurrection that the apostles came to understand that the same Spirit that filled Jesus, was also to be given to them, "...stay here in the city until you have been clothed with power from on high" (Lk 24:49). The Acts of the Apostles (2:2–4) describes the experience of the apostles and those others who had gathered in the upper room, waiting, as they had been instructed to do. "And suddenly from heaven there came a sound like the rush of a violent wind, and it filled the entire house where they were sitting....All of them were filled with the Holy Spirit...."

It was probably not until the experience of the feast of Pentecost that the apostles were able to fully comprehend and understand that Jesus intended the Spirit, which Christians today call the Holy Spirit, to be his gift to the Church. Just as the Holy Spirit had worked within

Jesus, that same Spirit would now work within the Church, enabling all that Jesus had promised to come to pass, and slowly guiding and directing the baptized in the way of the kingdom.

4. Confirmation Scripture References

Isaiah 11:2, "The spirit of the LORD shall rest on him...."

Isaiah 42:1, "...my chosen...I have put my spirit upon him...."

Isaiah 61:1, "...the LORD...has sent me to bring good news to the oppressed...."

Ezekiel 36:26, "...a new spirit I will put within you...."

Joel 2:28, "...I will pour out my spirit on all flesh...."

Acts of the Apostles 1:8, "...you will receive power when the Holy Spirit has come upon you...."

Acts of the Apostles 2:4, "All of them were filled with the Holy Spirit...."

Acts of the Apostles 8:17, "...and they received the Holy Spirit...."

Romans 5:5, "...God's love has been poured into our hearts through the Holy Spirit...."

Romans 8:26, "...the Spirit helps us...."

1 Corinthians 12:4, 6, "...but the same Spirit; (...) in everyone."

Ephesians 1:13, "...you also...were marked with the seal of the promised Holy Spirit."

Matthew 16:24, "...If any want to become my followers, let them deny themselves...."

Matthew 25:21, "...enter into the joy of your master."

Mark 1:11, "...You are my Son, the Beloved...."

Luke 4:18, "The Spirit of the Lord is upon me...."

John 7:38, "Out of the believer's heart shall flow rivers of living water."

5. Jesus and the Eucharist

Jesus, evidently, shared many meals with his friends and apostles. From the gospels, we know that Jesus shared meals with people from all walks of life, a practice that caused his enemies to comment, "This fellow welcomes sinners and eats with them" (Lk 15:2). We also have other examples from the gospels that clearly illustrate his concern that the people who accompanied him were cared for and adequately nourished; the wedding feast of Cana (Jn 2:1–10) and the multiplication of the loaves and the fish in the feeding of the five thousand (Mt 14:15–21) are just two examples. Finally, after the Resurrection, we know that Jesus ate at least twice with his disciples, once on the shore of the lake (Jn 21:9–13) and the second time when he appeared to them in the upper room (Lk 24:41–43).

These are all examples of Jesus sharing essential nourishment with his friends and apostles, but none of these occasions, as important and as pleasant as they might have been, compare to the meal he shared with his apostles on the night before he died. This meal, what we now call the Last Supper, was unique and special. At this meal Jesus took some bread, blessed it and broke it saying, "This is my body, which is given for you..." (Lk 22:19). At the end of the meal, he passed around the cup and said, "This cup that is poured out for you is the new covenant in my blood" (Lk 22:20).

Perhaps, this simple sharing of the bread and wine, because it took place the night before he died, is the primary reason it is remembered so clearly by the apostles, and understood to be important. Perhaps, it was because this meal took place within the context of the remembering associated with the Feast of the Passover, a ritual meal and action already understood to be important and necessary by those who were in attendance. Or perhaps, it was because of the fact that Jesus clearly identified his actions of blessing the wine and breaking the bread, with a command to his disciples, "Do this in remembrance of me" (Lk 22:19; Mt 26:26–29; Mk 14:22–25; 1 Cor 11:23–26). For whatever reason, or combination of reasons, the apostles remembered this occasion after the death and Resurrection of Jesus and comprehended that this action was to be repeated, again and again, until the Lord returned, as he had promised.

6. Eucharist Scripture References

Genesis 14:18–19, "King Melchizedek...brought out bread and wine... blessed him...."

Exodus 16:4, "Then the LORD said to Moses, 'I am going to rain bread from heaven for you....' "

Exodus 24:8, "...the covenant the LORD has made with you...."

Deuteronomy 8:3, "...by feeding you manna...to make you understand...."

1 Kings 19:8, "...then he went in the strength of that food...."

Proverbs 9:5, "...eat of my bread and drink of the wine I have mixed."

Acts of the Apostles 2:42, "The breaking of bread...."

Acts of the Apostles 10:41, "Not to all the people but to us who were chosen by God as witnesses, and who ate and drank with him after he rose from the dead."

1 Corinthians 10:17, "...there is one bread, and we who are many are one body...."

1 Corinthians 11:26, "For as often as you eat this bread and drink the cup, you proclaim the Lord's death...."

Hebrews 9:14, "...the blood of Christ...purify our conscience...."

Mark 14:22, 24, "Take; this is my body....This is my blood...."

Luke 9:17, "...all ate and were filled."

Luke 24:35, "...he had been made known to them in the breaking of the bread."

John 6:11, "...he distributed...as much as they wanted."

John 6:35, "...I am the bread of life. Whoever comes to me will never be hungry, and whoever believes in me will never be thirsty."

John 6:51, "...I am the living bread that came down from heaven."

John 6:55, "...for my flesh is true food and my blood is true drink."

7. Jesus and Sinners

Even people who do not believe that Jesus is the Son of God are, nevertheless, left with the impression that he was a person with an unusual capacity for forgiveness. Not only was he able to forgive sinners, he was also able to forgive those who had sinned against him (Lk 23:34). The gospels are filled with illustrations of his forgiveness in action: the story of the Prodigal Son (Lk 15:11-32), the story of the Lost Sheep (Lk 15:3–7), and the story of the Woman caught in adultery (Jn 8:3–11) are some obvious examples.

The message that Jesus preached, a message preached by John the Baptist (repent and believe), but completed by Jesus (because the kingdom of God is among you), was a message that called people to *metanoia*, a Greek word that means to change your life and your heart. His was more than a message to call people to repentance (which means to be sorry for what you have done), Jesus wanted people to be sorry, but he also desired that they be fundamentally changed by their sorrow and their personal experience of forgiveness. This fundamental change, the reordering of their life and their decisions, was to be understood as *gospel* (good news), because it would usher in a new way of life as well as a new way of living, which he called the kingdom of God.

Jesus was so insistent on *metanoia*, and the ramifications of this life-changing decision, that when his apostles asked him for further clarification, "how often" did they have to forgive (Mt 18:21), he answered, "not seven times, but, I tell you, seventy-seven times" (Mt

18:22). In other words, in the kingdom of God, there was no limit to what could be forgiven, and no limit to what needed to be forgiven; "forgive us our sins, / for we ourselves forgive / everyone indebted to us" (Lk 11:4).

After his Resurrection, Jesus appeared to his disciples, and spoke to them in the words that have traditionally been understood to be the words that instituted the sacrament of penance and reconciliation: "If you forgive the sins of any, they are forgiven them; if you retain the sins of any, they are retained" (Jn 20:23). Within the context of his life and ministry, it can be understood that although the power to "retain" someone is certainly a prerogative, the intention of Jesus was to not retain, but rather to set them loose, to free people from that which held them fast, and set them firmly on the path to the kingdom of God.

8. Reconciliation and Penance Scripture References

Isaiah 55:7, "...let them return to the LORD, that he may have mercy on them...."

Ezekiel 18:30, "Repent and turn from all your transgressions...."

Joel 2:12, "...return to me with all your heart...."

Jonah 3:10, "...they [Nineveh] turned from their evil ways...."

Romans 6:7–8, "For whoever has died is free from sin. But if we have died with Christ, we believe that we will also live with him."

1 John 1:7, "...the blood of Jesus cleanses us from all sin."

Psalm 51:1, "Have mercy on me, O God...."

Psalm 103:1, "Bless the LORD, O my soul...."

Psalm 130:1, "Out of the depths I cry to you...."

Revelation 1:5, "To him who loves us and freed us from our sins by his blood."

Matthew 9:5, "Your sins are forgiven....Stand up and walk."

Mark 1:15, "...repent, and believe in the good news."

Luke 7:47, "...her sins, which were many, have been forgiven; hence she has shown great love."

Luke 15:11–32: The parable of the prodigal and his brother.

Luke 24:47, "...repentance and forgiveness of sins is to be proclaimed in his name to all nations...."

9. Jesus the Healer

A distinct portrait of the gospel presentation of Jesus is the clear impression that Jesus was a healer. There seems to be little doubt that not only had the people of that time and place understood that Jesus was a healer but also that his ministry was one of the ways Jesus identified himself. When the disciples of John the Baptist came to Jesus and asked him, "Are you the one who is to come, or are we to wait for another?" (Lk 7:19), Jesus responded, "Go and tell John what you have seen and heard: the blind receive their sight, the lame walk, the lepers are cleansed, the deaf hear, the dead are raised, the poor have good news brought to them" (Lk 7:22).

The original meaning of the word *salvation* is derived from the Latin word *salus,* which means "health." One understanding of salvation, an interpretation construed from the root meaning of the word combined with the experience of those who have been "saved," is that salvation is the restoration of health not just to the physical being of a person but also to the spiritual. In the life and the ministry of Jesus, this connection between the physical and spiritual health of a person was understood by the people of the time. There was little distinction made between the physical and spiritual worlds, and people fully expected that if a person experienced something in one realm, there would be a parallel experience in the other. In a very real sense, it was a holistic approach to the meaning of life.

In the "miracle" stories of the gospels, Jesus cures the blind (Mk

10:51–52; Jn 9:1–7), the deaf (Lk 7:22), the deaf and mute (Mk 7:37), the paralyzed (Mk 2:3–9), as well as other physical ailments. In other instances, he cures spiritual ills by driving the devil out of people (Mk 9:25), restoring them to mental health. In some instances, he cures both a physical malady and a spiritual one at the same time (for example, in the story of the paralyzed man who is brought to Jesus). In that case, Jesus states first, "Your sins are forgiven," and then, secondly, "Stand up and walk" (Mt 9:1–8).

10. Anointing of the Sick Scripture References

2 Kings 20:5, "I have heard your prayer, I have seen your tears; indeed, I will heal you...."

Isaiah 53:4, "...he has borne our infirmities / and carried our diseases...."

Acts of the Apostles 28:8–9, "Paul...cured him...[and] the rest of the people...came and were cured."

2 Corinthians 4:10, "...always carrying in the body the death of Jesus...."

2 Corinthians 12:9, "My grace is sufficient for you...."

James 5:15, "The prayer of faith will save the sick...."

Psalm 102:1: "Hear my prayer, O LORD...."

Matthew 8:14–17: Jesus cures Peter's mother-in-law and many others.

Mark 16:18, "...the sick, and they will recover."

Luke 22:42, "...yet, not my will but yours be done."

John 15:1–2, "...my Father is the vinegrower. He removes every branch in me that bears no fruit. Every branch that bears fruit he prunes to make it bear more fruit."

11. Jesus and Marriage

In the time of Jesus, marriage was not so much a religious matter as it was a family one. This is not to say that marriage did not have religious meaning or consequence, but this is an attempt to discuss marriage within its proper sociological context, especially within the context of how Jesus may have seen marriage practiced and how he may have understood what he saw. For example, in the first century, marriage was a state in the life cycle, normally expected to occur in the course of events for all men and women. Marriage was understood to be an agreement, contract, or covenant that was arranged between two families; our modern notion of romance rarely influenced the choice of a spouse. The fathers of the bride and groom mutually agreed upon the union, determined the gifts that would be exchanged, and even presided over the ceremony.

In the culture of first-century Palestine, as in most of the Ancient Near East, marriage was understood to be a kind of partnership where each partner had specific duties and responsibilities they were expected to fulfill. The husband was expected to provide some kind of living for the family (either through a learned trade, or perhaps as a day laborer), give leadership, and make the necessary judgments and decisions. The wife was expected to bear children, as well as manage the household. No one assumed that the partnership was one of equality, but it was routinely understood and accepted by everyone that if the spouses performed their tasks and fulfilled their responsibilities, the marriage would be a successful partnership, effectively contributing to their eventual happiness as well as the stability of the society in which they lived. There were, without a doubt, religious concerns (for example fidelity to the requirements of the covenant and a regular practice of the traditions), but the overriding concern appeared to be the need for each partner's specific roles and functions to be fulfilled.

A core value within this kind of partnership was the assumption that both spouses would be faithful to both their appointed tasks, as well as to each other; if this was not the case, the partnership, and consequently, the stability of the family would be weakened. By extrapolation, the stability of the society would also be threatened. For this reason, a very severe penalty for adultery was imposed: death by stoning. If, despite the best efforts of the spouses, the marriage partnership became intolerable, a remedy would need to be applied. For this reason, divorce was accepted and could be initiated only by the husband. In such an instance, the wife would be sent back to her family, and certain gifts (her dowry) would be returned to her family. There was no remedy available to a wife who found herself in an intolerable situation; the best that she could possibly hope for would be to try to convince her husband to divorce her.

Within this cultural context, Jesus interacted with married men and women and, as someone from a very small and intimate village, without a doubt, participated in numerous marriage ceremonies. However, the gospels speak of only two occasions in which we can find Jesus directly involved in a wedding ceremony and commenting on some aspect of marriage. The first is at the wedding feast at Cana (John 2:1–10). Here, Jesus is portrayed as a wedding guest, and he performs the miracle of changing water into wine. The second, and perhaps the most important, is reported in both the Gospel of Matthew (5:31–32) and the Gospel of Mark (10:2–9) when Jesus is asked by the scribes and Pharisees to express his opinion about divorce. Jesus clearly states the following, "'For this reason a man shall leave his father and his mother and be joined to his wife, and the two shall become one flesh.'...Therefore what God has joined together, let no one separate" (Mk 10:6–9). The Gospel of Luke (16:18) makes Jesus' teaching even clearer: "Anyone who divorces his wife and marries another commits adultery, and whoever marries a woman divorced from her husband commits adultery."

12. Matrimony Scripture References

Genesis 1:27, "God created humankind... / male and female he created them...."

Genesis 2:24, "...a man leaves his father and his mother and clings to his wife, and they become one flesh."

Genesis 24:67, "Isaac...took Rebecca, and she became his wife; and he loved her. So Isaac was comforted...."

Tobit 7:11, "...it has been decreed from heaven that she be given to you....May the Lord of heaven...guide and prosper you both...and grant you mercy and peace."

Tobit 8:7, "Grant that she and I may find mercy / and that we may grow old together."

Song of Songs 8:6, "...for love is strong as death...."

Sirach 26:3, 14, "A good wife is a great blessing; / ...a gift from the Lord...."

Jeremiah 31:31, "...I will make a new covenant...."

Romans 8:35, "Who will separate us from the love of Christ?"

Romans 12:1, "...your bodies as a living sacrifice, holy and acceptable to God...."

1 Corinthians 6:19, "...your body is a temple of the Holy Spirit...."

1 Corinthians 13:2, "...if I have all faith...but do not have love, I gain nothing."

Ephesians 5:2, "...live in love, as Christ loved us...."

Colossians 3:14, "Above all, clothe yourselves with love, which binds everything together in perfect harmony."

1 Peter 3:8, "...have unity of spirit, sympathy, love for one another, a tender heart, and a humble mind."

1 John 3:18, "...let us love, not in word or speech, but in truth and action."

1 John 4:8, "...for God is love."

Matthew 19:6, "...what God has joined together, let no one separate."

Mark 10:8, "and the two shall become one flesh. So they are no longer two, but one flesh."

John 2:1–11, the wedding at Cana.

John 17:23, "...that they may become completely one...."

13. Jesus the Priest

In the Jewish experience of Old Testament priesthood, a traditional understanding of what the priesthood means would include the qualities of service, authority, and leadership. Within the Jewish tradition, being a member of the priesthood was hereditary, usually reserved to members of the clan of Aaron and the tribe of Levi (see Ex 28—29; 32:25–29). The priests of that era offered sacrifices, interpreted the Mosaic Law, took care of the holy places, and staffed the Temple in Jerusalem. Their role was not particularly exclusive however, because in addition to the priests, there were also scribes, rabbis, and elders, all of whom shared in the ministry of service, authority, and leadership.

Jesus' contemporaries recognized him to be a person who served, taught with authority, and someone who provided leadership, but they never identified him as a priest. The more common titles usually associated with Jesus included "Rabbi" (Mk 9:5), "Teacher" (Lk 11:45), "Lord" (Jn 11:39), "Messiah" (Mk 8:29), and "Prophet" (Lk 7:16). Although it can be asserted that the people recognized, in his ministry, certain functions and qualities that could be associated with the role of a priest, it can also be stated that they never made the connection. It was only later, years after his death and Resurrection, that the writer of the Letter to the Hebrews identified Jesus as the "high priest" (Heb 4:14; 5:10). This identification probably happened as a result of the early communities' reflection on the meaning of his passion and death, a reflection that led them to the conclusion that his death on a cross was a sacrifice, and since it was a sacrifice, Jesus was both priest (the person who offers the sacrifice on behalf of the people) and the victim.

Yet, perhaps it was the witness of his life of service that prompted people to accept the designation of Jesus as a priest, for it was from this example of service that the early Christian community determined directives and interpretations about their understanding and practice of ministry. The words of Jesus formed the core principle of this ministerial role: "But it is not so among you; but whoever wishes to become great among you must be your servant, and whoever wishes to be first among you must be slave of all" (Mk 10:43–44).

14. Holy Orders Scripture References

Acts 10:39, "We are witnesses of all that he [Jesus] did...."

Romans 12:6, "We have gifts that differ according to the grace given to us...."

2 Corinthians 4:5, "...we proclaim Jesus Christ as Lord and ourselves as your slaves for Jesus' sake."

2 Corinthians 5:18, "...has given us the ministry of reconciliation."

Ephesians 4:12, "... or building up the body of Christ...."

Hebrews 5:10, "...designated by God a high priest...."

1 Peter 4:10, "Like good stewards of the manifold grace of God...."

1 Peter 5:2, "...tend the flock of God that is in your charge...."

Matthew 9:38, "...ask the Lord of the harvest to send out laborers into his harvest."

Matthew 10:7, "...proclaim the good news, 'The kingdom of heaven has come near.'"

Matthew 20:27, "...whoever wishes to be first among you must be your slave...."

Luke 10:2, "The harvest is plentiful, but the laborers are few...."

Luke 22:19, "Do this in remembrance of me."

John 12:26, "Whoever serves me must follow me...."

John 17:17, 19, "...sanctify...in truth...."

John 20:22, "Receive the Holy Spirit."

John 21:17, "Feed my sheep."

SCRIPTURE REFERENCES FOR DEACONS

Acts of the Apostles 6:3, "...select...seven men of good standing, full of the Spirit...."

Acts of the Apostles 8:35, "...he proclaimed to him the good news about Jesus."

1 Timothy 3:8–13, qualifications of deacons.

SCRIPTURE REFERENCES FOR BISHOPS

Acts of the Apostles 20:28, "Keep watch over yourselves and over the flock, of which the Holy Spirit has made you overseers, to shepherd the Church of God...."

1 Timothy 3:1–7, Qualifications of bishops.

1 Timothy 4:14, "Do not neglect the gift that is in you, which was given to you through prophecy...."

2 Timothy 1:6, "...rekindle the gift of God that is within you through the laying on of my hands...."

PART SEVEN

Praying With Scripture

1. A Method for Prayer

It might seem that the way a person begins to pray with the Scriptures is to simply open up the Bible and begin reading. Although it is certainly possible that some people may well begin praying in this fashion, to do so might not be as fulfilling an experience as it could be.

The beginning posture, the necessary first step to pray with Scripture begins with a time of self-reflection and examination. A person begins by taking a "personal inventory" of one's values and beliefs in order to discover if, among those values and beliefs, there is the conviction and the belief that God has spoken to his people (CCC 51). To truly benefit from praying with Scripture, it is necessary to understand and appreciate this first principle of sacred revelation and communication. When a Christian claims, and then proclaims, one's personal conviction and belief that God has indeed spoken to his people, the next step is to personalize this belief and formulate a statement of intimate acknowledgment. This automatically moves one on to the second step in the process: an acceptance of a God that speaks not only to *people*, but even more importantly, a God that speaks to individual persons, to *me*, to the person that I am.

This second step leads to a deepening awareness and acceptance that God has spoken to me first, and has desired this intimate relationship with me, long before I was conscious that it was even happening. As the prophet Jeremiah once said, "Before I formed you in the womb I knew you, / and before you were born I consecrated you..." (Jer 1:5). The second step, over time, slowly leads a person to the realization that this intimate communication comes as a gift from God, initiated by God, and is not at all dependent upon personal talent or ability. Another way to understand the process is to recognize and accept it as *grace*.

God desires to communicate with us. This unmerited gift of grace is observed with the eyes of faith. It occurs when people make room in their lives for God and take the time to listen to God's voice. People of faith recognize the communication of God in the person of Jesus, God's Word, and in the experience of the Church, the Body of Christ. In addition, people of faith recognize the presence of God in other people, in creation, through the many different events and experiences of life, and through holy Scripture. In all these modes of communication, our response is to listen to what God is telling us: listening to God is the basic attitude of prayer.

Listening, however, is more than just an attitude, it is also a skill that takes preparation, time, and commitment in order to develop. To truly listen, to develop an "ear for the voice of God," means the individual chooses to develop a daily practice of *silence* and *solitude*. The First Book of Kings tells a wonderful story which illustrates the necessity of developing this basic posture for prayer:

> "He [the Lord] said, 'Go out and stand on the mountain before the LORD, for the LORD is about to pass by.' Now there was a great wind, so strong that it was splitting mountains and breaking rocks in pieces before the LORD, but the LORD was not in the wind; and after the wind an earthquake, but the LORD was not in the earthquake; and after the earthquake a fire, but the LORD was not in the fire; and after the fire a sound of sheer silence. When Elijah heard it, he wrapped his face in his mantle and went and stood at the entrance of the cave..." (19:11–13).

For most people, preparing to listen to the voice of God entails spending a few moments quieting themselves down, and settling into a comfortable and receptive prayer position. Before you begin to read the selected Scripture, you should also pause to remember that you are in the presence of God, that you have been called by God to this moment of the day, and that you are willing to listen to whatever it is that God might be calling you to do. In a very real sense, all of this preparation is done in imitation of the Lord, who would often seek out a quiet place in order to pray to his heavenly Father (Lk 6:12).

As you pray, become conscious of all that you bring to this moment of prayer. Your thoughts, feelings, actions, and experiences of the day are also present. These things will often become a very "vocal" presence as you begin the process of quieting down and preparing to listen to God. If you acknowledge all of these thoughts and feelings at the beginning of your prayer time, instead of dealing with them when they arrive as "uninvited guests," either in the middle of your prayer, or as distractions, you will be better prepared to listen and be present to the moment.

Once you feel that you are as quiet as possible at this particular moment, begin to read the selected Scripture slowly and attentively. Each Scripture passage needs to be approached in a particular manner. For example, if you are reading a story about an event in the life of Jesus, try to be as present to the moment as possible (try to put yourself into that time and place). Try to imagine what it would be like to have been an actual witness to the event about which you are reading. Respond to what Jesus says, and to how the individual, or crowd, in the story reacts. Savor each moment for as long as possible before moving on to the next point. Certain words are going to hold special meanings and importance for you, spend the extra time that may be required to let these words fill your heart and spirit.

As you read, if something strikes as you particularly important or significant, don't move on to another point, stay with the one that captured your attention: this may be well be the cherished moment of intimate communication between yourself and the Lord. If you feel loved, stay with the feeling. If you feel challenged, imagine accepting the challenge. If you feel peaceful, rejoice in the peace you have been given. If you find yourself struggling, or becoming disturbed by what you read, ask for the necessary insight to understand. Each of these occurrences are examples of when you should pause and resist the urge to move on. Do not leave this moment until it feels "complete" to you.

There will also be times in your prayer when you have done everything you can to be receptive to the word and nothing happens. You either feel nothing, nothing grabs your attention, or nothing feels important or significant to you. As difficult as it may be, discipline yourself to stay with these moments. Many times, God is profoundly present in such moments (Ps 139:7–8).

When your prayer period is concluded, don't just close the Scriptures and begin your next project. At the end of your prayer time, thank the Lord for whatever it may be that you experienced. If it was a consolation (a good feeling or insight), thank the Lord for the consolation; if it was not, try to thank the Lord for having given you the opportunity to be in his presence. Saint Alphonsus Liguori, for example, always concluded his prayer time with a type of prayer that he termed the "prayer of affection." An example of this kind of prayer follows, it is adapted from his classic work about prayer, *The Practice of the Love of Jesus Christ:*

> My God and my all, I wish to seek no other good but you, who are infinite goodness. You who take such good care of me, make me have no other care except to please you. Grant that all my thoughts may always be in pleasing you always. Drive far from me every occasion that distracts me from your love...I love you, infinite goodness, I love you my delight. O Word, Incarnate, I love you more than myself... I want nothing from you but yourself. Amen.

2. Suggested Scripture Passages

The Scripture passages that follow describe the experience of other people as they came to an understanding of the presence of the Lord in their lives. The column on the left lists an inner disposition, which may be descriptive of how a person might feel as he or she comes to the Scriptures to pray. The right column provides a Scripture passage that may be helpful.

Choose a Scripture passage and slowly, and prayerfully, read the Word of God. Gently permit the Word to wash over you, through you, and in you. Become refreshed and nourished by it.

A listening heart	1 Samuel 3:1–18
Trust	Luke 1:26–38
Weariness	Psalm 62
A desire to pray	Luke 11:1–13
Praise God	Psalm 96
Thankfulness	Psalm 92
Close to the Lord	John 15:15–17
Fear	Isaiah 44:1–5
Confusion	Psalm 25
Hope	Romans 8:28–39
A call to serve	Acts 22:3–16
Waiting	Psalm 40
Patience	James 5:7–11
Memory	Psalm 136
Healing	1 Corinthians 12:4–11
Thirst for God	Psalm 42
Blindness	Luke 18:35–43

3. An Eight-Day Retreat Experience

The directed retreat experience in which an individual retreatant meets once each day with a trained spiritual director is very popular. The popularity of the experience may be attributed to something as simple as the choice to gift oneself with eight full days of silence and solitude. On the other hand, the experience may be popular because of its profundity: it is not just the silence and solitude, it is also the communication and revelation of the presence of the Lord in the Word.

Ideally a directed retreat should include leadership, or direction, by a trained spiritual director, however, not all people have this opportunity. There is, nevertheless, great value in the act of committing oneself to the process, and entering into the experience of a retreat with the Word of God, even when a director, or leader, is not present.

What follows is an eight-day, thematic, scriptural retreat. It is envisioned that the person who chooses to use this retreat experience will commit to an extended period of silent prayer each day (a minimum of one hour every day is most beneficial). A theme is provided and introduced for each day of the retreat. A selection of Scripture passages (listed with an indication of the focus of each), all of which contribute to the process of prayerful reflection about the theme, is also suggested. At the end of the thematic presentation, a sampling of questions, appropriate for journaling (keeping a written record) and personal reflection, completes the experience.

The extended period of prayer is introduced by the directions, "Experiencing the Prayer," that follows below. The prayer period is concluded with the "Awareness in Prayer" exercise which poses some probing questions. It will lead to personal reflection and provide the opportunity for journaling the prayer experience. Both components are used each day during the eight-day retreat experience.

EXPERIENCING THE PRAYER

1. Choose a quiet place for prayer.
2. Become as comfortable and as relaxed as possible, fully realizing that the harmony of body, soul, and spirit is essential for the experience to be successful.
3. Slowly permit the Lord to bring himself to your awareness.
4. Ask the Lord for the necessary grace to receive whatever it may be that you are to graced and gifted with.
5. Select a Scripture passage and read it prayerfully and slowly.
6. Pause wherever you feel the Lord may be calling you.
7. Respond, with your heart, to whatever the Lord may be communicating.
8. Continue prayerfully reading and praying, until the prayer period comes to an end.
9. Conclude the prayer period with a prayer of your own making, or slowly pray the *Our Father* or some other favorite prayer.

AWARENESS IN PRAYER

1. Is there a feeling, or sense, that God has revealed something to me?
2. Can I clearly identify what it is that the Lord may be calling me to do?
3. What was my attitude in prayer, did I find my attitude changing, or remaining the same?
4. What particular passage of Scripture spoke to me the most?
5. What was enjoyable about the experience? What was difficult, or the most challenging?
6. How did I respond?
7. Did I remain faithful to the period of prayer?

For the person who does not have a director for their retreat experience, the time spent honestly answering and reflecting upon the journal questions provided is very important. Your recorded answers to the questions can be very useful whenever you have the opportunity to discuss your spiritual journey with your spiritual director. These recorded answers are also very useful, even if you do not have a spiritual director; your answers can be referred back to and reflected upon as your spiritual journey progresses. They can serve as a type of signpost, marking where you have been, and possibly, suggesting the next step(s) in your journey.

FIRST DAY OF RETREAT

God's love is expressed in me

As I enter this first day of retreat, I do so confident that God has loved me and called me into life, but also with an urgent sense for this truth to take even firmer root in my heart. I wish to know, with all of my heart and soul, that the Lord has created me out of love, that the Lord continually thinks of me, and that, in the eyes of the Lord, I am both precious and loved.

Isaiah 43:1–7	You are precious in my eyes
Psalm 8	Lord, who are we that you would think of us?
Psalm 139	Truly you have formed my inward being
Isaiah 55	Let all who thirst, let them come to the water
Romans 8:28–39	If God is for us, who can be against us?
Luke 1:26–38	My soul proclaims the glory of the Lord

JOURNALING QUESTIONS

- Do I have a conviction that God surrounds me with love?
- What are the events and experiences in my life that seem to confirm this conviction?
- What events and experiences seem to challenge it?

SECOND DAY OF RETREAT

God's love is expressed in creation

As I enter this second day of retreat, I will ask for the grace to see more clearly God's love expressed in creation. I am aware of the fact that the creative force and energy of God is present in all things, but I ask for an ever-deepening awareness and appreciation, an attitude of wonder and awe for all creatures, and for the entire created world.

Genesis 1:1–31	And God saw that it was good
Wisdom 11:21–27	Lord, you love all that exists
Psalm 104	Yahweh my God, you are great indeed
Psalm 148	Praise the Lord, all of the earth
Psalm 33:6	By the word of the LORD the heavens were made

JOURNALING QUESTIONS

- Have I come to a deeper awareness of the creative power of God at work in the world and in all of the creatures of the world?
- Have I been able to identify some of the gifts that God has given me for my use that I hold in high regard and treasure?
- Have I also become aware of those gifts that I might abuse or not fully respect?

THIRD DAY OF RETREAT

God's love expressed in Jesus, the Incarnate Word

As I enter into this third day of retreat, I do so, desiring to recognize, even more, the love of the Father as it is revealed through his Son. I acknowledge Jesus as my personal Lord and Savior, and I have accepted him into my heart and soul. I anticipate, in this period of prayer, an intimate and revealing communication with my Lord.

John 13:1–20	Jesus washes the feet of his disciples
John 14:1–7	Do not let your hearts be troubled, trust in me
John 14:8–13	To have seen me is to see the Father
Ephesians 2:11–18	Through Jesus we possess the way to the Father
John 15:1–6	I am the true vine
John 4:34–38	My food is to do the will of him who sent me

JOURNALING QUESTIONS

- In what ways have I been surprised in my relationship with the Lord?
- Looking at the events and the experiences of my life, were there certain ones I freely shared, and still others I was hesitant to bring to the Lord in prayer?
- What is the Lord asking of me today?

FOURTH DAY OF RETREAT

The Father's love and humanity's blindness

On this fourth day of retreat, I bring to my prayer, a desire for self-knowledge and gratitude for God's mercy. Self-knowledge helps me to see and to understand what prevents me from loving the Lord, which, in turn, prevents me from becoming my true self. Once I am aware of what blinds me, I experience that in the light of the Lord's abundant love and mercy.

Isaiah 44:9–20	In confusion humanity makes idols
Hosea 11:1–11	Israel seems to be helpless
Psalm 51	Have mercy, O God, have mercy
Ezekiel 36:25–29	I shall sprinkle clean water upon you
John 12:1–8	The woman who anoints the feet of Jesus

JOURNALING QUESTIONS

- Do I recognize and accept the call to the conversion of my mind and heart?
- On those occasions when I do not fully cooperate with the Lord, do I treat myself with gentleness, and permit the Lord to forgive me, and make me whole again?
- Is there any part of myself that I am withholding from the Lord, keeping in darkness, not permitting the Lord to bring into the light?

FIFTH DAY OF RETREAT

A time for sowing

On this fifth day of retreat, I petition the Lord to sow within my heart the seeds of his love and forgiveness. I ask that the Lord prepare within me a receptive ground for the Word that is to be implanted there. I pray that I might become, through the power of grace, not only a hearer of the Word of God but also a doer of the Word.

1 Samuel 3:1–18	Speak Lord, your servant is listening
Matthew 13:1–23	Parables of the seed and the sower
Luke 18:35–43	Lord, that I may see!
1 John 4:7–21	God has first loved us

JOURNALING QUESTIONS

- As I prayed, could I feel if there was any part of myself that was resisting the Word of God?
- What word(s) did I most need to hear today, and did I receive this grace in my prayer today?
- If I did not receive the word that I was hoping to hear, was it because I was trying to be the sower, not permitting the Lord to do the planting?
- Has something been planted by the Lord that needs to be cultivated so it can grow as the Lord desires?

SIXTH DAY OF RETREAT

Resisting fear and anxiety

On this sixth day of retreat, I present myself, in prayer, to the Lord just as I am. The Lord has worked with me for five full days, and there may still be a tendency on my part to pull back and try to assert control. More often than not, this desire is rooted in fear and anxiety; I may be asked to do something I feel I am not quite ready to do. In my prayer, I ask the Lord to rid me of fear, so that I may serve him with a full heart and spirit.

Isaiah 43:1–5	You have called me not to fear
Isaiah 43:10–21	Let me know your love and protection
Psalm 136	Remember how God has worked for you
Mark 5:25–36	Fear is useless, draw near to Jesus
Romans 8:28–39	God loves me
1 Thessalonians 5:23–25	You will do it

JOURNALING QUESTIONS

- In my prayer, was I able to recall other times in my life when I was either fearful or anxious?

- How did the Lord use this situation to help me grow and love?
- Is there anything that was revealed to me in prayer today that I feel I must protect?
- Is the fear of losing something I feel is important a stumbling block to my growth and development?

SEVENTH DAY OF RETREAT

The kingdom of God

On this seventh day of retreat, I reflect upon the Lord's call to join him in building the kingdom of God. I consider this invitation in the light of the previous meditations: the creative love of God, the personal call to holiness, the love of God made flesh in Jesus, and my own call to be a doer of the Word. My desire, in this prayer period, is to deepen my own awareness of the reality that "all things are possible in God."

Philippians 3:7–14	All I want is to know Christ Jesus
1 Corinthians 1:26–31	God chooses the weak to shame the strong
Psalm 40	To do your will is my desire
Psalm 42	My soul thirsts for the living God

JOURNALING QUESTIONS

- In my prayer, was I aware of the call to build the kingdom as well as the difficulties associated with this call?
- How easy is it for me to go my own way or follow my own path?
- What are the possible warning signs in my own life that signal I may be pulling away from the path of the kingdom?

EIGHTH DAY OF RETREAT

The Lord calls me forth

On this eighth and final day of retreat, we are called by the Lord to rejoice in our humanity. We celebrate the freedom we feel as sons and daughters of the Lord. At the same time, we realize that this freedom comes to us as an unmerited gift of God's grace. As free men and women, we understand that when the Spirit of the Lord touches our spirit, there is nothing and no one more satisfying, and more complete.

John 3:22–30	He must become greater
Psalm 40	To do your will is my only desire
Philippians 3:7–14	I want to know only Christ and his Resurrection
Romans 8:35–39	Who will separate us from the love of Christ?
Psalm 63	Thus I will bless you as long as I live

JOURNALING QUESTIONS

- What key graces did I experience during these days of retreat?
- What is the Lord asking me to do within the concrete, lived experience of my day-to-day life?
- How can I witness to others about the wonderful things the Lord has done for me?

PART EIGHT

Praying With Major Personalities of the Bible

Sometimes we may forget that all of the people in the Bible, their stories, struggles, concerns, defeats and victories, are stories of real people. Long before they were kings or queens, great prophets, apostles and disciples, or saints, they were normal everyday human beings. This may seem like an obvious point, but it is nevertheless a point that is worth reflecting on.

A second point, that complements the first, is that the Bible story of each of these real people is the "highlight" of their life, at least from the biblical perspective. The dramatic moment(s) that are portrayed in the Bible represent a very small sampling of their life experience. Often, the Bible story does not dwell on the individual struggle, the doubts, the wondering, and all those other human things that preceded the biblical event for which the person is revered today. As a result, we may, at times, get the feeling that these biblical heroes and personalities are too big, too unapproachable, too special, to be of any help to us in our spiritual journey.

In the prayer meditations that follow, an attempt is made to introduce what we know about the "real person" who is portrayed in the Bible. Once we get a possible insight into what this person might have been like (imagination plays an important role here), we then meditate and pray with them, using the Scriptures that are associated with their stories and other Scriptures that may be helpful and appropriate. In this way, the biblical characters become alive and real for us and hopefully a possible source of inspiration and guidance.

1. Abraham and Sarah

Abram (roughly the "father is exalted"), who would later change his name to Abraham ("father of a multitude"), was most probably a nomadic shepherd, a man of great wealth and some influence, living around 1900 B.C. He was born in the city of Ur (Gen 11:28), a city well known because it was centered around a ziggurat (stepped temple, which some attribute to the story of the Tower of Babel) and was heavily populated. It was in Ur that Abram married his first wife, Sarai (later to be known as Sarah), before leaving on one of his many nomadic journeys that eventually ended in Canaan, the Promised Land.

Abraham, who suddenly appears in the book of Genesis (Gen 11:26), is a central character in the Old Testament. According to Jewish legend, from the time he was a young boy he realized that there was only one God, and although he did not yet know the name of God, he nevertheless tried to remain faithful to this one God. Obviously, in a world in which monotheism had not yet taken root, this would have been an experience of God that would have been extremely unique, and probably not supported by his friends and neighbors. Whether or not the legend is true, the Scriptures reveal to us that when Yahweh spoke to Abraham, he found Abraham to be receptive to his call.

Sarah ("princess") shared Abraham's journey to the Promised Land and was the mother of Isaac (the name means "laughter"), through whom "offspring shall be named for you" (Gen 21:12). Reputedly she was a woman of great beauty (Gen 12), but in a culture that treasured fertility above beauty, she did not consider herself to be blessed or beloved. That is until the messenger of God announced that she would become a mother very late in life (Gen 18:1–15), news which at first startled Sarah and Abraham, but which they eventually came to understand as part of the plan of God (Gen 21).

Although there are many details in the story of Abraham and Sarah that are easily recalled, perhaps what is taken for granted are the drastic changes that took place in their lives as a result of their response to the voice of God. Obviously they were required to obey the agreements of the covenant, were tested by Yahweh in ways that they might not have imagined, and eventually had to learn what was appropriate in their relationship with Yahweh and what was not. Other changes are not as obvious but were nevertheless significant. One such change is the fact that they moved from a very fertile land in Mesopotamia teeming with water, to the land of Palestine where water was scarce. This fact may well help to explain why water plays such a significant role in the Bible—it was something that was difficult to find.

With the image of a wealthy, confident, and nomadic shepherd in your mind, accustomed to the culture and the expectations of a specific time and place, in a world where the idea of monotheism would not have been easily accepted, meditate on the Word of God as Abraham and Sarah experienced it.

Genesis 12:1–9
Genesis 15:7–20
Genesis 17:15–22
Genesis 21:1–21
Genesis 22:22
Sirach 44:19–21
Romans 4:1–25

2. Miriam

Miriam ("lady princess") was the sister of Moses, who saved Moses from the death that Pharaoh had ordered for all male Hebrew babies (Ex 2:1–8). Miriam watches after Moses as he is floated in the Nile in a basket of reeds and sees the Pharaoh's daughter discover him. Cleverly, Miriam suggests Moses' own mother as a nursemaid to the child.

Miriam also possessed the gift of prophecy (Ex 15:20–21) and was at the head of the women as one of the leaders of the crossing of the Red Sea (Mic 6:4), afterward singing the refrain to their hymn of thanksgiving. The fact that there are seven texts that speak of Miriam indicate her place as a woman leader in Israel. The prophet Micah says of her, "For I brought you up from the land of Egypt, / and redeemed you from the house of slavery; / and I sent before you Moses, / Aaron, and Miriam" (Mic 6:4). She is most probably the Miriam after whom all of the Marys of the New Testament were named.

With the image of a strong and faithful woman, open to the Word of God, a woman who used the gifts that God gave her in difficult and often trying circumstances, join your voice with her voice in prayer.

Exodus 2:4–8	Sirach 15:1–10
Exodus 15:20–21	Proverbs 7:1–4
Numbers 12	

3. Moses

Moses ("I drew him out of the water") is the dominant figure of the Pentateuch, Exodus through Deuteronomy. Moses is the great leader and giver of the law, who led the Chosen People out of Egypt and whose relationship with Yahweh was unparalleled. His is a story that is filled with drama, legend, and myth, all of which contribute to his "larger than life" status. At the same time, despite his status, he is also a man who exhibits a full range of human emotions: fear, anxiety, anger, frustration, a lack of confidence, humility and, of course, perseverance.

His life journey begins with him being fished out of the river Nile by the daughter of Pharaoh and then raised as a favored son in the imperial household. One day he noticed a Hebrew slave being beaten, and in a fit of rage he killed the assailant. Fearing for his life he fled into the desert where he encountered the Lord, speaking to him from a bush that seemed to be burning. At first reluctant, and then finally, agreeing to what the Lord was calling him to do, he returned to Egypt and confronted Pharaoh. A classic power struggle between Pharaoh and Yahweh, working through Moses, resulted in the Hebrew slaves being set free, thus beginning the migration to the land of Canaan which we today remember as the Exodus and the Passover.

Pray with Moses, not as the great and fearless leader, but rather as a man trying to discern the will of God. As you pray ask for the grace of a listening heart, a grace that will ease your fears and anxiety, in the hope that you too may discover the will of the Lord.

Exodus 3:1–6
Exodus 4:14–16; 7:1
Exodus 32:11–14
Numbers 11:10–15
Sirach 45:1–6
Hebrews 3:2; 11:24
2 Corinthians 3:12–13

4. King David

The story of the powerful and passionate king of biblical Israel (1010–970 B.C.) is told in 1 Samuel 16:13—1 Kings 2:12. He was the youngest of eight brothers (1 Sam 17:12) and was a shepherd, tending his father Jesse's flocks, when he was chosen by God to become the anointed and chosen one, to replace King Saul who had displeased Yahweh. As a result of this, Saul became very angry with David, and David had to flee Saul's wrath. Eventually, after the suicidal death of Saul, David became king at the age of thirty and ruled in Hebron, before eventually moving the capital to the city of Jerusalem.

As king in Jerusalem, David ruled for thirty-three years, a reign that was quite successful insofar that he subdued the traditional enemies of Israel: the Philistines, Canaanites, Moabites, Ammonites, Aramaeans, Edomites, and Amalekites, bringing peace and prosperity to the country. However, his time as king was also marked by personal tragedy, because of his weaknesses and sins. An adulterous relationship with Bathsheba (the mother of Solomon, later to be king), combined with the murder of Uriah the Hittite (2 Sam 11), are powerful stories of his lust and deceit, and the tremendous suffering David and others endured as a result of his sin. However, at the same time, his great remorse and repentance has inspired countless men and women throughout the ages.

Pray with David, not as king, but pray with him as a normal person, a man filled with many conflicting feelings, but a man who, despite his sins, or perhaps because of his sins, also enjoyed a deep and passionate relationship with God.

2 Samuel 1	Psalm 98
Psalm 63	Sirach 47:2–11

5. The Prophet Isaiah

Isaiah ("God is salvation") appears to have been from Jerusalem, perhaps a member of the nobility, a contemporary of the prophet Micah, and was preceded in his prophecy by Amos and Hosea. Biblical events seem to place him around 740 B.C. in the northern kingdom of Judah. He was a married man, a father of at least a couple of sons, a counselor to the king. There are some indications that he was also a scribe.

Isaiah's name tells it all. His prophecy was a prophecy that insisted on total reliance on Yahweh. Despite the difficulties and the threats that surround the Chosen People, it was only Yahweh who would save them. The kings of the time were busy making alliances with other kings, looking to them for protection and security, and in the process forgetting the promise and the covenant. Isaiah continued to try and call them back to the fidelity of their relationship with the Lord. It was a cry that went unheeded for the most part.

Isaiah seems to have been a favorite prophet of Jesus, who often makes reference to him. In addition, Isaiah provides the Christian community with powerful references in which that community was able to recognize the person of Jesus. Two such references are the suffering servant (Isa 42:1–7) and the prophecy that "the young woman...shall bear a son, and shall name him Immanuel" (Isa 7:14).

As you pray with Isaiah, pray with a prophet's attitude and insight, a conviction that it is only in the Lord that salvation can be assured. See if you can identify the underlining frustration that must have been present in his prayer to know the truth, to do your best to proclaim it, but to have the proclaimed truth ignored or quickly forgotten.

Isaiah 2:2–5	Isaiah 25:1–5
Isaiah 6:1–10	Isaiah 43:8–12
Isaiah 11:1–10	Sirach 48:23–25

6. The Prophet Jeremiah

Jeremiah ("Yahweh exalts") is the most clearly defined prophet in the Old Testament. Although all of the details of his life are most certainly not known, we can become very familiar with the emotions, feelings, convictions, and faith that animated him and of which his prophecy speaks.

He lived during the sixth and seventh centuries B.C., at a time when the kingdom of Judah continued to be unstable as a result of the disintegration of the Assyrian Empire and the continuing battle between Egypt and Babylon for dominance. The people of the time not only had to endure political instability but also the warping of moral and religious values in Judah as a result of the idolatrous reign of various kings who had followed King Hezekiah and the reforms that he had attempted to put into place (2 Kings 18:ff).

Jeremiah's prophecy reminded the people that Yahweh was the creator of heaven and earth, a powerful God, but also a God of tenderness and love. Yahweh was a faithful God, even when the people had wandered away and had turned instead to the idols of Baal and Moloch. It was to Yahweh that the people had to return to, away from their idol worship, if they were ever to know peace and tranquillity. All that they were suffering was the result of their unfaithfulness.

Jeremiah also had to lead the people through a great tragedy, the destruction of the city of Jerusalem, the Temple, and the exile of the people into Babylon. In the midst of this great torment, he reminded them that they were still the covenant people of the house of Israel and Judah, no matter where they were (Jer 29). Even in exile, they were still the Chosen People of God.

Pray with Jeremiah as he struggles to understand and accept what is happening to the Jewish people. Not only must he struggle to understand, but he must also listen carefully to the voice of the Lord so that he can speak to the people in the name of the Lord. It is often very difficult and challenging to accept those things that happen to us, but it is even more difficult in times of stress to be the person that others look to for guidance and direction. As a prophet and the anointed one of God, Jeremiah was such a person.

Jeremiah 1:4–10
Jeremiah 18:1–6
Jeremiah 20:7–18
Jeremiah 31:31–34

7. Esther

Esther (possibly from the Persian, "star") was queen of the Persian king Ahasuerus (486–465 B.C.), more than likely his second wife. By her courage and cleverness, she prevented the extermination of the Jews that had been planned by the evil Haman. Armed with faith in God, Esther went before the king at the risk of her very life and begged for her people's safety. Her beauty and goodness saved her and the Hebrew people.

Even though Esther was a queen, she was first and foremost a woman, and as a woman in a patriarchal society she had very little standing. Her fears were very real in light of what Haman had planned. Perhaps her first response was the response of the powerless, wondering what she could possible do. However, as a result of prayer and because of an inner courage that she may well have been initially unaware of, she confronted the evil directly, and in the end prevailed.

Pray with Esther from a position of weakness and powerlessness.

Pray with the realization that your own gifts, talents, and abilities may not be enough. Pray, grateful for all that you have been given, but pray also with a growing awareness of your complete and total dependence on the Lord.

Esther 14:1–9
Wisdom 3:9
Sirach 51:1–12
Hosea 14:9

8. Ruth

Ruth ("female companion") was the Moabite daughter-in-law of Naomi who returned with her to Bethlehem after her husband had died. Ruth went to the barley fields to glean grain where Boaz, a wealthy kinsman of Naomi, noticed her and made sure that she was protected in the field and had adequate water to drink. Boaz and Ruth married and had a son of whom was said, "He shall be to you a restorer of life and a nourisher of your old age; for your daughter-in-law who loves you, who is more to you than seven sons, has borne him....They named him Obed; he became the father of Jesse, the father of David" (Ruth 4:15, 17).

Ruth is considered one of the mothers of Israel, since she is the great-grandmother of King David. She is also listed in the Gospel of Matthew in the genealogy of Jesus, the last of the five mothers of Israel named (Mt 1:1–16).

Pray with Ruth as the proud grandmother, who rejoices in her children but who also rejoices in her children's children. Pray with her as a woman who is grateful to the Lord for all that she has been gifted with.

Ruth 1:16–17
Ruth 4: 13–22
Psalm 17:1–7
Sirach 50:22–24
Luke 1:46–55

9. John the Baptist

John, born of elderly parents, Zechariah and Elizabeth around 7 B.C., is a major personality of the New Testament. All four gospels introduce John as being present at the beginning of the public ministry of Jesus. Other references to John suggest that his ministry of calling people to repentance was well received, and as a result of this ministry, suggest that John "prepared the way" for the ministry of Jesus. At the same time he was a controversial figure and was also perceived as a threat by King Herod and by the priests and the scribes of the Jerusalem Temple.

Pray with John, not as the popular baptizer or the prophet who drew great crowds, but rather with John the man, struggling with the Word of God as he understood it. Imagine what it must have been like for him to arrive at the decision that "he must increase and I must decrease," as he became more and more aware of his role in God's plan. It is never easy to change and it is not always easy to accept God's will.

John 1:6–9
Matthew 3:1–12
Matthew 17:10–13
Malachi 3:1–5
Sirach 48:10–11

10. The Blessed Virgin Mary

Mary (or Miriam) of Nazareth was the daughter of Joachim and Anne, the spouse of Joseph, and the mother of Jesus. Our primary information about her is found in the Infancy Narratives of the gospels of Luke and Matthew, which tell of the birth of Jesus. Other Scripture references place her at the wedding feast of Cana (Jn 2:1ff), at the foot of the cross (Jn 19:25), and with the apostles after the Resurrection, devoting herself to prayer (Acts 1:14). All other references to the Blessed Mother are references that come to us through various pious legends.

Pray with the Blessed Virgin as she moves from her first *fiat* (yes), to the plan of the Lord announced to her by the angel, through all the other moments in her life where she had to confirm that first *fiat*. Pray with her as a woman who did not understand all that was happening, who did not know all of the details and who was never sure of what might happen next, but who nevertheless remained completely faithful.

Luke 1:26–38
Matthew 1:18–25
Luke 2:1–38
Matthew 2:1–23
Luke 2:39–52
Matthew 3:13
James 2:1–12
Matthew 10:35–39
Luke 14:25–35
Matthew 12:46–50
John 19:25–27
Acts of the Apostles 1:12–14
Revelation 12:1–6, 13–17

11. Mary of Magdala

Although very little is absolutely known about Mary Magdalene, that which seems to be of the utmost importance has been preserved in the gospels: Jesus released her from possession of "seven demons" (Mk 16:9) and she was one of the women present at the foot of the cross (Mt 27:55ff). Perhaps most important of all, she is one of the first witnesses to the Resurrection of the Lord. It is her testimony and witness that provide the necessary "push" to the apostles Peter and John to come out of hiding and to go the empty tomb of the Lord (Jn 20:2).

A persistent story about Mary Magdalene, none of which can be proved, is that she often accompanied the Lord and his apostles on some of his journeys. It would seem that this relationship with the Lord might well explain her presence, and therefore also her pivotal role, as a witness to the crucifixion and as a witness to the Resurrection.

Pray with Mary, devoted to the Lord. Pray with her as she listens to the good news of the kingdom of God. Pray with her as she struggles to comprehend what the gospel is calling her to do. Pray with her as she watches Jesus die and as she receives the overwhelming news of his Resurrection.

Mark 15:40–41	Luke 24:1–10
Matthew 27:55–56	John 20:11–18
Mark 16:1–6	

12. Saint Peter

A Galilean and one of the twelve apostles called by Jesus, little is actually known about Saint Peter, but the gospels do agree that he was the brother of Andrew, was a fisherman, a resident of Capernaum, and he was married. We also know that his mother-in-law lived with him, which was not necessarily a common occurrence at the time. The gospels also report his many follies and sins, far more than any other apostle or disciple, all of which may well be an indication of his status as the "rock" and his designation in the letters of Paul as a respected and important leader of the Church.

There are many traditions and stories about Saint Peter, but perhaps the most significant can be found in the writings of Clement of Rome who reports that "Peter and Paul were persecuted and put to death in Rome." Archaeological discoveries under the basilica of St. Peter's in Rome seem to support the assertion that it is the burial place of Saint Peter.

Pray with Peter as he struggles with his weaknesses and as he is moved to faith and belief. Feel the contrasting moments of generosity and love as they come into conflict with real feelings of anxiety and fear. Finally, recognize with Peter in his journey of faith, through the power of grace, his movement from resistance to the call of the Lord to his final acceptance of all that the Lord has required of him.

Luke 5:1–11
Mark 10:23–31
Luke 9:28–36
John 6:66–69
Luke 22:31–34
John 20:1–10
Acts of the Apostles 15:1–21
1 Peter 1:3–9
1 Peter 1:16–19

13. The Apostle Paul

Paul, born in Tarsus somewhere between A.D. 1–10, was a Jew but he was a Jew born outside of Israel, which made him distinctly different from the other apostles, all of whom were born in Israel. As a Jew born outside of Israel, he was at home not only in the Jewish world but also in the dominant culture of the time, known as the Hellenistic or Greek culture.

Paul, by his own reckoning, was a Pharisee and a zealous observer of the Mosaic Law. He did not encounter the historical Jesus but rather powerfully encountered the risen Christ on the road to Damascus (A.D. 37–40) which changed his life forever. For the next thirty years, until his martyrdom under the emperor Nero in A.D. 67, he preached the gospel.

Paul's gift to the Church are the letters that he wrote, some of which are now collected for us in the New Testament. These are important letters because they are the oldest record for us of the early Christian community and theology in which Paul ministered and preached. It might be important to recall that these letters are older than the gospels, which were not written until after Paul's death.

There are many ways to pray with Paul and many different themes suggest themselves as important. For our purposes we pray with Paul as he puts on "the mind of Christ" and teaches us to do the same.

Romans 3:21–23
1 Corinthians 12:12–27
1 Corinthians 13:1–13
Philippians 2:5
Philippians 3:17–21

PART NINE

A Scriptural Rosary

The rosary (from rosarium, "a rose garden") is a popular devotional prayer that according to pious tradition can trace its origin back to Saint Dominic in the thirteenth century. Although it cannot be proven, despite the popular legends surrounding it, that the rosary can be attributed to Saint Dominic, it can be asserted that at least various elements of the rosary as we know it today were practiced by the faithful during the lifetime of Saint Dominic. There was great interest in the life of Jesus and Mary, especially among simple people who did not have access to books or the ability to read any of the literature that might have been available. The simple stories illustrated by what came to be the fifteen mysteries of the rosary were easily remembered.

The essential elements of the rosary consist of meditations on significant moments in the life of Jesus and Mary, recitation of a series of Our Fathers, Hail Marys, the *Gloria Pater*, the Apostles' Creed, and, in some countries, a prayer attributed to the Blessed Mother from the Fátima apparitions in 1917: "O my Jesus, forgive us our sins, save us from the fires of hell, lead all souls to heaven, especially those in greatest need."

Thirteen of the fifteen mysteries of the rosary are securely anchored in the Scriptures, particularly in the Gospel of Matthew. Two of the glorious mysteries have no direct scriptural reference, the Assumption of the Blessed Virgin Mary and the Crowning of Mary as Queen of the angels and the saints; these mysteries come to us from the tradition of the Church, and in the case of the Assumption of Mary is a dogma of the Church (CCC 966).

The rosary is prayed beginning with the Sign of the Cross. Then we say the Apostles' Creed, one Our Father, three Hail Marys, and one Glory to the Father on the small chain. Then we recall the first mystery, say one Our Father, ten Hail Marys, and one Glory to the Father. This completes one decade. All the other decades are said in the same manner with a different mystery meditated upon during each decade. At the end of the rosary, the prayer Hail, Holy Queen is sometimes recited.

Although any of the mysteries may be prayed at anytime, some people adhere to the following tradition when praying the rosary:

Sunday	The Glorious Mysteries (in honor of the Resurrection)
Monday	The Joyful Mysteries
Tuesday	The Sorrowful Mysteries
Wednesday	The Glorious Mysteries
Thursday	The Joyful Mysteries
Friday	The Sorrowful Mysteries (in remembrance of Good Friday)
Saturday	The Joyful Mysteries

The Apostles' Creed
The Our Father
The Hail Mary
The Glory to the Father
The Hail, Holy Queen

1. The Joyful Mysteries

The Annunciation (Lk 1:26–38)
The Visitation (Lk 1:39–45)
The Birth of Jesus (Lk 2:6–14)
The Presentation in the Temple (Lk 2:22–24; 29–32)
The Finding in the Temple (Lk 2:42–50)

2. The Sorrowful Mysteries

The Agony in the Garden (Jn 18:1; Mt 26:42)
The Scourging at the Pillar (Mt 27:26)
The Crowning With Thorns (Mk 15:17–19)

The Carrying of the Cross (Jn 19:16–17)
The Crucifixion (Lk 23:33)

3. The Glorious Mysteries

The Resurrection (Mk 16:1–7)
The Ascension (Lk 24:51)
The Descent of the Holy Spirit (Acts 2:1–4)
The Assumption of the Blessed Virgin Mary (Rev 12:2–9)
Mary is crowned queen of heaven and the saints (Rev 12)

4. The Biblical Rosary

This rosary is made up of fifty descriptors of the Blessed Virgin Mary taken from biblical passages. Begin the rosary in its usual way with the Apostles' Creed, the Our Father, three Hail Marys, and the Glory to the Father. Meditate on each of the following biblical passages and then say the Hail Mary. Conclude the rosary in the usual way, with the Glory to the Father, the Fátima Prayer, and the Hail, Holy Queen.

Greeted by the Angel Gabriel: Luke 1:28
Favored One: Luke 1:28
Mother of Jesus: Luke 1:31
Mother of the Son of the Most High: Luke 1:32
Mother of the Son of David: Luke 1:32
Mother of the King of Israel: Luke 1:33
Mother by act of the Holy Spirit: Luke 1:35, Matthew 1:20
Servant of the Lord: Luke 1:38
Virgin, Mother of Emmanuel: Matthew 1:23
You in whom the Word became flesh: John 1:14

You in whom the Word dwelt among us: John 1:14
Blessed among all women: Luke 1:42

Mother of the Lord: Luke 1:43
Happy are you who have believed in the words
uttered by the Lord: Luke 1:45
Lowly handmaid of the Lord: Luke 1:48
Called blessed by all generations: Luke 1:48
You in whom the Almighty worked wonders: Luke 1:49
Heiress of the promises made to Abraham: Luke 1:55
Mother of the new Isaac: Luke 1:37, Genesis 18:14
You who gave birth to your firstborn at Bethlehem: Luke 2:7

You who wrapped your Child in swaddling clothes
and laid him in a manger: Luke 2:7
Woman from whom Jesus was born: Galatians 4:4, Matthew 1:16, 21
Mother of the Savior: Luke 2:11, Matthew 1:21
Mother of the Messiah: Luke 2:11, Matthew 1:16
You who were found by the shepherds
with Joseph and the newborn Christ Child: Luke 2:16
You who kept and meditated all things
in your heart: Luke 2:19
You who offered Jesus in the Temple: Luke 2:22
You who put Jesus into the arms of Simeon: Luke 2:28
You who marveled at what was said of Jesus: Luke 2:33
You whose soul a sword shall pierce: Luke 2:35

Mother who was found together with the Child
by the Wise Men: Matthew 2:11
Mother whom Joseph took into refuge in Egypt: Matthew 2:14
You who took the child Jesus to Jerusalem
for the Passover: Luke 2:42
You who searched for Jesus for three days: Luke 2:46
You who found Jesus again in His Father's House: Luke 2:46–49
Mother whom Jesus obeyed at Nazareth: Luke 2:51

Model of widows: Mark 6:3
Jesus' companion at the marriage feast of Cana: John 2:1–2
You who gave rise to Jesus' first miracle: John 2:3–11
Mother of Jesus for having done the will
of the Father in heaven: Matthew 12:50

Mary who chose the better part: Luke 10:42
Blessed for having heard the word of God
and kept it: Luke 11:28
Mother standing at the foot of the cross: John 19:25
Mother of the disciple whom Jesus loved: John 19:26–27
Queen of the Apostles, persevering
in prayer with them: Acts of the Apostles 1:14
Woman clothed with the sun: Revelation 12:1
Woman crowned with twelve stars: Revelation 12:1
Sorrowful Mother of the Church: Revelation 12:2
Glorious Mother of the Messiah: Revelation 12:5
Image of the New Jerusalem: Revelation 21:2

PART TEN

For Further Study

1. Glossary of Terms

Aaron Brother of Moses and the sister of Miriam. He is portrayed as a capable helper to Moses, serving as a prophet (Ex 7:1) and a judge of the people when Moses was absent (Ex 24:14). Along with Hur, Aaron held up Moses' hands during the battle with Amalek (Ex 17:12). Like Moses, he was denied entrance into the Promised Land (Deut 32:48–52).

Abba Aramaic word for *father,* properly translated as "my father" or "our father." Young children often used this familiar form of address. Jesus used the intimate address *Abba* when he invoked his Father in the greatest crisis of his life (Mk 14:36). Two other New Testament occurrences of *Abba* also are used in the context of prayer, Romans 8:15 and Galatians 4:6 (CCC 2605).

Abel Second son of Adam and Eve who offers an acceptable sacrifice to God (Gen 4:1–16). According to the Genesis account, Abel was murdered by his brother Cain.

Abraham An extraordinary person whose story is told in the book of Genesis, chapter 12 to 25. Abraham ("father of a multitude") was born almost two thousand years before Christ, probably in the city of Ur of the Chaldeans, now in modern-day Iraq. He responded to the call of Yahweh and entered into a covenant with God. Because of his special calling, he is known as the "Father of the Jewish people," and, by extension, the spiritual father of all believers. Faith, especially in the sense of absolute trust in God and fidelity to God's will, was his outstanding characteristic (CCC 145–146, 705–706, and 2570–572). Abraham is also considered a great prophet in Islam.

Absalom One of the sons of King David, Absalom rebelled against his father and was executed as he hung by his hair in the branches of an oak tree. His story is told in 2 Samuel 13—20.

abyss The abode of the dead (Rom 10:7), the watery deep (Ps 77:16), and the place where evil spirits are confined (Lk 8:31). According to the book of Revelation, the abyss is the place from which the Antichrist will come (Rev 11:7; 17:8).

Acts of the Apostles Book of the New Testament, attributed to the writer-editor known as Luke, written about A.D. 80–85, after the destruction of the Temple in Jerusalem. It describes the faith and the way of early Christians and the evangelical efforts of Saint Paul and other missionaries. The writer-editor is not as much concerned with historical details as he is with the action of God in history, especially through the preaching of the apostles. He is also concerned with the Church as a human organism compelled to adapt itself to actual circumstances in order to carry out its mission to other places and cultures.

A.D. This designation for the Christian era is derived from the Latin words *anno Domini*, meaning "the year of the Lord." Time is measured on a calendar before and after the year in which tradition assumed that Jesus was born. A date followed by the abbreviation A.D. means so many years after the birth of Jesus. In consideration for those of other faiths, many now favor the designation C.E. for "Christian Era" in place of the traditional A.D.

Adam and Eve According to Genesis, Adam (in Hebrew "earthly" or "a human") and Eve are the first human beings created by God (Gen 1 and 2). They were expelled from the Garden of Eden because they disobeyed God's command not to eat of a certain tree. The Christian doctrine of original sin is traced back to these "first parents" (CCC 399).

Adonai Jews, out of reverence for the name of God, often did not pronounce the name of Yahweh and substituted the word *Adonai*, an Old Testament Hebrew term for God meaning "Lord" or "my Lord" in its place (CCC 209).

agape This Greek term occurs in the synoptic Gospels in Matthew 24:12 and Luke 11:42. It is used several times in the Gospel of John and in the letters of John and Paul to refer to love, specifically the love of God for us and our love for God and one another. It is the most singularly Christian form of love. Christ instructed his disciples to have this kind of love for one another (Jn 13:34–35). Agape is totally selfless love, which seeks not a person's own interest but only the concern for the well being of another. Among the earliest followers of Jesus, the agape was a holy meal celebrated as a memorial of the Last Supper (1 Cor 11:20–22, 33–34). The custom of sharing agape-style meals in Christian settings is often linked to the festive spirit of the Seder or Passover meal.

alms Gifts to the poor. In the Old Testament, alms for the poor was recommended (Isa 58:6–8) and required every three years (Deut 14:28–29). In the New Testament, it is further recommended (Acts 6; 2 Cor 8—9) and can be viewed as required for salvation (Mt 25:31–36) (CCC 1969).

amen A Hebrew word meaning "truth, certainty, and faithfulness." It is often used in prayer as a way of concluding the prayer with emphasis, such as "may it be so," or "I believe."

anawim From the Hebrew word meaning "remnant." Many of the prophets prophesied that only a small remnant of people would remain faithful to God and to his covenant and would therefore be saved from destruction. It is from this faithful remnant that a new people would come forth (Isa 10:20).

angel From the Greek word for "messenger," angels are often spoken of in the Bible. There are many Old Testament references to them (Gen 32:1; Isa 6; Tob 5). Of special note is the gospel assertion that angels are spiritual beings (Mt 22:30), who always enjoy the vision of God in heaven (Mt 18:10) and who will accompany Jesus at his Second Coming (Mt 16:27). In the course of the centuries, theologians have described angels as created spirits without bodies, endowed with intellect and free will, inferior to God but superior to human beings. The Catholic Church professes that angels exist, but does not define any details about them (CCC 328–336).

Antichrist A term used to describe the chief of Christ's enemies, the final opponent. The term is used in the New Testament only in 1 John 2:18; 24:4:3; and 2 John 7. Historically, the Antichrist has been identified with individual persons (for example, the Roman emperor Caligula and Hitler) or with social institutions. Some non-Catholics preach that the Catholic Church is the Antichrist. We have no definite identification of the Antichrist from the Bible or from the Church (CCC 675).

Antioch City on the river Orontes, now in modern-day Turkey. In ancient times it was a great city on par with Rome and Alexandria. According to the Acts of the Apostles (11:26), it is the city where the designation "Christian" was first used. This is also the city that was visited by Saint Paul and Barnabas, as described in Acts 13:14–52.

apocalypse Name given to the last book of the New Testament, the book of Revelation as it is more commonly known today. It means an "uncovering" or "revealing." The book of Revelation, written sometime after A.D. 90, is a highly symbolic work dealing with things to come and the struggle between the Church and the powers of evil; although it contains dire warnings, it is fundamentally a message of hope to the Church concerning the final triumph of Jesus Christ (CCC 1137).

apocalyptic From the Greek, literally meaning to "unveil" or to "reveal." Today, when the word is used, it more often than not refers to a world-view and a type of biblical literature that comes from times of suffering and persecution. Two such examples of apocalyptic literature would be the book of Daniel and the book of Revelation. See also **dispensational premillennialism.**

Apocrypha From the Greek meaning "hidden." Some Old Testament books written in Greek are included in Catholic Bibles and are often omitted in Protestant bibles because they are not considered to be canonical, that is, inspired Scripture. These books are collectively known as the Apocrypha and include Tobit, Judith, Sirach, Wisdom, and 1 and 2 Maccabees. See also **pseudepigrapha**.

apostasy In the Old Testament, the word *apostasy* is understood as "unfaithfulness to God" (Jer 2:19) and in the New Testament generally used to describe the situation of a person who abandons the Christian faith (Heb 6:6) (CCC 2089).

apostle From the Greek word meaning "one who is sent," this term is used often in the New Testament. It is specifically used to describe the twelve men whom Jesus gathered around him for instructions. Eleven of the twelve apostles are considered the prime witnesses of the Resurrection and served in various leadership roles in the Christian community. The apostles were commissioned by Christ to preach the Gospel throughout the world (Mt 28:19–20) (CCC 75–76).

apple Fruit that is widely believed to be the fruit from the tree of knowledge in the Garden of Eden, the apple is never mentioned by name (Gen 2:9; 3:6).

Aramaic Primary language spoken by Jesus and his apostles. It is a Semitic language, related to biblical Hebrew. Aramaic words that have found there way into the New Testament include *maranatha,* meaning "Come, Lord, come!" (1 Cor 16:22) and *mammon*, meaning "wealth" (Mt 6:24).

Ark of the covenant People of Israel carried a small box made of precious wood in their wanderings, which they placed in the Temple at Jerusalem. The two tablets of the Law (the Ten Commandments) that were given to Moses by God, a golden dish of manna, and the rod of Aaron, which blossomed, were enclosed in this sacred chest made of acacia wood. The Ark came to be regarded as the sign of God's abiding presence and protection. The book of Exodus, chapter 25, provides explicit instructions for the construction of the Ark.

Armageddon Mountain of Megiddo bordering the Plain of Esdraelon in present-day Israel. This mountain was the great battlefield of ancient Palestine where the fortunes of kings and nations were decided. In the New Testament, Armageddon is a symbol of the struggle between good and evil that goes on in the world and in every person (Rev 16:16). It has also come to be synonymous with the place of the final cosmic battle between God and Satan, where good will finally prevail over evil.

Athens Great city in Greece, the capital of Attica. It was considered a city where great literature, art, and civilization flourished. The apostle Paul preached a famous sermon here on the Areopagus hill while on his second missionary journey.

Atonement, Day of In Hebrew, *"Yom Kippur."* A festival observed ten days after the beginning of the Jewish New Year (Lev 16:29) to atone for the sins of the people and, in Old Testament times, the particular sins of the high priest committed during the previous year.

Baal A Canaanite god. The Semitic word means "owner" or "lord." He was thought to be the god of the weather and god of thunderstorms, and as such, lightning was his weapon. Opposition to Baal is persistent in the Scriptures, a circumstance which indicates that the god maintained a fervent following for many years. Many of the Old Testament prophets struggled against his followers.

Baalzebub Originally, a god worshiped by the Philistines in the time of the Old Testament (2 Kings 1:2–16). In the New Testament, Jesus denies that he casts out devils in the name of Baalzebub, the "prince of demons" (Mk 3:22–26), which may indicate the development of the so-named deity from god to demon over the centuries.

Babylonian Captivity Also known as the Babylonian Exile. The period in Jewish history when the Jewish people were removed from the Promised Land and sent to Babylon, first in 597 and then in 586 B.C. They returned to a decimated Jerusalem and a destroyed Temple in 538 B.C.

Bathsheba Wife of Uriah the Hittite, she was coveted and seduced by King David, who arranged the murder of Uriah in order to enable his adultery (2 Sam 11:1–4). She became the mother of King Solomon (2 Sam 12:24).

B.C. This designation for the Christian era is the abbreviation for "before Christ." Time is measured on a calendar before and after the year in which tradition assumed that Jesus was born. A date followed by the abbreviation B.C. means so many years before the birth of Jesus. In consideration for those of other faiths, many now favor the designation B.C.E., "Before the Christian Era," in place of the traditional B.C.

Beatitudes The promises of Christ concerning happiness or blessedness as proclaimed in the Sermon on the Mount. Matthew lists eight beatitudes (5:3–12); Luke mentions four (6:20–23). God considers them basic qualities of Christian holiness that will be generously reward (CCC 1716–1719).

Bel and the Dragon One of the additions to the book of Daniel that is found in the Greek translations of the Hebrew Old Testament. Protestants include it among the Apocrypha, while Catholics include it with the canonical text of the book of Daniel (Dan 14:1–42).

Beloved Disciple A disciple mentioned only in the Gospel of John, and then never identified by name. Some scholars associate the Beloved Disciple with the traditional author of John's Gospel, the apostle John, the son of Zebedee (Jn 19:25–27; 21:20–24).

Benedictus A poetic exclamation, attributed to Zechariah, the father of John the Baptist (Lk 1:68–79). The Benedictus is named for the first word of the prophetic hymn in its Latin translation.

Bethany A village on the east slope of the Mount of Olives, less than two miles from Jerusalem. It was the village of Martha and Mary and the place where Lazarus was raised.

Bethel With the exception of Jerusalem, Bethel (in Hebrew "house of God") is mentioned more than any other city in the Scriptures. In existence probably before 2000 B.C., it is a city associated with Abraham, Jacob, and the prophet Elijah.

Bethlehem Today, a suburb in the metropolitan city of Jerusalem about six miles southwest of the ancient city, Bethlehem (in Hebrew, "house of bread") is home to the shrine that holds the cave where Jesus Christ was born. The shrine is located under the eastern end of the Church of the Nativity. The present basilica was built at the direction of the emperor Constantine in the fourth century and restored by Justinian around A.D. 545.

Bible A term used to describe the sacred Scriptures of Christianity, from the Old French word *"bible,"* which is based on the Latin and Greek word *"biblia."* The Bible has been passed on from generation to generation in different forms. The authoritative and canonical text of the Bible is based on the original Hebrew Bible often referred to as the Masoretic Text which forms the Old Testament, and the approved twenty-seven books which form the New Testament. In Catholic tradition later Greek texts have also been accepted as part of the authoritative text of the Old Testament. See **Apocrypha**.

biblical criticism The study of biblical texts, from the Greek word *"krino,"* which means to "judge" or "discern." The purpose of biblical criticism is to arrive at an informed opinion about a text being studied using at least five distinct "tools of discernment." The five tools of discernment include textual criticism (to establish the original wording), historical criticism (the attempt to reconstruct the circumstances in which the text was written), literary criticism (examination of the words and the style of the text), form criticism (determining the oral and written stages of the text), and redaction criticism (determining the manner in which the text was edited). Modern biblical scholarship has further refined and expanded these original critical tools, but the traditional five types of criticism referenced here are useful for understanding the concept.

bishop from the Greek word *"episcopos,"* which may be translated as "overseer" or "guardian." First used in the Philippians (1:1). In the letter of Timothy (1 Tm 3:1–7) and the letter of Titus (1:5–9), the qualifications of a bishop are explained (CCC 1590).

blasphemy The contempt or lack of due reverence for God or for something that is accepted as sacred (Lev 24:16) (CCC 2148).

Body of Christ A term used to describe the Church. Saint Paul speaks of the Church as the Body of Christ; Christ is the Head and we are the members (Col 1:18; 1 Cor 12:27) (CCC 787–795).

body, resurrection of According to Scripture and the formal teaching of the Church, the body will be resurrected and reunited to the soul after death, on the last day, the Final Judgment. Christ taught the resurrection of the body (Mt 22:29–32; Lk 14:14; Jn 5:29). The doctrine was preached as a fundamental mystery of the Christian faith (1 Cor 15:20; Rev 20:12) and was included in all of the early creeds (CCC 998–1001).

bread, breaking of The most ancient reference for the celebration of the Eucharist. The Acts of the Apostles (2:42) describes the earliest Christian communities as devoting themselves "to the teaching of the apostles and to the communal life, to the breaking of the bread and to the prayers."

Caiaphas High priest during the time of Jesus from A.D. 18 until he was disposed by Vitellius, the successor of Pontius Pilate, probably in A.D. 36–37 (Mt 26:3; Jn 18:13).

Cain Firstborn son of Adam and Eve (Gen 4:1), he later killed his brother Abel (Gen 4:8). Although the book of Genesis identifies Cain as a farmer, in Hebrew the name means "metalworker."

Calvary Place where Jesus was crucified, Calvary is a Latin translation of the word *Golgotha,* meaning "place of the skull." Calvary was the place outside of the city walls of Jerusalem where criminals were usually executed.

Cana Village in Galilee, mentioned only in the Gospel of John, as the site of the miracle in which Jesus turned water into wine (Jn 2:1–11).

Canaan, Canaanites Land located between the Jordan River and the Mediterranean Sea, including a small sliver of modern-day Syria, as it extends on the coast. This is the land which is known as the Promised Land. By 2000 B.C. the Canaanites seemed to have an established and advanced society based on agriculture but also including some merchants and also seamen. It was to this land and this people that the Hebrew people came on their exodus from Egypt.

canon From the Greek word "*kanon,*" which is derived from the Semitic word meaning "reed." Originally understood to mean a straight rod, a tool that was used for measuring by a carpenter or a mason. As such, canon came to be understood as meaning the "norm" or the "rule."

canon of Scripture The list or collection of books of the Bible officially recognized and accepted by the Catholic Church as the inspired Word of God and therefore to be accepted by all believers as the rule or norm of faith (CCC 120). There is a difference between the Roman Catholic canon of Scripture and the Protestant canon of Scripture insofar as the Roman Church accepts certain books, primarily written in Greek, that have not been accepted by Protestant churches. Such books are designated as "deutero-canonical" (second canon) by the Catholic Church and as "apocrypha" by the Protestant churches. See also **Apocrypha**.

Capernaum In the time of Jesus a village located on the northwest coast of the Sea of Galilee. This town seems to be the center of Jesus' Galilean ministry (Mt 4:13). The village is in ruins today.

charism Extraordinary gifts or graces of the Holy Spirit given to individuals for the sake of others. Saint Paul lists nine of these graces (1 Cor 12:4–11); he also insists that the virtue of charity is above all other charisms (1 Cor 13) (CCC 799–801).

children of God Term often used by the early Christian community to identify themselves and to define their understanding of their relationship with God (Rom 8:16–17; Phil 2:15). Some scholars believe that the name was used by the Johannine community as the special designation for all Christians (1 Jn 3:1) (CCC 1692).

Christ A title of Jesus, from the Greek *"Christos,"* meaning the "anointed one," identical to the Hebrew word for messiah, that is, savior or deliverer. To acknowledge Jesus as the Christ is to acknowledge him as savior (CCC 436–440). Isaiah contains so many messianic prophecies that it has sometimes been referred to as "the gospel within the Old Testament."

circumcision The removal of the foreskin of the male penis. From a religious viewpoint, circumcision was very important to the people of Israel: it was a "mark of the covenant" between Yahweh and his people (Gen 17:10–14), routinely performed on infants eight days after birth (Gen 17:12; Lev 12:3). Jesus himself was circumcised on the eighth day after his birth (Lk 2:21), and the early Christians were sometimes referred to as simply "the circumcised" (Acts 11:2). It was soon recognized, however, that the Mosaic Law need not be imposed on gentile Christians and that circumcision was no longer a religious requirement for the baptized (Gal 5:6; 6:15 and Rom 3:30) (CCC 527).

Christian Name first used by Pliny the Younger in A.D. 112 in a report to the emperor Trajan. The designation Christian is used only three times in the New Testament (1 Pet 4:16; Acts 11:26 and 26:28), more often than not the early communities described themselves as "believers," "disciples," or "followers of the way."

Colossae City in Asia Minor located approximately 110 miles east of Ephesus. The city was known for its wool and cloth. A Christian community was established here, and it was to this community that Paul's letter to the Colossians was written.

commandment Written or verbal directive, requirement, or expectation usually attributed to God but occasionally attributed to a king in relationship to his subjects. The word appears 180 times in the Old Testament.

conversion In the New Testament the Greek word "*metanoia,*" often translated as "conversion" or "repentance," means something very profound and personal: not merely a change of manners but a change of heart, a turning away from sin, a return to the Father's love. Jesus insisted on metanoia; he wanted people to be sorry but he also desired that they be fundamentally changed by their sorrow and their personal experience of forgiveness (Lk 11:4; Mt 18:21–22) (CCC 1427–1429).

Corinth A city in Greece, approximately forty miles southwest of the city of Athens. Destroyed by the Romans in 146 B.C., it was reconstructed by Julius Caesar one hundred years after its destruction. An important city in the life of the apostle Paul, it was home to an early Christian community and also home to Aquila and Priscilla, who were great supporters and benefactors of Paul. Letters to the Christian community in Corinth were written by Paul while he was in Ephesus around A.D. 57.

cosmology A particular understanding and interpretation of the universe peculiar to an individual person, culture, or society. Ancient cosmologies that are represented within the Scriptures are significantly different from modern cosmologies. For example, in the Scriptures it is assumed that the earth is flat and that there are three "levels" in the known universe: the upper level (heaven), the middle level (earth), and the lower level (the underworld, Sheol, hell).

covenant A formal agreement, pact, or contract; in religious terms it describes the special relationship between God and his people. The Old Testament gives many examples of God's covenant with the Israelites: for example, with Abraham (Gen 15ff), with Noah (Gen 6:18), and with Moses (Deut 5—7). In the covenant, God promised to be faithful to his people; they in turn promised to be faithful to him alone and to keep his commandments. One of the dominant themes of the Old Testament is that while God is always faithful to his part of the covenant, the people are not always faithful to theirs. The New Testament describes the new covenant: that is, the special relationship between God the Father, Jesus his beloved Son, and each Christian in and with Jesus. The new covenant does not annul the old but, in Jesus, brings it to fulfillment (Gal 3:15–29). In the new covenant, Jesus expresses unconditional love for his people, instructs them, forgives them, and lays down his life for them, thus sealing the new covenant in his own blood (1 Cor 11:25) (CCC 1961–1974).

creation The act of God, as described in the book of Genesis (Gen 1:1—2:4) by which God created the entire universe and all that is in it. A second story of creation, that differs markedly from the first story of creation and which is viewed by Scripture scholars as perhaps an older tradition, follows the first story of creation (Gen 2:4b–25). Regardless, in each story God is presented as the creator, making all things out of nothing (CCC 198; 296).

cross A word from the Greek *"stauros,"* a term that describes the instrument of suffering on which Jesus died for the salvation of the world (Mt 27, Mk 15, Lk 23, Jn 19). In the ancient world, the use of an upright stake (sometimes a crossbar was also added) that was used to execute or torture a victim, or to display the corpse of an enemy, was widespread. Today, the cross is a symbol of the redeeming love of Jesus, profoundly respected by Christians throughout the world. Also, a term that describes the suffering or mortification of a Christian, especially when accepted lovingly in union with the sufferings of Christ: "If any want to become my followers, let them deny themselves and take up their cross and follow me" (Mk 8:34) (CCC 616–617).

cuneiform writing One of the earliest forms of written communication, cuneiform writing is made up of a series of wedgeshaped marks. Originally, each mark represented a particular concept ("to stand," or "orchard," for example) and eventually came to represent a particular sound. When writing became phonetic, the form of communication could become much more complex, relating full records of a particular event or circumstance rather than as an aid to memory, which seemed to have been its original purpose.

Damascus Present-day capital city of Syria, it is one of the most continuously occupied cities in the world. The city figures prominently in both the Old Testament (1 Kings 11:23–25; 2 Sam 8:5–6) and in the New Testament, where the conversion of the apostle Paul took place (Acts 9:2–30; Gal 1:17).

Dead Sea The body of water at the mouth of the Jordan River. The Dead Sea is approximately fifty miles long and ten miles wide and at some points reaches a depth of thirteen hundred feet. It is composed of 25 percent salt (in comparison, the oceans are only 5 percent). In the Bible the Dead Sea is often referred to under a variety of different names including "Salt Sea" (Gen 14:3), "Sea of the Arabah" (Deut 3:17), and "Eastern Sea" (Ezek 47:18), to name just a few.

Dead Sea Scrolls A collection of manuscripts and fragments of manuscripts discovered between 1947 and 1956 at the site of the ancient Qumran community west of the Dead Sea. They have been dated from approximately one hundred years before and after Christ. Among the scrolls are portions of many Old Testament books and writings about the Essene community (an ascetical community or sect living in Palestine during the first century A.D.). The scrolls, which are still being studied, have been of great value to biblical scholars in reconstructing the textual history of the Old Testament.

Decalogue See **Ten Commandments.**

demythologizing Concept vigorously debated by scholars in the 1950s and attributed to the twentieth-century New Testament biblical scholar Rudolf Bultmann, who proposed that the language and the conceptual framework of the New Testament was primarily mythological. Bultmann argued that since modern people hold a scientific view of the world, a mythological view of the New Testament became increasingly problematic. He wanted the mythological elements of the New Testament clearly identified, not eliminated, so as to enhance the truth of the New Testament and make it more acceptable to all. The concept is rarely if ever used today.

deuterocanonical texts Books or parts of books that are found in the Greek Septuagint (LXX) translation of the Old Testament but are not found in the Hebrew text (MT). These texts are accepted in the Roman Catholic and Orthodox communities but are not accepted in the Protestant communities. See also **Apocrypha, Septuagint, and Vulgate.**

devil; Satan An evil spirit or fallen angel; specifically, the term often applies to Satan, the chief of the fallen angels (Mt 12:24) who tempts the human person to sin. In this teaching and ministry, Jesus Christ opposes the evil spirit with the Spirit of God (CCC 391–395).

diaspora From the Greek word meaning "scattered abroad," this term refers to members of the Jewish community who lived outside the land of Palestine after the Babylonian Exile of 586 B.C.

disciple A word from the Greek which means "learner," it is used to describe those who hear and follow the teaching of Jesus (Mt 10:1), not only in New Testament times but in every age (CCC 645, 647).

dispensational premillennialism A system of biblical interpretation, used by some evangelical Protestant theologians and popularized by British writer John Nelson Darby in the early nineteenth century. In this system, world history is divided into six or seven time periods in which God deals with the human race in distinctly different ways. Biblical prophecy (in this system no single book contains the entire picture and so prophecies need to be pieced together for the truth to emerge) is understood as a literal prediction of events in world history. The book of Daniel and the book of Revelation are of central importance in this system.

Divided Kingdom, Divided Monarchy The two-hundred-year period (922–722 B.C.) that followed the reign of King Solomon in which the people of the Old Testament were divided into the kingdom of the North (Israel) and the kingdom of the South (Judah).

Easter A movable feast, celebrated on a Sunday between March 22 and April 25, commemorating the Resurrection of Jesus Christ from the dead (Mk 16:1–7). It is considered the greatest of all Christian feasts and holds a central place in the liturgical year. The celebration of the Resurrection continues for a period of fifty days from Easter Sunday to the feast of Pentecost.

economy of salvation The great plan of God by which his will and work is accomplished even without the help of human beings. This plan of salvation is described in Ephesians 1:3–14.

Eden According to the book of Genesis (Gen 2:8–15), the garden associated with paradise. In Hebrew, Eden is often translated as "luxury" or "delight." However, in ancient Sumerian it could also mean "plain," or "steppe." Also referred to in the book of the prophet Ezekiel in which he refers to Eden as the "garden of God" (Ezek 28:11–19).

El An ancient name for God, used either to identify the god El who was a god in the pantheon of the Canaanites or often in conjunction with another name, such as in El Shaddai, the name by which Yahweh may first have been known (Ex 6:2–8). The prominence and importance of the name El can also be seen since it is used so often in personal names such as *El*ijah, *El*i, *El*eazar, and *El*isha, for example.

elders In the Old Testament, elders were senior members of the twelve tribes who often served in roles of leadership (Ex 18:13–17; Num 11:16–30). In the New Testament, elders were people who served in important roles within the Christian community (Jas 5:14; 1 Pet 5:11; Acts 15:2).

Eleven, the Refers to the apostles of Jesus during the brief period of time after the death of Judas Iscariot (Mt 28:16; Mk 16:14) and before the choice of Matthias to replace him (Acts 1:23–26).

Emmanuel Hebrew for "God is with us," or "May God be with us." The name is given to Jesus in the Gospel of Matthew (Mt 1:23). May also be spelled "Immanuel."

Emmaus From the Hebrew word meaning "warm wells," it refers to a town that plays a prominent role in the post-Resurrection story of Jesus in the Gospel of Luke (Lk 24:13–35).

English Bible According to tradition, the first attempt to translate the Bible into English was probably made by the Venerable Bede (d. 735), but there are no surviving manuscripts or parts of manuscripts from this attempt. The *Wessex Gospels* of the tenth century was a second attempt to at least translate the Gospels into English but the oldest surviving manuscript is from John Wycliffe (1324–1384), who translated his edition of the Bible from the Latin Vulgate. However, it was William Tyndale (1484–1536) who is known as the "Father of the English Bible." It is estimated that at least 80 percent of the King James Version of the Bible, first published in 1611, is the result of his efforts. Other notable early English Bibles would include the Rheims-Douai Bible (1582–1610), the Bishops' Bible (1568), and the Geneva Bible (1557–1560).

Ephesus A city in Lydia, Asia Minor, which was noted for its magnificent temple to Diana and also for its great theater. A city that Paul visited on his second and third missionary journeys.

Epiphany From the Greek word *epiphaneia,* which means "manifestation." The term refers primarily to the feast of the Epiphany on January 6 (or the Sunday closest to this date in some countries) and celebrates the manifestation of the Lord to the entire world as represented by the Magi or the Three Kings (Mt 2:1–12).

Eretz Israel The territory we would understand today as the Holy Land. Most biblical scholars would agree that in his adult life Jesus of Nazareth never left this territory, the religious land that circled around the Jerusalem Temple.

eschatology *Eschata* is Greek for "last things"; eschatology is that part of theology that studies the "last things," such as death, judgment, heaven, hell, the resurrection of the body, and the Second Coming of Christ (CCC 1020–1041). Many biblical books contain eschatological assertions and ideas, all of which are not meant to be understood and interpreted literally in their every detail.

Essenes A rigorous Jewish sect existing from around the second century B.C. through the Roman destruction of the second Temple in A.D. 66–70. Clearly identified with the Qumran community which produced the Dead Sea Scrolls. The Essene community was apocalyptic in their thoughts and practices, patiently waiting for God to come and to destroy the evil around them.

Euphrates River Largest river in western Asia, it served as the northern boundary of the kingdom of Israel during the time of King David. According to the book of Genesis, the Euphrates was one of the four rivers (also the Pishon, Gihon, Tigris) that flowed from the Garden of Eden (Gen 2:14).

evangelist From the Greek meaning "one who bears good news"; this word appears three times in the New Testament (Acts 21:8; Eph 4:11; 2 Tim 4:5). By the third century, the traditional authors of the four canonical gospels—Matthew, Mark, Luke, and John—were commonly identified as evangelists, and the four living creatures from the book of Revelation (Rev 4:7) were assigned to them. As a result, Matthew is known as the lion, Mark as the ox, Luke as the man, and John as the eagle.

exegesis The practical application of hermeneutics to a biblical text. See also **hermeneutics, biblical criticsm.**

Ezekiel In Hebrew, a word meaning "God strengthens." Ezekiel was a prophet from approximately 593–570 B.C. He was one of the captives deported from Israel to Babylon by King Nebuchadnezzar in 597 B.C.

faith One of the three (faith, hope, and charity) theological, or God-given and God-directed, virtues or powers, grace, by which, in the words of the First Vatican Council, "a person is enabled to believe that what God has revealed is true—not because its intrinsic worth is seen with the rational light of reason—but because of the authority of God who reveals it, that God who can neither deceive nor be deceived." See Romans 1:5; 16:26; and 2 Corinthians 10:15–16 (CCC 1814–1816).

Feast of Weeks, or the feast of the harvest, was held on the fiftieth day or seven weeks after the second day of the Passover celebration. The feast was limited to a single day in the sanctuary of the Temple in Jerusalem. Two loaves of unleavened bread, ten suitable animals for a burnt offering, one kid for a sin offering, and two lambs for a peace offering were designated.

Feast of Tabernacles Also known as the Ingathering or the Feast of Booths, this was the last of the three annual feasts celebrated in Israel. This feast was celebrated in the seventh month when the agricultural season had been completed. The feast stretched over a period of seven days in which the daily offering in the Temple in Jerusalem included the sacrifice of bulls, two rams, fourteen lambs, and a he-goat.

firmament According to the book of Genesis, the division created by God between the waters of the earth and the waters of the heavens. In order to fully understand the biblical concept, a person needs to imagine that the earth is flat and that a kind of dome is created in the sky, separating the earth from the heavens. The firmament, or in some translations the "vault of heaven," is the dome (Gen 1:6–8).

Gabriel One of the archangels who appears in Jewish and Christian literature. Gabriel appears only in the book of Daniel (8:15–26; 9:21–27) and in the Gospel of Luke (1:11–20, 26–38). The other two archangels that frequently appear are Raphael (Tob 12:15) and the patron angel of Israel, Michael (Dan 10:13; Rev 12:7) (CCC 328–336).

Galatia A Roman Province in central Asia Minor. The southern portion of the province was visited by Saint Paul in his missionary journeys.

Galilee The region between Samaria on the southern border, the river Leontes on the north, and the Sea of Galilee (thirteen miles long and eight miles wide) on the east. The whole Galilee area, the primary area of Israel in which Jesus lived and ministered, is approximately fifty miles long and thirty-five miles wide. The land has some mountains (the highest of which is four thousand feet) and is filled with many areas of trees and fields.

Gehenna A valley south of Jerusalem known for its worship of the god Moloch. It is used in the New Testament to denote hell (Lk 12:5; Mk 9:45; and Mt 5:22).

gentiles Word used frequently in the Bible to mean "pagans" or "foreigners" or simply "people who were not Jews." In the Old Testament, there is evidence of hostility and distrust between Jews and Gentiles. In the New Testament it is clear that Jesus first directed his disciples to preach the Good News only to "the lost sheep of the house of Israel" (Mt 10:6), but gradually the mission was extended to "all nations" as well (Mt 28:19). The extension of the Church to the Gentiles is spoken of in the Acts of the Apostles (Acts 8–12) and in many of the New Testament letters (CCC 58, 60).

Gethsemane From either the Hebrew or the Aramaic word meaning "oil press." It was the place on the Mount of Olives that Jesus prayed after the Last Supper, the garden in which he was arrested by the temple guards (Mk 14:32; Mt 26:36).

gifts of the Spirit A concept found in the New Testament in the writings of Saint Paul, but also a concept with some foundation in the Old Testament (Judg 3:10; Num 11:29). The gifts of the Spirit (*pneuma* and *charismata*) are gifts of divine grace, and they vary from one person to another (Rom 12:6; 1 Cor 12:4–11). There are four separate listings of the gifts of the Spirit found in the letters of Paul: Romans 12:6-8, 1 Corinthians 12:8-10, 1 Corinthians 12:28, 29–30.

Gnostic/gnosticism From the Greek word *gnosis* meaning "knowledge." Gnosticism was an early Christian heresy that emphasized the need to possess "secret knowledge" in order to be saved. Gnosticism was a very complex set of ideas, and some Scripture scholars believe that some of the Gnostic ideas have influenced later Christian writings while others believe that it would be more accurate to state that Christian writing influenced Gnostic ideas.

golden rule First popularized in the seventeenth century, the golden rule is found in Matthew 7:12 and Luke 6:31: "Do to others as you want them to do to you."

Golgotha In Hebrew, the "place of the skull." This is the place where Jesus was crucified.

Good Samaritan Samaritan man who in the parable of Jesus was offered as an example of what it means to live in the kingdom of God, a good neighbor (Lk 10:29–37). When Jesus first told this parable there was probably no one in his audience who would have been able to imagine such a thing as a "good Samaritan" since Jews and Samaritans had nurtured a centuries-old disdain for each other.

Gospel From an Old English word *god-spel* meaning "good news," a Gospel is one of the four divinely inspired accounts of the life, teaching, suffering, death, and Resurrection of Jesus Christ. It is customary to describe the gospels of Matthew, Mark, and Luke as "synoptic Gospels" because they give a "synopsis" or similar view of the life and teaching of Jesus; the Gospel of John reflects a different apostolic tradition. The Church holds the gospels in high esteem; passages from them are proclaimed in the eucharistic liturgy and in the formal celebration of all of the sacraments (CCC 125–127).

Habakkuk Prophet in Judah during the last days of the reign of King Josiah (648–609 B.C.) and the reign of King Jehoiakim (609–598 B.C.).

Hail Mary The best-known and most popular prayer in honor of the Blessed Virgin Mary; it is composed of verses from the Gospel of Luke (Lk 1:28, 42) and a centuries-old petition formulated by the Church (CCC 2676–2677).

heaven The dwelling place of God and the angels and the place of eternal happiness for all those who have been saved; it consists primarily of the face-to-face vision of God and the possession of eternal peace.

hell Hebrew word in English used to translate *"Sheol"* and *"Gehenna"* and the Greek *"Hades."* Hell is the dwelling place of Satan and the evil spirits and of all those who die deliberately alienated from God. The primary punishment of hell is the pain of loss; the deprivation of the face-to-face vision of God and eternal happiness with him. There is also the pain of sense caused by an outside agent, described as fire in the New Testament (Mt 25:41; Mk 9:43). Hell is the dire destination for one who freely chooses his or her own will against the will of God (CCC 1033–1037).

Hellenism, Hellenists Term used in reference to people and cultures who assumed the Greek language and culture, usually as a result of conquest set in motion by Alexander the Great (d. 323 B.C.). Also commonly used to identify Greek-speaking Jews of the Diaspora and any and all Gentiles. See 2 Maccabees 4:10; Acts of the Apostles 6:1; 9:29.

hermeneutics Understood in the broadest possible sense, it is the field of theological study that deals with the interpretation of sacred Scripture. It includes a study of the principles that are used in biblical interpretation and the process that is used. See also **exegesis, biblical criticism.**

Hexateuch First six books of the Old Testament, in contrast to the first five books of the Old Testament identified as the Pentateuch. Some biblical scholars suggest that the inclusion of the book of Joshua completes the story of the conquest of the Promised Land, thus giving the reader a more balanced view of the biblical tradition.

historical literature The Old Testament books of Joshua, Judges, Ruth, 1 and 2 Samuel, 1 and 2 Kings, 1 and 2 Chronicles, Ezra, Nehemiah, Tobit, Judith, Esther, and 1 and 2 Maccabees. These books give us the history of Israel, from the settlement in the Promised Land (around the twelfth century B.C.) to the Babylonia exile (587–539 B.C.) and beyond. They are concerned with the themes of Israel's faithfulness to God and God's plan for the salvation of all people.

Hosea In Hebrew a word meaning "may Yahweh save," and also meaning "salvation." Hosea was the last of the prophets of the Northern Kingdom (721 B.C.).

INRI An abbreviation that stands for the Latin words "*Iesus Nazarenus Rex Iudaeorum*," or "Jesus of Nazareth, King of the Jews," which was a phrase Pontius Pilate had ordered affixed to the cross of Jesus (Jn 19:19–20; Lk 23:38).

inspiration, biblical The teaching of the Church, as expressed in Vatican II, that "the divinely revealed realities, which are contained and presented in the text of sacred Scripture, have been written down under the inspiration of the Holy Spirit. For Holy Mother Church relying on the faith of the apostolic age, accepts as sacred and canonical the books of the Old and New Testaments, whole and entire, with all their parts, on the grounds that, written under the inspiration of the Holy Spirit (Jn 20:31, 2 Tim 3:16; 2 Pet 1:19–21, 3:15–16), they have God as their author, and have been handed on to the Church herself. To compose the sacred books, God chose certain men who, all the while he employed them in this task, made full use of their powers and facilities so that, though he acted in them and by them, it was as true authors that they consigned to writing whatever he wanted written, and no more" (Dogmatic Constitution on Divine Revelation, 11) (CCC 106).

Isaac In Hebrew, a name meaning "he laughs," or "laughter." Isaac is the son of Abraham and Sarah and half-brother of Ishmael. Later married Rebekah and became the father of Jacob and Esau. He is the second of the three patriarchs of the Israelites (Ex 2:24; Jer 33:26).

Isaiah Hebrew name meaning "Yahweh is salvation." Isaiah is the son of Amoz; he prophesied in Judah between 740–701 B.C. The book of Isaiah is the longest prophetic book in the Old Testament.

Ishmael Hebrew word meaning "may God hear." Ishmael is the son of Abraham by Hagar and the half-brother of Isaac.

Israel Hebrew word meaning "he who strives with God," or possibly "may God rule." Israel is the name assumed by Jacob after his struggle as told in Genesis 32:28 (also Gen 35:10 which suggests another understanding). In the Old Testament not only is it the name of the patriarch but also the name of the people who are descended from the patriarch. As a political designation the name refers to the nation as a whole and during the period of the Divided Monarchy (922–722 B.C.), it refers to the Northern Kingdom, distinct from the Southern Kingdom in Judah.

Israelites Name given to the descendants of Jacob, collectively, the twelve tribes (CCC 62–64, 218).

JB Abbreviation used to designate the Jerusalem Bible. Also, NJB which is used to identify the New Jerusalem Bible (1985).

Jacob In Hebrew, a name meaning "heel grabber" (Gen 25:26). Jacob is an Old Testament patriarch, the son of Isaac and Rebekah, the brother of Esau, and the father of Dinah and of twelve sons who names are the names of the twelve tribes of Israel. There is disagreement about the period of time in which Jacob lived. Some scholars prefer between 1950–1550 B.C., while others believe it is much later between 1200–900 B.C. His death and burial is described in Genesis 49:28–33.

Jacob's well The setting for the encounter between Jesus and the Samaritan woman that is related in the Gospel of John (Jn 4).

Jehovah A name for Yahweh, used in the King James Version of the Bible. It is actually a mistaken use of the four Hebrew consonants YHWH and is, in fact, not a name used in the Old Testament. Regardless of the mistake, it is nevertheless a name used for God in some Protestant Evangelical traditions.

Jeremiah Hebrew name meaning "may Yahweh lift up." Jeremiah seems to be a somewhat common name in the Old Testament with at least ten distinct references. The most prominent reference is to the prophet Jeremiah who prophesied during the reign of King Josiah, beginning in 626 B.C. He was well connected and was a frequent counselor to the king, who did not always follow his advice. The last years of his life were lived in exile with Baruch, who was his friend and secretary.

Jericho An ancient city dating from the period of 8000–7000 B.C., located on the south end of the Jordan Valley. In ancient times the city was well known for its palms and for its extensive gardens.

Jerusalem In Hebrew, a term meaning "foundation of the god Shalem," referring to the Ugaritic twin gods of twilight (Shalem) and dawn (Shahar). An ancient city, there are references to it as early the nineteenth century B.C. in Egyptian texts although archeological evidence suggests that it was an inhabited area as far back as the fourth millennium. It is considered a holy city to Christians and to Jews, while Islam considers it the third most holy city.

Jerusalem Temple First construction began by King Solomon in the 960 B.C. period to provide a permanent structure for the Ark of the covenant, the place where Yahweh was physically present (Ex 29:42; 33:9). Destroyed by the Babylonians between 587–586 B.C. and then rebuilt on a much smaller scale in 538 B.C. and the years that followed. This Temple was completely replaced by the building efforts of Herod the Great, beginning in 20–19 B.C. and became perhaps the largest religious building in the Western World. Final touches were still being applied to the Temple in A.D. 60, just a few years before the Romans ultimately destroyed it during the siege of Jerusalem in A.D. 70. The Temple has never been rebuilt.

John, the apostle and evangelist Also known as the Beloved Disciple, he was the brother of James and a son of Zebedee. Present at Jesus' Crucifixion, Jesus committed his mother to the care of the apostle. Tradition, which is by no means certain, suggests that he lived in Ephesus until A.D. 100, while other traditions have him exiled to Patmos. Still other traditions contend that he was martyred much earlier, along with his brother James. He is often credited with writing the Gospel of John, the letters of John, and also the book of Revelation.

John the Baptist A significant person in each of the four gospels, seemingly John conducted a successful ministry long before Jesus, a ministry that called people to repentance and a change of life. Baptism was the sign of their willingness to convert. The New Testament proclaims that John is a prophet who emerges from the desert to announce the coming of Jesus (Mt 3:1–12; Mk 1:4–8; Lk 3:1–20), and some parallels to the prophet Elijah are also proposed (Mt 17:10–13; Mk 9:11–13). According to tradition, John was the son of Zechariah and Elizabeth, a member of the priestly class, and a cousin to Jesus (Lk 1:5–80). Matthew (3:4) and Mark (1:6) inform us that his ministerial diet consisted of locusts and wild honey and that he wore a cape made of camel's hair. Herod beheaded him (Mt 14:3–12). There is some indication that John's ministry and influence continued after his execution; in the Acts of Apostles, Christians encounter disciples of John who are unaware of Jesus but who eventually are accepted into the Christian community (Acts 18:24–28; 19:1–7) (CCC 719).

Johannine literature Designation by modern biblical scholars for the five books of the New Testament that are traditionally attributed to John the Evangelist: the Gospel of John, 1, 2, and 3 John, and the book of Revelation. Only the book of Revelation actually credits the writing to John (Rev 1:4). All the books are very similar in style, but there are enough differences for biblical scholars, as far back as Origen in the third century A.D., to doubt if they are in fact the effort of a single author.

Jordan River River that runs from north of the Sea of Galilee to the Dead Sea, it occupies two-thirds of the valley between the modern-day countries of Israel and Jordan. Part of a river system that runs for approximately thirty-five hundred miles from southern Turkey to the Zambesi in southeast Africa, it is the world's lowest river, flowing mainly well below sea level. The average width of the river does not usually exceed ninety feet, and it varies in depth from approximately three feet at the river fords to about ten feet deep in its normal flow. The current is very swift. It was in the waters of the Jordan River that Jesus was baptized by John the Baptist.

Joseph Also written as Josephus, Josech, Joses, a name in Hebrew meaning "may Yahweh add." The name appears fourteen times in the Scripture most prominently given to Joseph, the son of Jacob, who rose to power and authority in Egypt, Joseph, the husband of Mary who was the mother of Jesus, and Joseph of Arimathea in whose tomb Jesus was laid after the Crucifixion.

Judaism The oldest known monotheistic religion of the Western world, it was revealed by God and originated with the Mosaic covenant (Ex 19:5–6) and was identified with the land of Israel (Deut 11:8–9). Judaism does not have a formal creed, but traditionally expresses belief in God who reveals himself through the law, the prophets, and the events of history; the faithful Jew is one who lives justly according to the law and who worships God by prayer, reflection upon the sacred writings, and the observance of Sabbath and other festivals. According to the Second Vatican Council, there is a relationship between the Church and the Jewish people, "That people to which the covenants and promises were made and from which Christ was born according to the flesh (Rom 9:4–5)...for the sake of the fathers, for the gifts of God are written repentance..." (Dogmatic Constitution of the Church, 16) (CCC 62–64).

judgment According to Catholic teaching, there is a distinction between general judgment and the particular judgment. The general, or Last Judgment, is the final judgment of the human race by Jesus Christ (Mt 25:31; 2 Thess 2:3–10) who "will come in glory to judge the living and the dead" (Nicene Creed). The particular judgment is the judgment that takes place immediately after an individual's death and determines whether the person will spend eternity in either heaven or hell (CCC 678–679).

justification Process by which a sinner is made right with God; in the teachings of Saint Paul, God makes a person "just," free from sin and pleasing to God through grace, attested by faith (Rom 3:2–30). According to the Council of Trent, "Justification is the change from the condition in which a person is born as a child of the first Adam into a state of grace and adoption among the children of God through the second Adam, Jesus Christ our Savior." Thus, justification includes a true removal of sin by the power of God and a true supernatural sanctification through the gift of sanctifying grace or participation in the life of God (CCC 1266).

kerygma Word from the Greek meaning "proclamation"; in the Christian sense, it refers especially to the preaching of the Good News of salvation, the proclaiming of the essential elements of God's salvific plan in Christ, the passing on of the core message of the gospel (CCC 2–3).

keys Symbol of spiritual power and authority conferred on Saint Peter and his successors by Jesus Christ, "I will give you the keys of the kingdom of heaven" (Mt 16:19). The "power of the keys" is an expression used to describe the authority of the Bishop of Rome, the pope, over all the faithful and all the churches. It is also used to describe the Church's authority to "bind" and "loose" (forgive or retain) sins in the sacrament of penance (CCC 551–553).

kingdom of God A rich biblical term, often translated as "the reign of God." The coming of the kingdom of God was foretold in the Old Testament and was especially revealed in the person of Christ, Son of God and Son of Man (Mk 1:15; Mt 4:17); in the words, works, and miracles of Jesus, the kingdom is described (Lk 11:20; Mt 12:28).

KJV Common abbreviation used for the King James Version of the Bible which for centuries was the standard Protestant Bible in English. Also sometimes identified as the Authorized Version of the Bible.

Lamb of God Title which John the Baptist uses to greet Jesus at the beginning of the Gospel of John (Jn 1:29; 35).

Last Supper Traditional name given to the Passover meal, which Jesus ate with his apostles in Jerusalem on the night before he died (Mk 14:15; Lk 22:12). According to Catholic teaching, it was on this occasion that Jesus instituted the Holy Eucharist and the holy priesthood. The Church celebrates the Lord's Supper on Holy Thursday evening (CCC 610–611).

Lazarus Name that features prominently in the New Testament. Lazarus was a beggar in the story Jesus told about the beggar and the rich man (Lk 16:19–31) and he was also Lazarus of Bethany, brother of Mary and Martha, and a very close friend of Jesus. The story told of his death and his rising (Jn 11:1–44) from the dead through the intercession of Jesus seemed to have been a major factor in the decision to seek Jesus' death. At the very least this action of Jesus seemed to infuriate the high priests and the Pharisees.

Leviathan Great, mythological sea monster, from the Canannite stories about Baal. In the Old Testament, Yahweh is portrayed as the victor over such sea monsters (Ps 74:13–14). In Isaiah, the Leviathan is a symbol of the death of the wicked (Isa 27:1).

Life, Book of In the book of Revelation, a list of those who will be able to enter the New Jerusalem (Rev 21:27). In the Old Testament (Mal 3:16—4:3) it indicates a scroll in heaven, a roster, on which the names of those who will be saved from the wrath of God have been inscribed.

Lord's Day First day of the week, Sunday, the day of the Resurrection of Jesus. The only direct New Testament usage of the word is found in Revelation 1:10 (CCC 2174).

Lord's Prayer In Latin, *Pater Noster,* this term refers to the prayer Jesus taught his disciples to pray and found in Matthew 6:9–13 and Luke 11:2–4 (CCC 2765–2766).

Lord's Supper Another name for the Eucharist (1 Cor 11:20). Other names include the "breaking of bread" (Acts 2:42), "sharing in the blood of Christ" and "sharing in the body of Christ" (1 Cor 10:16), and the Lord's table (1 Cor 10:21).

Luke, evangelist Traditionally, Luke is a companion to the apostle Paul and author of the third synoptic Gospel and also the Acts of the Apostles. Some traditions hold that he was a physician and an educated man. He was not an eyewitness to the events he records in the gospels, but certainly a participant in some of the events in the Acts of the Apostles. Modern-day scholarship holds that he wrote sometime during A.D. 70–90, with the dates of A.D. 80–85 as probably accurate.

LXX The Latin numeral equivalent for the number seventy. Also a rounded number used to identify the Septuagint (Greek translation) of the Old Testament which, according to a long-standing tradition, was the work of seventy-two translators who worked from the Hebrew and Aramaic in Alexandria in Egypt from the third to the first century B.C. See also **Septuagint.**

Magnificat From the Latin word meaning "magnify." Mary's canticle of prayer and thanksgiving found in the Luke 1:46–55. It is the response of the Blessed Mother to the invitation of the angel to become the mother of Jesus, "My soul magnifies the Lord." Some scholars cross-reference the *Magnificat* to Hannah's Canticle (1 Sam 2:1–10).

Mark, evangelist Mark, the son of Mary in whose home the early Christian community met in Jerusalem, accompanied Paul and Barnabas on missionary journeys. Tradition also places Mark in Rome with Peter, serving as his interpreter. This same tradition suggests that the Gospel of Mark, accepted by all Scripture scholars as the first gospel, records the stories about Jesus that he heard Peter preach. Further traditions have identified Mark as one of the seventy disciples of Jesus (Lk 10:1), as the owner of the house where Pentecost took place (Acts 2:1–4), and as the first to preach the gospel in Egypt. He is regarded as having suffered a martyr's death.

Masorah From the Hebrew word meaning "transmission," this term refers to the traditional Hebrew text of the Bible. This text is preserved within the Rabbinic tradition and contains not only the texts of the Scriptures but additional detailed notes and annotations. Sometimes it is referred to as the Masoretic Text or the Hebrew Scriptures. The text includes the following books:

The Law: Genesis, Exodus, Leviticus, Numbers, Deuteronomy.
The Prophets:
(Former) Joshua, Judges, Samuel, Kings
(Latter) Isaiah, Jeremiah, Ezekiel
(The Twelve) Hosea, Joel, Amos, Obadiah, Jonah, Micah, Nahum, Habakkuk, Zephaniah, Haggai, Zechariah, Malachi
The Writings: Psalms, Job, Proverbs, Ruth, Song of Songs, Ecclesiastes, Lamentations, Esther, Daniel, Ezra-Nehemiah, Chronicles

Matthew, apostle The name of Matthew appears in all of the listings of the apostles and by tradition Matthew is identified as a tax collector at the time when he was called by Jesus (Mt 9:9). Traditionally, Matthew is also identified as the writer of the gospel that bears his name. However, modern biblical scholarship tends to believe that the gospel, perhaps written in A.D. 90, is probably not written by the apostle but by an unnamed Christian who was a member of the community founded by the apostle.

Melchizedek King of Salem (Jerusalem) and priest who blessed Abraham on his return from a battle (Gen 14:17–20). Held in high esteem by later commentators as an example of an ideal priest.

midrash A Jewish commentary on the Old Testament clarifying a passage from a legal, homiletic, or narrative point of view. Midrashim is the plural form of midrash.

miracles of Jesus The gospels recount a large number of miracles performed by Jesus Christ: for example, miracles of healing, miracles of raising the dead, and miracles exhibiting control over natural forces. In the New Testament sense, they are signs and wonders, events that are naturally unexplainable, which serve as a confirmation of credibility by manifesting the power of Christ and inviting those who witness them to faith in Christ himself (Jn 2:11) (CCC 517, 1507).

NAB Abbreviation used to designate the New American Bible. Also the NABR which designates the New American Bible with the revised New Testament (1986).

NIV Abbreviation used to designate the New International Version of the Bible.

NRSV Abbreviation used to designate the New Revised Standard Version of the Bible.

Nag Hammadi documents Over three hundred Coptic Christian documents were discovered in Egypt in 1945, including some noncanonical gospels (for example, the Gospel of Thomas). These documents are important because they illustrate the influence of Gnostic thought on some Christian ideas and concepts.

names for God There are many names for God used in both the Old Testament and the New Testament. In the Old Testament, the most common name for God is Yahweh, which is used 6,828 times. Other names include Elohim (2,600 times), Yahweh Sabaoth (279 times), El Shaddai (48 times), and *Adonai* (Hebrew for "my great Lord"), which came into use after the Exile and was used in place of Yahweh. In the New Testament, which was written in Greek, the most common name for God is *"theos"* which is the Greek word for the "deity" (1,318 times). *"Kyrios"* which translates "lord" in the Greek, is used 100 times in reference to God (Lk 1:66) but is used 719 times to refer to Jesus. The name that Jesus used for God was "Father." Other New Testament names for God would include the God of the Fathers, the Almighty, and the Holy One.

Nazareth Town in northern Israel near Haifa, the site of the Annunciation, the home of the Holy Family, and the place where Jesus was rejected. An imposing modern basilica, the Church of the Annunciation, is built over the spot where tradition says that the home of the Blessed Mother stood.

Negeb, the Term in Hebrew meaning "dry, parched," referring to the southern part of biblical Judah, now the largest region in the modern state of Israel. The Hebrews spent a large portion of their time wandering through the southern Negeb during the wilderness sojourn experience of the Exodus (Deut 1:19).

Nile Great Egyptian river (Nile means "dark" or "blue") extremely important to the economy of Egypt. The overflowing of the Nile, caused by the intense rains in the south, ensures the fertility of the land. The river flows north from its sources in Lake Victoria in Uganda for 4,037 miles. One of the signs and wonders performed by Moses as a demonstration to the Pharaoh of the power of Yahweh was to turn the waters of the Nile into blood (Ex 7:14–22).

Numbers Some numbers used in the Bible have symbolic significance: the number seven, for example, because it refers to the seven days of creation and the seven-day week which ends on the Sabbath. The number three can also signify "completion" while the number four is significant because of the four corners of the earth (Isa 11:12), the four winds (Jer 49:36), and the four living creatures that surround God (Rev 4:6–7). The number forty often can be read as meaning "a long time." See also Proverbs 30:18–19.

Nunc Dimittis Latin term meaning "now let us depart," it is the hymn of joy that is attributed to Simeon, a pious man who had been waiting patiently for the coming of the Lord, and who recognized Jesus. The hymn has a secure place in the Liturgy of the Hours, the praying of Compline, or Night Prayer (Lk 2:29–32).

oil In the Bible, the most common oil is olive oil. Oil was a basic part of the diet (1 Kings 17:12–16) and was used for cosmetic purposes (Esth 2:12), as well as used in the religious anointing of persons and objects (Gen 28:18; 1 Kings 1:39). In the New Testament, oil is used in the healing rituals (Mk 6:13; Jas 5:14).

Olivet, Mount Also known as the Mount of Olives, this mountain is east of Jerusalem. Gethsemane, the garden in which Jesus was arrested, is on the lower slope of the mountain.

papyrus A plant that grows in water and grew abundantly in the shallow waters of the Nile (Job 8:11). The plant is used not only for making scrolls (paper), but is also used for rugs, sails, rope, and even food.

parable A short story drawn from everyday life, used to point out a spiritual lesson. Jesus used parables extensively (more than twenty are recorded in the gospels) to express some truth about the reign of God (Mt 13:11). In reflecting upon parables, the main point—not the particular details—should be especially noted (CCC 546). It is interesting to note that the majority of the parables are recorded by Matthew and Luke, while Mark records only the parables having to do with sowing and planting. The Gospel of John records no parables.

The parables of Jesus include:

Mustard seed (Mk 4:30–32; Mt 13:31, 32: Lk 13:18–19)
Sower and the seed (Mk 4:3–8; Mt 13:3–8; Lk 13:18–19)
Landlord and his wicked tenants (Mk 12:1–11; Mt 21:33–42; Lk 20:9–18)
Plentiful harvest (Mk 4:26–29)
Yeast (Mt 13:33; Lk 13:20–21)
Wedding feast (Mt 22:1–4; Lk 14:16–24)
Lost sheep (Mt 18:12–13; Lk 15:4–6)
Talents (Mt 25:14–30; Lk 19:11–27)
Wheat and the weeds (Mt 13:24–30)
Treasure and the pearl (Mt 13:44–46)
Dragnet (Mt 13:47–48)

Rich fool (Lk 12:16–20)
Unforgiving servant (Mt 18:23–24)
Workers in the vineyard (Mt 20:1–15)
Foolish and wise bridesmaids (Mt 25:1–12)
Good Samaritan (Lk 10:30–35)
Barren fig tree (Lk 13:6–9)
Renouncing possessions (Lk 14:28–32)
Lost coin (Lk 15:8–9)
Prodigal son (Lk 15:11–32)
Unjust steward (Lk 16:1–8a)
Rich man and Lazarus (Lk 16:9–31)
Unjust judge (Lk 18:2–5)
Pharisee and the publican (Lk 18:10–13)

Paraclete Word meaning "Consoler," "Defender," or "Advocate," it is used in the Gospel of John to refer either to Christ himself, who fulfilled this role for the disciples, or to the Holy Spirit who continues to fulfill this role in the community of the Church (Jn 14:16) (CCC 692).

paradise Word meaning "garden," with special reference to the Garden of Eden (Gen 2:15) and to the eternal abode of the just (Lk 23:24); often used as a synonym for heaven.

Parousia Greek word meaning "coming," or "arrival." The Second Coming of Christ to earth (1 Cor 15:23), when his triumph over evil will be complete and his kingdom definitively established (1 Thess 4:15–17; Lk 23:3–14) (CCC 671–674).

Passover Solemn Jewish feast, celebrated annually on the fourteenth of Nisan (the first month of the postexilic Hebrew calendar, occurring during our March or April), commemorating the deliverance of the Israelites from the bondage of Egypt (Ex 12); its main feature was the sacrificial meal, ending with eating the paschal lamb, in later days celebrated in conjunction with the weeklong feast of Unleavened Bread. The Christian Passover is the sacrifice of Christ, the Lamb of God, by which humankind was freed from the bondage of sin and led into the freedom of the sons and daughters of God (CCC 1164).

pastoral letters Also known as the pastoral epistles. They are the three letters written by Paul to Timothy and to Titus, providing instructions for their ministry.

Patmos Small island, about ten miles long and six miles wide, located in the Aegean Sea, one of the Sporades Islands. This was one of the islands that according to Pliny and Tacitus (Roman historians) Roman authorities would often banish political prisoners or those people judged guilty of practicing magic and astrology. This is the island where John says that he was "on account of the Word of God and the testimony of Jesus" (Rev 1:9). Since prophecy was considered by Roman authorities as a type of "magic," it would make sense that this is the island where John served his sentence of banishment.

patriarch Male head of a family or a clan. When used in the Old Testament, it usually refers to Abraham (Gen 12-24), Isaac (Gen 25—36), and Jacob (Gen 25—36). More and more this term and the religious connotations that seem to be part of its use are giving way to the inclusion of the pivotal and essential roles of the wives of the patriarchs in the story of salvation. As a result Sarah (Gen 11:30), Rebecca (Gen 25:21), and Rachael (Gen 29:31) are assuming a more prominent consideration.

Pentateuch From the Greek *pentateuchos* meaning "five containers," this term, referring to the cases in which scrolls would be kept, is applied to the first five books of the Old Testament (Genesis, Exodus, Leviticus, Numbers, and Deuteronomy), also known as the book of the Law or the Torah. They tell the stories of creation, of God's promises to Abraham and his descendants, of the Exodus from Egypt, of the giving of the Law on Mount Sinai, and of how God brought the people of Israel to the Promised Land.

Pentecost Christian feast day, celebrated fifty days after Easter to commemorate the descent of the Holy Spirit upon the apostles as described in the Acts of Apostles (Acts 2:14). It is considered the "birthday of the Church," the day of its empowerment to bring the good news of Jesus Christ to all nations (CCC 731–732).

Pharisees Religious sect of the Jews that sought to protect the Jews from contamination by foreign religions and that strove for strict separation from the Gentiles: they insisted on absolute loyalty to the Scriptures and to the traditions of the rabbis. In the Scriptures, Jesus continually takes them to task and often rebukes them as "hypocrites" and as "blind guides" (Mt 23:25; Lk 11:39). As a result of the Jewish-Roman war (A.D. 67–70), in which most of the Sadducees and Zealots were killed, the Pharisees stepped into the leadership vacuum that resulted. Judaism from this time on was basically a form of Pharisaical Judaism.

phylacteries Small containers (black boxes) in which selected Scripture quotations were recorded and stored on parchment paper. According to Jewish tradition, the phylacteries were then bound to the arm and forehead during prayer. The tradition is based on Exodus 13:9, Deuteronomy 6:8 and 11:18.

Pilate, Pontius Roman prefect of Judea and the fifth governor of the province who held the office for over ten years (A.D. 26–36). He was governor during the ministry and execution of both John the Baptist and Jesus.

Polytheism The belief in the existence of many different gods. In the time of both the Old and the New Testaments, most of the societies and cultures of the day, with the notable exception of the monotheistic Jewish people (Isa 40–55), were polytheists (CCC 2112).

prophets Men and women who served as a channel of communication between God and humanity. The Bible portrays prophets as people who experienced the "hand of the Lord" (1 Kings 18:46; 2 Kings 3:15; Jer 15:17), or people who had the Spirit of God "rest upon them" (Num 11:25–26). Such people were then compelled to speak to the people about God and his relationship with them (Amoa 3:8; Jer 20:9). The experience was not necessarily one that was always appreciated or understood and more than one potential prophet tried unsuccessfully to avoid it (Jer 1:6, 11:18–12:6; Ezek 2:1—3:15; Jonah 1:1–10) (CCC 64; 218).

prophetic literature The Old Testament books of Isaiah, Jeremiah, Lamentations, Baruch, Ezekiel, Daniel, Hosea, Joel, Amos, Obadiah, Jonah, Micah, Nahum, Habakkuk, Zephaniah, Haggai, Zechariah, and Malachi. Prophecy was a feature of many religions during the Old Testament period. The true prophets were not merely concerned with predicting the future but were also called to speak to the people of God's behalf and remind them of their true calling.

proselyte A person who converts from one religious tradition to another. In the Bible the term is generally used to reference people who were Gentiles who became Jews (Acts 2:10).

Proverb Short, easy to remember, saying or popular truth, usually drawn from human experience, that is often witty, insightful, and sometimes even humorous.

pseudepigrapha Term meaning "false writings," and used to designate a variety of writings that emerged from the time of the Old Testament that were not accepted as canonical or inspired writings when the biblical canon was formed. Writings would include the Odes of Solomon, and the Testaments of the Twelve Patriarchs. In reference to the New Testament, "false writings" would be designated as the apocrypha and would include the Gospel of Thomas and the Acts of Peter. See also **Apocrypha.**

Q Commonly accepted, though speculative, hypothesis that an independent manuscript circulated in some of the early Christian communities, that contained a collection of the sayings of Jesus. The collection was used in the Gospel of Matthew and the Gospel of Luke and disappeared with the appearance of the gospels.

Qumran Scrolls See **Dead Sea Scrolls.**

Rapture, the Based on 1 Thessalonians 4:16–17 from the viewpoint of biblical prophecy as understood by some evangelical Protestants, the Rapture is believed to be an event that will occur during the "end times." When the Rapture occurs, Christ will raise all believers who have died and all living Christians will also be caught up and taken immediately up to heaven. The Rapture is to be followed by seven years of great tribulation until Christ returns again for the Last Judgment. See also **dispensational premillennialism.**

reconciliation Act of reestablishing a damaged or destroyed relationship between two parties. Reconciling humankind to God was the primary work of Jesus Christ and is an essential part of the Good News (2 Cor 5:17–20). According to Catholic teaching, reconciliation with God after one has gravely sinned against him and reconciliation with the Church, which is wounded by sin, are basic results of the sacrament of penance (CCC 1468–1469).

redeemer Person who buys back something of significance that has been sold or, in ancient times, a member of the family who would purchase back another member of the family from slavery. The biblical concept of purchase from slavery and the attribution of the action to God is found in Job 19:25, Proverbs 23:11, and Isaiah 47:14. The designation is never used for Jesus Christ, although "redemption" is applied to him (1 Cor 1:30).

Red Sea A large, although narrow, body of water between the Arabian Peninsula and Africa. The sea is twelve hundred miles long and between one hundred thirty and two hundred fifty miles wide. At its deepest point, the depth of the sea is more than seventy-two hundred feet. According to the book of Exodus, this is the sea that the Israelites crossed as they were fleeing from the Egyptians. However, that scenario is problematic, and it is not at all certain that the biblical reference is to the Red Sea. Some would argue that it is more probably a reference to the "Sea of Reeds" since ancient Hebrew does not distinguish between a sea and a lake.

Among biblical scholars, there is no agreement; and no one explanation is generally accepted.

Resurrection of Christ Fundamental Christian belief that Jesus Christ arose from the dead (Mk 16:1–7); it is the cornerstone of the Christian faith, the central theme of apostolic preaching (1 Cor 15:13–14), the guarantee of the Christian's final resurrection with Christ (Rom 6:5–8). The Resurrection of Christ is celebrated on Easter Sunday (CCC 648–655).

Revelation, divine Manifestation of God and his plan of salvation to humankind; in Catholic theology, a distinction is sometimes made between the body of revealed truth given to us by God ("divine revelation") and the process by which Christ revealed it (CCC 74–79).

Rosetta Stone A granite block discovered by the soldiers of Napoleon in the Nile Delta in 1799. The stone had inscribed on it a decree from the Egyptian Pharaoh Ptolemy V (203–180 B.C.) in hieroglyphic Egyptian, demotic Egyptian, and Greek which became extremely useful in decoding ancient Egyptian hieroglyphics.

RSV Abbreviation used to designate the Revised Standard Version of the Bible.

Sabbath The seventh day of the week (Saturday), prescribed in the Decalogue as a day to be kept holy, a day of rest and religious observance (Deut 5:12–14), held in special reverence by religious Jews; the manner of observing it became a source of conflict between Jesus and some of the Pharisees (Mk 2:28); in apostolic times Christians transferred the Sabbath to the first day of the week in honor of the Resurrection of Christ and designated it the "Lord's Day" (CCC 2168–2173).

Samaritans Group of people who shared a common heritage with the Jews, but who differed with them over the place of worship (Jn 4:12) and as a result of this difference were in conflict with each other. There is only one mention of the Samaritans in the Old Testament (2 Kings 17:29) and there is some doubt that this is anything more than a reference to the people who lived in the Samarian region, but who had not yet developed a distinct religious tradition.

Sanhedrin Greek term meaning "a council of leaders." Although the term is used in many different ways to designate difference groups of people, in the New Testament it usually refers to the chief court of chief priests and elders in Jerusalem (Mt 26:59).

scribe Person with the ability to read and to write. Scribes would often specialize in a certain area of expertise, such as the law or finance, and were usually associated with the task of record keeping and administration.

Septuagint From the Greek word for "seventy," it is the name of the Greek translation of the Hebrew Scriptures, composed for Jewish communities in the Diaspora in Egypt, around 250 B.C. It became the basis for the Roman Catholic canonical Old Testament and influenced many writers of the New Testament. According to tradition, seventy-two different scribes produced the translation in a period of seventy-two days. The text of the Septuagint includes the following:

Law and History: Genesis, Exodus, Leviticus, Numbers, Deuteronomy, Joshua, Judges, Ruth, 1 and 2 Samuel, 1 and 2 Kings, 1 and 2 Paralipomena (Chronicles), 1 Esdras, 2 Esdras (Ezra-Nehemiah), Esther, Judith, Tobit, 1–4 Maccabees.

The Poetic and Prophetic Books: Psalms, Odes, Proverbs, Ecclesiastes, Song of Songs, Job, Wisdom of Solomon, Sirach (Ecclesiasticus), Psalms of Solomon, Hosea, Amos, Micah, Joel, Obadiah, Jonah, Nahum, Habakkuk, Zephaniah, Haggai, Zechariah, Malachi, Isaiah, Jeremiah, Baruch, Lamentations, Letter of Jeremiah, Ezekiel, Susanna, Daniel, Bel and the Dragon.

seraphim Fiery supernatural beings with six wings who guard the divine throne, usually associated with the cherubim (Isa 6:1–7 Ezek 1:27).

Sermon on the Mount Comprehensive presentation of the teachings of Jesus as presented in the Gospel of Matthew, chapters 5—7; a brief version is also found in the Gospel of Luke 6:20–49. The sermon includes the teaching of Jesus on true discipleship and an explanation of the Beatitudes, the Lord's Prayer, and the relationship of the old law to the new law in Christ (CCC 2764).

seven last words of Christ Words spoken by Jesus on the cross: (1) "Father, forgive them; for they know not what they do"; (2) to the repentant thief, "Truly I say to you, today you will be with me in paradise"; (3) to the Blessed Mother and the apostle John, "Women, behold your son…Behold your mother"; (4) "My God, my God, why have you forsaken me?"; (5) "I thirst"; (6) "It is finished"; (7) "Father, into your hands I commend my spirit."

showbread Also known as the Bread of the Presence (Num 4:7), holy bread (1 Sam 21:6), or sometimes simply as the bread (Ex 40:23). It refers to the twelve loaves of unleavened bread that were placed in the Temple tabernacle as an offering to God. The bread was replaced every Sabbath and the old loaves were then eaten by the priests (Lev 24:5–9). This is the same bread consumed by David and his men (1 Sam 21:5) when he was being pursued by King Saul.

synagogue From a Greek word meaning "a meeting." A synagogue was the Jewish meeting place or center, less sacred and formal than the Temple, used for religious worship, biblical readings and study, prayer and other community affairs. Jesus often taught in synagogues (Mk 1:21; Lk 4:16) as did the apostle Paul and the other apostles (Acts 14:1; 18:19).

Talmud The Jewish compilation containing the Mishnah or oral interpretation of the law in written form; Jews (and some

Christians too) still consider it an authoritative guide and aid to the spiritual life.

Ten Commandments Commandments given by God to Moses on Mount Sinai as found in Exodus 20:1–21 and Deuteronomy 5:2–33 and interpreted by Jesus (Mt 5:17–48). As given in the book of Exodus, the Ten Commandments are as follows: (1) I am the Lord your God and you shall have no other gods before me; (2) You shall not take the name of the Lord your God in vain; (3) Remember to keep holy the Sabbath; (4) Honor your father and your mother; (5) You shall not kill; (6) You shall not commit adultery; (7) You shall not steal; (8) You shall not bear false witness against your neighbor; (9) You shall not covet your neighbor's house; (10) You shall not covet your neighbor's wife.

testament Binding agreement or covenant. In biblical understanding, the term refers to the special relationship that God entered into with the Chosen People. In the Old Testament, it is understood as the agreement that God entered into with the people of Israel. In the New Testament, it is understood as the agreement that God entered into with the Church. The Old Testament is compromised of forty-six books, detailing the relationship between God and Israel before Jesus, while the New Testament has twenty-seven books that are concerned with Jesus and the early Church.

Tetragrammaton, the Sacred From the Greek word meaning "four letters." This term designates the four letters YHWH, "I am who I am" (Ex 3:14), the name of the God of the Old Testament. In English, the name is usually pronounced "Yahweh," although some mistakenly pronounce it as "Jehovah." Other Old Testament names for God would include *Adonai* (Lord) or the Canannite expressions for God, El or Elohim.

Torah From the Hebrew word meaning "to study," "to learn." This is a term commonly used to refer to the Mosaic Law as contained in the Pentateuch or first five books of the Bible, namely, Genesis, Exodus, Leviticus, Numbers, and Deuteronomy (CCC 1961).

tradition According to Catholic teaching, one of the sources (together with the sacred Scripture) of divine Revelation; it is, as Vatican II points out, the Word of God which has been entrusted to the apostles by Christ the Lord and the Holy Spirit; unlike many Christian communities that teach Scripture alone is the source of divine Revelation, the Catholic Church professes that "sacred tradition and sacred scripture form one sacred deposit of the word of God, which is committed to the Church" (Dogmatic Constitution on Divine Revelation, 10).

Transfiguration of Christ The appearance in glory of Jesus Christ during his earthly life, as recorded in Matthew 17:1–3, Mark 9:2–13, and Luke 9:28–36. The Transfiguration is understood as a significant event that showed the Lord to be the Messiah, reaffirmed his sonship with the Father, and foreshadowed his future glory; this event is commemorated on the First Sunday of Lent each year and there is a special feast of the Transfiguration designated for August 6 on the Roman Liturgical Calendar (CCC 554–556).

Vulgate The Latin version of the Bible translated by Saint Jerome from the Greek and the Hebrew in the fourth century. This version of the Bible is the one commonly used in the Catholic Church and was declared authentic by the Council of Trent in 1546.

Wisdom literature Job, Psalms, Proverbs, Ecclesiastes, Song of Songs, Wisdom of Solomon, and Sirach (also known as Ecclesiasticus). The wisdom books are concerned with practical living. They give the sort of advice that is passed on from generation to generation. Later wisdom passages also begin to ask about the origin of wisdom herself and come to see her as an agent of God's divine activity in the world (in biblical literature, wisdom usually is portrayed as feminine).

word of God An expression used to describe several different realities; notably, Jesus Christ as the Word of God (Jn 1:1, 14); and the Bible as containing "the Word of God in the words of men."

worship Adoration given to God that expresses itself in praise, thanksgiving, self-offering, sorrow, and petition. Worship is an interior activity, which often expresses itself in bodily gestures or postures: singing, kneeling, prostrating, dancing, and other forms of movement. Worship is also expressed in rites and ceremonies. Private worship of God can occur anywhere and at any time (Jn 4:21–24). Public worship is liturgy centered on Christ.

wrath of God The ancient Israelites used this metaphor of anger to describe God's attitude toward sin. This is an anthropomorphism that occurs in the Old Testament to describe God as punishing sinners (Ps 2:11). Jesus employs this anthropomorphism when he says, "You brood of vipers! Who warned you to flee from the wrath to come?" (Mt 3:7). The apostle Paul describes the Day of Judgment as the "day of wrath" (Rom 2:5). The author of the book of Revelation refers to "the wrath of the Lamb" and "the wrath of God the Almighty" (Rev 19:15; 6:16).

Yahweh A Hebrew name for God meaning approximately "I Am Who Am" (Ex 3:13–14). It especially designates God as creator of the universe and source of all life (CCC 206–207).

Yeshua The Hebrew name of Jesus of Nazareth, the name by which he was called by his family and friends. Jesus is a Hellenized form of his name, as is Mary (Miriam), Joseph (Yosef), James (Yacov), Judas (Yudah), and Simon (Shimon).

2. Reference Guide to Biblical Names and Places

Readers of the Bible often want a quick reference guide to common biblical names, terminology, and places referenced in the Bible. In addition to names and places, a representative sampling of specific events of importance in the life of prominent personages of the Old

Testament and New Testament are provided below. The listing is alphabetical and provides a quick scriptural reference point.

Abba	Mk 14:36	Rom 8:15	Gal 4:6
Abel	Gen 4:1–2	Lk 11:51	Mt 23:35
Abigail	2 Sam 3:3		
Abner	1 Sam 14:50		
Abraham	Gen 11:26	Gen 17:5	Heb 11:8–12
Absalom	2 Sam 3:3	2 Sam 13:1–18	
abyss	Lk 8:31	Rom 10:7	
Adam	Gen 1:27	Gen 2:7	Lk 3:38
Ahaz	2 Kings 16:2	2 Chr 28:1–4	
amen	Num 5:22	Deut 27:15–26	1 Cor 14:16
anathema	1 Cor 12:3		
Andrew	Mk 1:29	Jn 1:44	
angel	1 Sam 29:9	Heb 1:14	
Annunciation	Lk 1:26–38		
anointing	Ex 30:32	Ex 28:41	Acts 10:38
Antichrist	1 Jn 2:18		
apostasy	Josh 22:22	Acts 21:21	
apostle	Heb 3:1	Mk 3:14–15	Lk 11:49
ark	Deut 10:8	Ex 25:16	2 Sam 15:24–29
Armageddon	Rev 16:16		
Artemis	Acts 19:28		
ascension	Acts 1:4–11	Lk 24:50–51	
ashes	Isa 58:5	Jer 6:26	2 Sam 13:19
Babel	Gen 10:1–10		
Babylon	Dan 4:30	Isa 14:3	Jer 50—51
Barabbas	Jn 18:40		
Barnabas	Acts 4:36	Col 4:10	
Bartholomew	Mt 10:3	Mk 3:18	Lk 6:14

Bathsheba	2 Sam 11:3	1 Kings 2:19–21	
Benjamin	Gen 35:18	1 Sam 22:7	
Bethany	Mk 14:3–9	Jn 1:28	
Bethel	Gen 12:8	Josh 18:13	Zech 7:2-3
Bethesda	Jn 5:2		
Bethlehem	Gen 35:19	Josh 19:15	
Bethphage	Mt 21:1	Lk 19:29	
blasphemy	Lev 24:10–13	Acts 6:11	2 Sam 12:14
blessing	Deut 11:26	Rom 15:29	Heb 6:7
Boanerges	Mk 3:17	Lk 9:54–56	
brimstone	Gen 19:24	Deut 29:23	Isa 30:33
burning bush	Ex 3:3	Gen 15:17	Ex 19:18
Caiaphas	Mt 26:57–68	Jn 11:49	
Cain	Gen 4:1	Gen 4:4–16	
Caleb	1 Chr 2:9	Num 14:24	
Calvary	Lk 23:33		
Cana	Jn 2:1		
Capernaum	Mt 4:13	Mk 2:1	Lk 7:1–10
cherubim	Ex 25:18-22	Heb 9:5	Ps 80:1
Christian	Acts 11:26	Acts 26:28	1 Pt 4:16
Claudia	2 Tim 4:21		
Clement	Phil 4:3		
conversion	Mt 18:3	Jn 12:40	Lk 22:32
covenant	Gen 6:18	2 Sam 7	Mic 6:1–8
Damascus	2 Kings 5:12	2 Cor 11:32–33	
Dead Sea	Gen 14:3	Deut 4:49	Zeph 14:8
Deborah	Gen 35:8	Judg 4:4	
Dinah	Gen 30:21	Gen 34	
disciple	Isa 8:16	Lk 6:17	Acts 6:7
Ebenezer	1 Sam 7:12		
Eden	Gen 2:10–14		
Eli	1 Sam 1—4		

Elizabeth	Lk 1:5–80		
Emmaus	Lk 24:13–35		
Enoch	Gen 5:18–24	Heb 11:5	
ephphatha	Mk 7:34		
Esau	Gen 25:21–26	Rom 9:13	
Eunice	2 Tim 1:5	Acts 16:1	
Euphrates	Deut 11:24		
evangelist	2 Tim 4:5	Lk 20:1	Acts 21:8
Eve	Gen 4:1	Gen 3:1–16	
excommunication	Mt 18:15	1 Cor 5:5	Titus 3:10
Gabriel	Dan 8:16	Dan 9:21	Rev 8:2
Gamaliel	Num 1:10	Acts 5:33–40	
Gaza	Josh 15:47	Judg 16:21–31	
Gethsemane	Mt 26:36	Mk 14:32	
Gideon	Jdgs 6—8		
Goliath	1 Sam 17	2 Sam 21:19	
Gomer	Gen 10:2–3	Hos 1:3	
Goshen	Gen 47:1–6	Josh 10:41	
hallelujah	Ps 104—106	Rev 19:1	
Hananiah	Jer 28	Dan 1:6–7	
Hebron	Num 13:22	2 Sam 2:11	2 Chr 11:10
hell	Mt 5:22	Mk 9:43	Jas 3:6
Hermes	Acts 14:12		
Herod	Mt 2:1–18	Lk 3:19	Mk 6:14–28
hosanna	Mt 21:9	Mk 11:9	Jn 12:13
hypocrite	Mt 7:5	Lk 12:56	Mt 23:27–28
Iconium	Acts 13:51		
idolatry	Ex 32	Deut 4:15–18	Eph 5:5
Jabez	1 Chr 2:55	1 Chr 4:9–10	
Jacob	Gen 26—50		
James	Mt 4:21	Mk 14:33	Lk 9:54
Jason	Acts 17:5-9	Rom 16:21	

Jebusite	Num 13:29	Gen 10:16	
Jehoshaphat	2 Sam 8:16	2 Kings 8:14	
Jericho	Josh 3:14–17	Mk 10:46	Lk 19:1–11
Jesse	1 Sam 16:20	Lk 3—22	
Jethro	Ex 3:1	Ex 4:18	
Jezebel	1 Kings 18:19	1 Kings 21	
Lamb of God	Jn 1:29	Jn 1:35	
Laodicea	Rev 3:14–22	Col 4:12–13	Col 2:1
Lappidoth	Judg 4:4		
Lazarus	Jn 11:1–44	Lk 16:19–31	
Leah	Gen 29:21–30		
Leviathan	Ps 104:26	Job 3:8	Ezek 29:3–5
Linus	2 Tim 4:21		
Lion of Judah	Rev 5:5	Gen 49:9	
Logos	Jn 1:1	1 Jn 1:1	Rev 19:13
Lord's Day	Rev 1:10		
love feast	Jude 12	2 Pet 2:13	1 Cor 11: 17–34
Lucifer	Is 14:12	Rev 9:1	
Luke	Col 4:14	2 Tim 4:11	
magi	Acts 8:9	Mt 2:1–12	Ps 72:10
Magnificat	Lk 1:46–55		
Mammon	Mt 6:24	Lk 16:13	
Manasseh	Gen 41:51	Josh 22:7	
manger	Prov 14:4	Lk 2:7	
manna	Ex 16:35		
Massa	Gen 25:14	1 Chr 1:30	Prov 30:1
Matthias	Acts 1:15–26		
mediator	Gal 3:19–20	Heb 8:6	2 Sam 14: 1–23
Megiddo	Josh 12:21	1 Chr 7:29	
Melchizedek	Heb 7:22	Gen 14:18	

Methuselah	Gen 5		
Michael	Dan 12:1	Rev 12:7	
Mizar	Ps 42:6		
Moriah	Gen 22:2	2 Chr 3:1	
Nain	Lk 7:11–17		
Nathan	2 Sam 7	1 Kings 1:13–14	
Nathanael	Jn 1:45	Jn 21:2	
Nazarene	Mt 2:23	Acts 24:5	
Nazareth	Lk 2:39	Lk 4:16	Jn 1:46
Nebuchadnezzar	Jer 27:8	Jer 49:28–33	Dan 1:1
Nicodemus	Jn 3:1–21	Jn 7:50–52	
Ninevah	Gen 10:11	Jon 3:3	
Nimrod	Gen 10:8–10	Mic 5:6	
Nod	Gen 4:16		
Olivet	2 Sam 15:30	Zech 14:4	Mk 13:3–37
Onesimus	Philem 10	Col 4:9	
Ophir	2 Chr 8:18	Ps 45:9	
Ophrah	Josh 18:23	Judg 6:11	
Pamphylia	Acts 13:13	Acts 15:38	
Patmos	Rev 1:9		
perdition	Ps 18:4		
praetorium	Mt 27:27	Mk 15:16	Acts 23:35
predestination	Acts 4:28	Rom 8:28–30	Eph 1:5
Promised Land	Heb 11:9	Gen 12:1–2	
Rabboni	Mk 10:51	Jn 20:16	
Rachel	Gen 29:17	Gen 31:19	Mt 2:18
Rahab	Josh 6:17		
Rebecca	Gen 24	Gen 27:5–17	Rom 9:10
Rechabites	1 Chr 2:55	Jer 35:2–3	
regeneration	Mt 19:28	Titus 3:5	
restoration	Acts 3:21		
Reuben	Gen 29:32	Gen 42:37	

Rome	Acts 1:7	Rev 17:18	Rev 18:9
sabbath	Gen 2:2	Ex 16:21–30	Mt 12:1–14
Sadducees	Mk 12:18	Lk 20:27	Mt 22:23
Salem	Gen 14:18	Heb 7:1	
Samaritans	Jn 4:39		
Samson	Judg 13—16		
sanctuary	Ezek 5:11	Mt 23:16	Heb 9:24
Sanhedrin	Mt 26:59	Mk 14:55	Acts 4:15
satyr	Lev 17:7	Isa 13:21	
Seraphim	Isa 6	2 Chr 11:15	
Serpent, bronze	Num 21:4–9	1 Cor 10:9	
Sheba, Queen of	1 Kings 10:1–10		
Shechem	Gen 34	Josh 24:32	
Sheol	Ezek 31:15	Ps 86:13	Job 7:9
Shiloh	Judg 21:19	Jer 7:14	
Sidon	Gen 10:19		
Siloam	Jn 9:7–11	Lk 13:4	
Sinai, Mount	Ex 19:1	Judg 5:5	
Stephen	Acts 6:1–6		
steward	Gen 43:19	Isa 22:15	Gal 4:2
stumbling block	Lev 19:14	Rom 9:32	
Succoth	Ex 12:37	Gen 33:17	
tabernacle	Ex 26:7–11	Ex 40:34–35	
Tabor	Josh 19:22	1 Chr 6:77	
Thaddaeus	Mt 10:3	Mk 3:18	
Theophilus	Lk 1:3	Acts 1:1	
Thomas	Mt 10:2–4	Mk 3:16–19	Lk 6:14–16
thorns, crown of	Mt 27:29	Mk 15:17	Jn 19:2
Transfiguration	Mt 17:1–8	Mk 9:2–8	
unknown god	Acts 17:23		
Ur	Gen 11:28	Neh 9:7	
virgin birth	Mt 1:23	Lk 1:34	

yoke	Lk 14:19	Mt 11:29	Acts 15:10
Zacchaeus	Lk 19:1–10		
zealot	Lk 6:15	Acts 1:13	
Zeus	Acts 14:12		

3. Favorite Bible Stories: A Quick Reference List

The Bible contains many familiar stories that have proven to be beloved throughout the years. These stories tell us of the exploits of men and woman whom we have come to identify as the "heroes of the Bible." The chart that follows provides a quick reference point in locating these stories.

OLD TESTAMENT STORIES

Adam and Eve	Gen 2:7–25
Abraham and Isaac	Gen 22:1–14
Bel and the Dragon	Dan 14:1–30
Cain and Abel	Gen 4:1–16
Call of Isaiah	Isa 6:1–9
Call of Samuel	1 Sam 3:1–10
Creation of the World	Gen 1:1–31
David and Bathsheba	2 Sam 11:2–17
David and Goliath	1 Sam 17:20–52
David and the prophet Nathan	2 Sam 12:1–7
Daniel in the lion pit	Dan 14:31–42; Dan 6:17–25
Dead bones and dry bones	Ezek 37:1–14
Elijah and the fiery chariot	2 Kings 2:1–13
Jacob wrestles with God	Gen 32:22–32
Joseph and his coat of many colors	Gen 37:2–36
Moses and the burning bush	Ex 3:1–6
Naaman cured of his leprosy	2 Kings 5:1–14
Noah and the Ark	Gen 6:9—8:22

Samson and Delilah	Judg 16:4–21
Queen of Sheba	1 Kings 10:1–10
Shadrach, Meshach, and Abednego	Dan 3:8–23, 91–97
Susanna	Dan 13:1–64
The Seven martyred brothers	2 Macc 7:1–41
Ten Commandments	Ex 20:1–18; Deut 5:1–22
Tower of Babel	Gen 11:1–9
Walls of Jericho come tumbling down	Josh 6:1–16
Wisdom of King Solomon	1 Kings 3:16–28

NEW TESTAMENT STORIES

(Note: in this listing the parables of Jesus are not provided. For a complete listing of the parables see the glossary of terms.)

Adulterous woman	Jn 8:3–11
Annunciation of the Blessed Mother	Lk 1:26–38
Ascension of the Lord	Acts 1:6–11
Baptism of Jesus	Mt 3:13–17
Behold your mother	Jn 19:25–27
Beheading of John the Baptist	Mt 14:3–12
Birth of Jesus	Lk 2:1–20
Birth of John the Baptist	Lk 1:5–58
Conversion of Saint Paul	Acts 9:1–19
Cure of the paralytic	Mk 2:1–12
Golden Rule	Mt 7:12
Good Shepherd	Jn 10:1–17
Good Thief	Lk 23:39–43
Holy Innocents	Mt 2:16–18
Jesus walks on the water	Mk 6:45–52
Lord's Prayer (Our Father)	Lk 11:1–4

Magi	Mt 2:1–12
Man born blind	Jn 9:1–38
Martyrdom of Saint Stephen	Acts 7:55–60
Michael the Archangel	Rev 12:7–9
Miracle of the loaves and fishes	Mt 14:13–21
Moneychangers in the Temple	Mt 21:12–17
Palm Sunday	Mt 21:1–11
Passion and death of Jesus	Mk 14—15
Pentecost	Acts 2:1–13
Road to Emmaus	Lk 24:13–35
Transfiguration of Jesus	Lk 9:28–36
Washing of the feet	Jn 13:1–15
Wedding feast at Cana	Jn 2:1–10
Widow's mite	Lk 21:1–4
Woman at the well	Jn 4:1–42
Woman clothed with the sun	Rev 12:1–6
Zacchaeus	Lk 19:1–12

4. Bibliography of Reference Sources

Paul J. Achtemeier. *HarperCollins Bible Dictionary,* rev. ed., New York: Harper Collins, 1996.

Advent Scripture Service from *Manual of Community Prayers for the Baltimore and St. Louis Provinces.* Esopus, New York: Mount Saint Alphonsus Seminary, 1971.

Donald Harman Akenson. *Saint Saul: A Skeleton Key to the Historical Jesus.* New York: Oxford University Press, 2000.

Alphonsus Liguori, *Lord of My Heart: Affections and Prayers From the Practice of the Love of Jesus Christ,* Thomas M. Santa, C.Ss.R., ed. Liguori, Mo.: Liguori Publications, 1997.

Archdiocese of Denver. The Denver Catholic Biblical School Program: Second Year. *New Testament Foundations*. Mahwah, N. J.: Paulist Press, 1995.

William J. Bausch. *Pilgrim Church.* Mystic, Conn.: Twenty-Third Publications, 1998.

Bible Basics: An Introduction to Scripture for Catholics. A Redemptorist Pastoral Publication, Liguori, Mo.: Liguori Publications, 1994.

Raymond E. Brown. *An Introduction to the New Testament.* New York: Doubleday, 1997.

Raymond E. Brown, Joseph Fitzmyer, Roland E. Murphy. *The New Jerome Biblical Commentary,* Englewood Cliffs, N.J.: Prentice-Hall, 1990.

Catholic Encyclopedia for School and Home, St. Joseph's Seminary and College, Dunwoodie, Yonkers, NY. New York: McGraw-Hill Book Company, 1965.

David Chidester. *Christianity, A Global History.* San Francisco: HarperSF, 2000.

Bruce Chilton. *Rabbi Jesus: An Intimate Biography.* New York: Doubleday, 2000.

Penitential Psalms from the *Christian Community Bible,* Catholic Pastoral Edition, Claretian Publications (Philippines) and Liguori Publications, Liguori, Mo., 1995

Paul John Coury, C.Ss.R. *A Prayer Service for Those Near Death.* Liguori, Mo.: Liguori Publications,1999.

A. Colin Day. *Roget's Thesaurus of the Bible.* San Francisco: HarperSF, 1992.

Jared Diamond. *Guns, Germs, and Steel: The Fates of Human Societies.* New York: W. W. Norton Co., 1999.

Some definitions from *The Essential Catholic Handbook,* A Redemptorist Pastoral Publication, Liguori, Mo., 1997. Additional definitions from *The Essential Catholic Handbook of the Sacraments,* A Redemptorist Pastoral Publication. Liguori, Mo.: Liguori Publications, 2001.

Gordon D. Fee and Douglas Stuart. *How to Read the Bible for All Its Worth: A Guide for Understanding the Bible.* Grand Rapids, Mich.: Zondervan Publishing House, 1993.

Bruce Feiler. *Walking the Bible: A Journey by Land Through the Five Books of Moses*. New York: William Morrow, 2001.

Richard Elliott Friedman. *Who Wrote the Bible?* Englewood Cliffs, N.J.: Prentice-Hall, 1987.

Kenneth Hagen, et al. *The Bible in the Churches: How Different Christians Interpret the Scriptures*. Mahwah, N.J.: Paulist Press, 1985.

Susan Haskins. *Mary Magdalen, Myth and Metaphor.* New York: Harcourt Brace & Company, 1993.

Joseph F. Kelly, ct.al. *The World of the Early Christians,* A Michael Glazier Book. Collegeville, Minn.: The Liturgical Press, 1997.

Jerome Kodell, O.S.B. *The Catholic Bible Study Handbook, A Popular Introduction to Sacred Scripture.* Ann Arbor, Mich.: Servant Books, 1985.

"The Litany of Penitence: Episcopal" from The Liturgical Conference, *Liturgy: Ritual and Reconciliation,* Vol. 9, No. 4, Fall 1991, pp. 56–57.

The Liturgical Conference. *Liturgy: From Ashes to Fire,* Vol. 10, No. 2, Summer 1992.

Teresa Malcolm. "Fearful Faith in End Time Novels," *The National Catholic Reporter,* (Vol. 37, No. 32), June 15, 2001.

Howard Marshall, A. R. Millard, J. I. Packer, and D. J. Wiseman. *New Bible Dictionary,* 3rd Edition, Downers Grove, Ill.: InterVarsity Press, 1996.

Richard P. McBrien. *Catholicism*. SanFrancisco: HarperSF, 1994.

Richard P. McBrien, general ed. *Encyclopedia of Catholicism,* New York: HarperCollins, 1995.

Mary Reed Newland. *The Family and the Bible.* New York: Random House, 1963.

Mary Nutting Ralph. *And God Said What? An Introduction to Biblical Literary Forms for Bible Lovers,* Mahwah, N.J.: Paulist Press, 1986.

Etymologies of Latin and Greek words, unless otherwise noted, are from *The Random House Dictionary of the English Language.* Unabridged Edition. New York: Random House, Inc., 1966.

Redemptorist Pastoral Publication. *"The Biblical Rosary"* from *The Essential Mary Handbook.* Liguori, Mo.: Liguori Publications, 1999.

Excerpts from the English translation of *The Roman Missal,* copyright 1973, International Committee on English in the Liturgy, Inc. (ICEL), are used with permission. All rights reserved.

Thomas M. Santa, C.Ss.R. "The Bible and the Sacraments," adapted from *The Essential Catholic Handbook of the Sacraments,* Liguori, Mo.: Liguori Publications, 2001.

Peter M. J. Stravinskas, ed. *Our Sunday Visitor's Catholic Encyclopedia,* Huntington, Ind.: Our Sunday Visitor Publishing Division, 1991.

Gerd Theissen and Annette Merz. *The Historical Jesus: A Comprehensive Guide.* Minneapolis, Minn.: Fortress Press, 1998.

Ronald D. Witherup. *The Bible Companion, A Handbook for Beginners.* New York: Crossroad, 1998.

5. Publishers of Catholic Biblical Resources

Note: The names and addresses of Catholic publishers or publishers whose list contains a representative sampling of Catholic books follows. Not all Catholic publishers are included, but rather only those publishers whose publications are referenced in *The Essential Bible Handbook.* This listing is provided as a service and is intended only as a beginning resource for those who desire to learn more about some of the Catholic resources that are available for Bible study and devotion. A web address is also provided whenever possible.

Ave Maria Press
Notre Dame, IN 46556
Web site: www.avemariapress.com

Doubleday (Random House)
1540 Broadway
New York, NY 10036
Web site: www.randomhouse.com

Liguori Publications
One Liguori Drive
Liguori, MO 63057–9999
Web site: www.liguori.org

The Liturgical Press
Collegeville, MN 56321
Web site: www.litpress.org

Our Sunday Visistor
200 Noll Plaza
Huntington, IN 46750
Web site: www.osvpublishing.com

Paulist Press
997 Macarthur Blvd.
Mahwah, NJ 07430
Web site: www.paulpress.com

Prentice-Hall
Upper Saddle River, NJ 07458
Web site: www.prenhall.com

St. Anthony Messenger Press
28 West Liberty St.
Cincinnati, Ohio 45210
Web site: www.americancatholic.org

St. Mary's Press
702 Terrace Heights
Winona, MN 55987–1320
Web site: www.smp.org

Servant Publications
P. O. Box 8617
Ann Arbor, MI 48107
Web site: www.catholicity.com

Twenty-Third Publications/Bayard
P. O. Box 80
Mystic, CT 06355
Web site: www.twentythirdpublications.com

United States Conference of Catholic Bishops
Publications Office
1312 Massachusetts Ave. N.W.
Washington, DC 20005
Web site: www.nccbuscc.org/publishing/index.htm